The Sieges of Rhodes, 1480 and 1522

Jonathan Davies

HELION & COMPANY

Helion & Company Limited
Unit 8 Amherst Business Centre
Budbrooke Road
Warwick
CV34 5WE
England
Tel. 01926 499 619
Email: info@helion.co.uk
Website: www.helion.co.uk
Twitter: @helionbooks
Visit our blog http://blog.helion.co.uk/

Published by Helion & Company 2024
Designed and typeset by Mary Woolley, Battlefield Design (www.battlefield-design.co.uk)
Cover designed by Paul Hewitt, Battlefield Design (www.battlefield-design.co.uk)

ISBN 978-1-804514-51-1

British Library Cataloguing-in-Publication Data.
A catalogue record for this book is available from the British Library.

Dedicated to
Professor Jonathan Riley-Smith and Dr R. C. (Otto) Smail

War is an opera. It requires an elaborate set, a large cast, an impresario and panache.[1]

The sieges of Rhodes were 'Grand Opera' indeed. There could be no better stage set than the City of Rhodes, set in the azure blue of the Aegean. The large cast consisted of, amongst others, Ottoman Janissaries playing opposite the Knights of St John, the last true crusaders. Suleiman the Magnificent, Pierre d'Aubusson and Phillipe Villiers de l'Isle Adam produced and directed these most extraordinarily bloody but mesmerising conflicts which aroused the wonder of Christendom. They were played out at a critical moment when the systems of attack and defence were transforming the nature of siege warfare. They have been largely forgotten in the history of the conflict between Christendom and Islam, overshadowed by those other magnificent set pieces the Siege of Malta and the Battle of Lepanto, yet they were not only important in the history of that conflict but in the history of warfare.

1 Quentin Hughes, 'Errors of Judgement: The Sieges of Rhodes and Malta,' in *Fort*, vol.31 2003, p.61.

Contents

Acknowledgements

I must mention the assistance that I have received from the librarians at the University of Birmingham Library, the University of Heidelberg, the Burgerbibliothek Bern and the Bodleian Library Oxford for the speed and politeness that they have demonstrated on every occasion. I should also apologise to as well as thank my typesetter who will have to have achieved the impossible once more, by turning my manuscript into a real book. My thanks to Stephen Ede-Borrett for his thoroughness in his editing and kindness to the author, thereby bringing this book into the world.

I would like, once more, to thank Pauline Asher for her painstaking work in correcting my drafts with remarkable patience and good humour. Any errors that remain are entirely my own and for which I humbly apologise. My great thanks go to Dr Catharine Davies for putting up with me and yet another damn book, that has taken up so much of our time as well as precious shelf space. I should conclude by thanking my many, many former pupils, who in their own way taught me far more about history than I taught them. I would like to thank the owner and staff at Efchi Suites 1904 for making us so welcome and comfortable during our stay, the breakfasts were especially delicious.

I conclude with the apology from the first printed account of the siege of 1522.

Go little book and woeful tragedy.
Of the Rhodian fearful oppugnation[1]
To all estates complaining ruefully
Of thine estate and sudden transmutation
Excusing me if in thy translation
Ought be amiss in language or in work
I me submit with their supportation
To be correct that am so small a clerk.[2]

1 *Oppugnacyon* or *oppugnation* is derived from the Latin *oppugnatus* meaning an attack or assault.

2 The concluding doggerel accompanied Robert Coplande's 1524 edition of Jacque de Bourbon's account of the siege.

The clerk at his work. His inkwell and pen holder sit beside him as he adds to or amends his text. Note that his quills do not have the feathery flourish associated with most (incorrect) modern interpretations. There is a counting board on the table, with which he can calculate his pitiful reward. He like all authors is a weary soul. (He is also sitting on the wrong side of the table!) *De Casu Regis Zyzymy* (The Case of Sultan Djem) printed in Ulm by Ioannem Reger in William Caoursin's *Obsidionis Rhodiae Urbis Descriptio*, 1496.

Preface

I first entered the harbour of Rhodes at the age of 17, perched on the stern of a fishing boat, arriving after a slow and wet journey on a distinctly choppy sea from the Turkish port of Bodrum. Fortified by cheap brandy and seasickness pills my legs were little more stable on land than they had been at sea. It took some time to convince the Greek authorities that I was a legitimate traveller protected by Her Majesty's Principal Secretary of State, but they eventually, grudgingly admitted me. However perverse my arrival I fell in love with Rhodes. The walls, streets and churches had survived the centuries remarkably well and retained their beauty and medieval atmosphere; this was of course before it had become the tourist 'hot-spot' of today. At university I was taught by the two leading scholars of the Hospitallers and crusading warfare, Professor Riley-Smith and Dr R. C. Smail. I was one of the students on the Cambridge Marqab Expedition where we studied a number of Byzantine, Hospitaller, Templar and Arab castles and surveyed the massively impressive fortification of Marqab in Syria. There after much study and cogitation we developed an entirely new interpretation of its development. Since those days I have always wanted to return to Rhodes and reacquaint myself properly with this Hospitaller fortress.

The sieges of Rhodes have been long forgotten. The island remained under Ottoman rule until 1912, when the Italians took control and brought a large number of emigrants. In the 1930s they attempted to make Rhodes the capital of their Dodecanese 'empire' and built a new Palace of the Grand Master as well as new civic buildings in their distinctive fascist style. The Second World War led to the defeat of the Italians by the Germans after their surrender in 1943 to the Allies and then to the extermination of the Jewish population by the Nazi occupiers. After the war the Italians were expelled and the island became truly Greek for the first time since 1309. Mass tourism has made the Island a popular destination for those seeking the sun but little is made of the two sieges by the tourist authority.

The 'Great Siege' of Malta in 1565 has far eclipsed these earlier and 'lesser' sieges, where the 'Holy Religion' also faced the might of the Ottoman Empire. In contemporary Europe the sieges of 1480 and 1522 were recognised and lauded as the magnificent and heroic defence of Christendom against the threat of a triumphant Islam. One of the first books printed in England in

1482 was an account of the first siege and the first opera in English was based on this heroic tale.

The sieges of Rhodes are particularly relevant to the 'Retinue to Regiment series' as the 40 years that separate the sieges saw a very significant change in the technologies of attack and defence. The sieges have been seen as demonstrating the transition from a traditional 'medieval' siege to a 'modern' one, an over-simplistic but not entirely unhelpful analysis. The first siege was very definitely 'late medieval' in character, with large bombards shooting stone balls against tall and comparatively thin medieval walls. It also saw the last recorded successful construction and use of trebuchets – by the defenders as well as the attackers. By 1522 the defences had been almost completely transformed on the latest and most modern principles. Artillery had also undergone a revolution. Many of the pieces were now bronze guns of comparatively narrow bore, shooting iron balls at much higher velocities than the larger stone-throwing bombards.

Other aspects of the siege which deserve study are the use of mining and counter-mining. This was particularly important in the 1522 siege when the remarkable engineer Tadini almost completely negated the massive tunnelling programme of the Ottomans. His career is worth a chapter in its own right. The extensive use of pyrotechnic and flame weapons is also an aspect which will be reviewed, as quite clearly they played an important part, especially in defence.

Most of all, the story is filled with great characters on both sides. Ambition and self-sacrifice, treachery and loyalty, cowardice and bravery are all features of the personalities of the time that make this far more interesting than simply a story about gunpowder versus stone.

Glossary

Ashlar – blocks of smooth, squared stone
Barbican – an outwork or forward extension of a castle gateway.
Bastion – a small tower at the end of a curtain wall, or in the middle of the outside wall.
Batter/Talus – a sloping part of a curtain wall. The sharp angle at the base of all walls and towers along their exterior surface.
Battlement – narrow wall built along the outer edge of the wall walk
Caponier – covered passage usually within a ditch useful for enfilading fire
Crenelation – a battlement made up of alternate crenels (openings) and merlons (square 'saw-teeth').
Curtain – those portions of a fortified wall which connect adjacent flanking towers.
Embrasure – the low segment of the alternating high and low segments of a battlement.
Enfilade – to fire along the length of an enemy's battle line.
Fausse-braye – a low wall with a wall walk, built a short distance in front of the principal curtain wall thereby producing a concentric fortification.
Gabion – wicker basket filled with earth and/or stone, used in fortifications, sometimes substituted with earth filled barrels
Hoarding or **brattice/breteche** – a temporary wooden balcony suspended from the tops of walls and towers before a siege, from which missiles could be dropped or arrows shot accurately towards the base of the wall.
Machicolation – a projection in the battlements of a wall with openings through which objects can be dropped directly onto besiegers at the base of the wall.
Mantlet/shutter – moveable device for closing the crenel or other opening.
Merlon – the high part of the square 'saw-tooth' between crenels in a battlement.
Palisade – a sturdy wooden fence usually built to enclose a site until a permanent stone wall could be erected.
Parapet – protective wall around the outer side of the wall walk, at the top of a fortification.
Postern or **Sally-port** – secondary gate or door to allow secret egress or a sally by the garrison.
Rampart/Terreplein – a protected fighting platform for castle defenders.
Relieving arch – arch built up in a wall to relieve thrust on another opening.

Tenaille – earth or masonry structure, built in the ditch to protect the curtain.
Terreplein - surface of rampart behind the parapet where guns are mounted.
Trebuchet – war engine using counterweight principle.

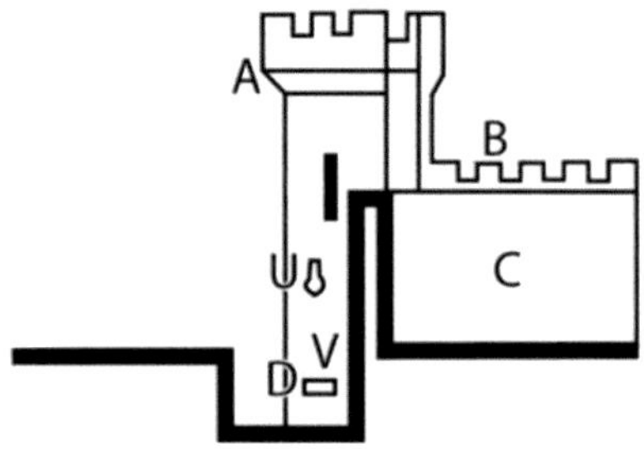

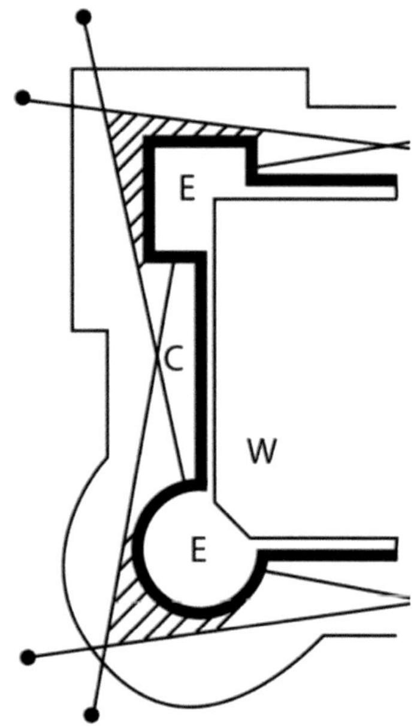

A: Machicolations, from which defenders could drop objects on attackers at the base of the wall.
B: Crenels and Merlons, the gap between could be provided with moveable wooden shutters.
C: Curtain wall.
D: Ditch.
E: Towers, hatching indicates dead ground where defensive fire could not reach attackers.
U: Keyhole, early style of gunport.
V: Letterbox gunport, usually found at low level.
W: Enceinte, the area enclosed by fortifications.

Introduction
Jerusalem to Rhodes

The Crusades, Triumph and Disaster

The Crusades are still with us. The use of the term 'Crusade' by President George W. Bush to describe the invasion of Iraq by predominantly Christian forces was a monumental disaster for relations between the West and the Moslem world. To the Islamic world, the Christian Crusades were exemplified by the massacre of the population of Jerusalem in 1099, followed by the establishment of 'Western' states in the Middle East, the oppression of the people and the desecration of their holy places. To this was added the nineteenth century experience of foreign rule in the form of direct or indirect colonial conquest in North Africa and later, after the destruction of the Ottoman Empire, the mandated territories whose governors had little regard for the rights and feelings of their diverse populations. This perception of the 'Crusading West' was reinforced by the events of this century which have hardly improved the reputation of the 'Christian' West in the Arab world.

In the West the Crusade did not develop pejorative associations, quite the opposite. A Crusade was a heroic attempt to improve or reform, not to destroy and enslave. In the West, the Crusade was part of a heroic, even romantic, ideal. It was also possible to coopt some of the major 'enemy' players into this, especially Saladin, whose bravery, leadership and generosity was so admired. It was understandable but still surprising that the British Army in the 1950s introduced new armoured vehicles, named the Saladin and Saracen. To Christendom, the Crusades provided Godfrey de Bouillon a hero of the stature to stand alongside the 'Nine Worthies', these were primarily Classical and Biblical heroes who were represented on the pediments and in the paintings on the walls of great houses and palaces. Godfrey, Raymond of Toulouse and King Richard the Lionhearted provided heroes for Christendom as well as for their own people, up to the present day. It is important to appreciate these two radically different perspectives of the idea of the Crusade. The sieges of Rhodes were some of the final manifestations of the original Crusades and counter Crusades.

The Crusade was created by the Church in order to achieve its own ends, exploiting the needs and attitudes of the time. To say it was not a Christian Act because it encouraged and directed violence is to assert that the Christian Church and the Pope at its head who proclaimed it were also not 'Christian'. When Pope Urban II preached the Crusade at the Council of Clermont in 1095 he had prepared the ground well politically, psychologically and emotionally. He grafted the well understood and much practised concept of the pilgrimage onto a military expedition. He coopted the chivalry of Christendom into its service where they would gain great spiritual benefits as well as in some cases great material ones. The papacy gained great authority in the secular world for its role in leading the crusading movement and coopted secular rulers and western knighthood in its service. It also diverted some of the endemic viciousness in the West beyond its borders for a 'good' cause, as well as giving the Normans an outlet for their penchant for aggressive acquisition.

Gustave Doré (1832–1883), The Discovery of the True Cross. Although a nineteenth century engraving, this highlights the importance of relics to the catholic Christian mind up to the present day. The processional cross made for the coronation of King Charles III contained a splinter from the 'true cross,' a gift from the current Pope. The possession of powerful relics imbued their possessor with an authority that impressed all true believers. The original True Cross was lost at the disastrous Battle of Hattin in 1187. The Hospitallers possessed an impressive treasury of relics that attracted pilgrims and further added to their status as the defenders of Christendom. (Public domain via Wikimedia Commons)

The language used resonated with the feudal classes as well as too many simple believers. Those who 'took the cross' were acting in the service of their spiritual Lord to restore his patrimony which had been taken by a common enemy. The well-known 'Just War' theory supported this argument as the Pope possessed the authority to order a military act to recover territory. Secondly, this land had once belonged to Christ by virtue of his presence and because it had once been part of the (Orthodox Christian) Byzantine Empire. Finally, it was a war to recover land that belonged to Christendom and not a war of conquest or conversion. It was also a war in defence of Christendom which had been in fear of the encroachment of Islam for centuries. It was so successful as a concept because it matched the medieval zeitgeist. To contemporaries, it was both intellectually and theologically sound, although this was and remains a serious source of embarrassment. The papacy has yet to explicitly apologise for the Crusades generally but has apologised for the Fourth Crusade that resulted in the sacking of Orthodox Christian Constantinople in 1204.

At the same time as the Latin States were being established in the East, the West, especially Venice and Genoa, was engaging in a vastly profitable trade in spices that were already being traded through the Arab world. Spices were not used in the West to hide the taste of rotting meat as so often reported; this is nonsense. As an aside, it must be said that spices were very expensive, if you could afford spices, you could certainly afford good quality, fresh meat. Eating putrid meat would kill you and there were strict regulations in medieval market places concerning standards of hygiene and waste disposal. In addition to spices, silks, cotton cloth, metalwork and high quality timber were also exported. There was also the lucrative pilgrim trade, providing shipping and accommodation for them in the East. The principal beneficiaries were the Italian city states, who with their fleets and territorial acquisitions played an important part in the development of the western economy. Venice came into conflict with the other major Christian power in the East, the Byzantine Empire. By the perverse manipulation of the papacy and the western leaders of the Fourth Crusade, Venice managed to divert the Crusade to besiege and capture Constantinople in 1204, in order to crush and humiliate a longstanding rival.

In the Latin East the early successes, explicable because of the power vacuum in the region at the time and the extraordinary violence of the Crusaders, led to the capture of Jerusalem and the establishment of the Latin States. They were not Crusader States since the Crusades were an entirely separate series of events. These Latin States had to develop a *modus vivendi* with their neighbours if both were to survive and thrive. A foolish attack on Damascus in 1148 as part of the second Crusade proved how damaging and difficult such ill-considered ventures could be. The Latin States depended for their defence upon their own domestic nobility and the power of the two principal military orders, the Templars and Hospitallers. The beginning of the end for the Latin States was the disastrous loss of the Latin field army at the Battle of Hattin in 1187, where they were out-thought and out-fought by Saladin and his army. Jerusalem was lost, and as there was no force that could come to its aid, so was almost the rest of the Latin Kingdom. The Third Crusade of 1191 led to the recapture of Acre and the consolidation of a 'rump' Kingdom but without Jerusalem which had always been a strategic outlier, difficult to defend but at the very heart of the crusading enterprise.

As Arab, and later Turkish, power waxed, that of the West waned. Christendom had neither the resources nor the will to provide the reinforcements in money and men needed to sustain the remaining Christian territories in the East. The success of Qualawūn in capturing the last strongholds, such as Marqab in 1284, achieved by undermining the principal tower, indicated that there was little future for a Christian state in the East. The fall of Acre in 1291 despite the best efforts of the Hospitallers and Templars, now assisted by the Teutonic Knights, was the end of almost two centuries of occupation. It was a humiliation for Christendom, but not one it seems deeply felt. The Genoese and Venetians were free to continue their lucrative trade with the Islamic world and without the costs and embarrassment of conflict, except when in their own interests. What however would be the future of the military orders, whose only *raison d'être* had been the existence of the Latin States?

The Hospitallers and the Crusades, to 1291

The origin of the order and its earliest days are unclear. The knights themselves dated it to a foundation by Judas Maccabeus, long before the birth of Christ. It is certain that there was a Christian 'hospital' in Jerusalem prior to the First Crusade as the flow, sometimes flood, of pilgrims meant that there were many in need of care, respite and consolation. The Benedictine Abbey of St Mary of the Latins seems to have established a hospital near to the Holy Sepulchre in about 1080. The Hospital appears to have seceded from the Abbey by 1113, under the leadership of one Gerard, about whom little is known. The function of the Hospital at that point was to care for the sick and the poor to whose service the Knights remained loyal. The Master of the Order still retains the Latin title *Custos Pauperum* (Guardian of the Poor). Thus, the maintenance of a hospital and the treatment of all poor, irrespective of faith or gender, remained at the heart of their faith and service.

To serve the poor and the sick was to serve the person of Christ. It was therefore essential to provide them all with the best possible care and comfort available. A regime of cleanliness, spacious and airy wards, a healthy and plentiful diet and the use of silver vessels was a demonstration of this and perhaps one of the reasons for their success in treating the sick. The Hospital in Jerusalem could accommodate 2,000 patients and the brothers would be displaced from their dormitories if more space was required. Their organisation was on a military basis, in the best possible sense of the word, with a Brother responsible for a ward with the assistance of a dozen paid servants. There was an obstetric ward, provision for the treatment of feet, as well as barbering. Each patient had a bed to his or her self and their linen was changed every fortnight (whether it needed to be or not!). The management and treatment of the poor was an indication of the level of organisation, commitment and wealth of the order, and it was these characteristics which were to make them such a powerful military force when they took up arms.

The Templars, in contrast, were created as a military order from their inception in 1119/20. Founded by Hugh of Payns, a knight from Champagne, in response to recent reverses in the East, the Order's purpose was to provide an armed escort to pilgrims from the relatively safe coastal ports to Jerusalem. The Templars were formally recognised by the Church at the Council of Troyes in 1129. The 'militarisation' of the Hospitallers was rather later than might be expected since their origin preceded that of the Templars. In 1136 the Hospitallers received the Castle of Bait Jibrin from King Fulk and in 1144 they received the former Byzantine fortification at Krak des Chevaliers. It was Master Gilbert who was to include a formal military obligation on the lives of the brothers, who belonged to a religious order which was clearly becoming central to the strategic security of the Latin States. It was in 1153 that the wearing of the cross by all brothers in the order's rule, and the Order's military role were established.

The military orders had two principal functions: the first was to build, modernise and maintain a series of strategically important castles to control territory and which would act as bases for operations and help preserve the states in the face of invasion. Their second role was to provide about half of the effective field army of Jerusalem. The disaster at the Battle of Hattin, where the members of both military orders were either killed or executed, led to the collapse of the Kingdom of Jerusalem, and the capture of its capital. Marqab and Krak des Chevaliers, both garrisoned by a few of the remaining Hospitallers, held out in the hope of a relief army from the West – this did arrive in the form of the 'Third Crusade' of 1191. The Latin States were saved but Jerusalem was lost and although it left a territory that was easier to defend, it was inevitable that when an able Moslem leader appeared, the Christian possessions in the East would come under threat again.

Matthie de Clermont Défend Ptolémaïs en 1291, by Dominique Papety (1815–49) at the Salles des Croisades in Versailles. A nineteenth century representation of the heroic but doomed defence of Acre. The Templars survived this disaster only to experience a much worse fate at the hands of the French monarchy and the Papacy. The Crusades were part of the prevailing Christian narrative and represented an ideal of devotion and suffering that would re-emerge as late as the two World Wars.[1](The Pilgrimage and the Crusade were closely connected and required no justification to most Christians. War between Christendom and Islam continued wherever there was contested territory. Granada was not finally recovered, by King Ferdinand of Aragon and Queen Isabella of Castile, until 1492, 200 years after the Latin States in the East had been finally crushed by Islam. (Public domain via Wikimedia Commons)

The establishment of a new headquarters in Acre, the new capital of the Kingdom, allowed for a period of consolidation. There were only about 300 Hospitaller brothers-

1 The Spirit of the Crusaders by Gertrude Meredith Williams (NMW A 2645) https://museum.wales/collections/online/object/3743db4e-4412-3247-ad42-41f1ee902543/The-spirit-of-the-crusaders.

at-arms and the order relied upon mercenaries and volunteers to provide the garrisons needed for their numerous fortifications, Marqab for example could have had a garrison of a thousand men. This was only possible because both Orders were major international institutions drawing manpower and wealth from across much of Christendom. The Order contained both Brothers and Sisters in the same Convent, although by the late twelfth century the sisters were to be found in separate nunneries. In the case of the Templars, they had become the de facto bankers for the French Crown, which was to lead to their catastrophic demise. Although both Orders were enormously wealthy on paper, converting this into manpower, money and the resources to sustain what was an expeditionary force far from the West, was a constant challenge. The resurgence of Mameluke power led to the capture of the 'Jewel in the Crown' of Hospitaller defences, Krak des Chevaliers, by Sultan Beybars in 1271. Marqab, which in many respects was as strong if far less beautiful, fell in 1285 and Acre succumbed in 1291.

The loss of the Christian possessions in the East, although an embarrassment and a humiliation for Christendom, was a calamity for the military orders. Their failure to defend the Patrimony of Christ, when they themselves were so obviously and embarrassingly wealthy required both explanation and expiation. The Teutonic Knights were to eventually find a new role for themselves fighting pagan tribes in the Baltic, becoming a major power in the region.[2] The Templars and Hospitallers first found a home in Cyprus, although they maintained control of the tiny Island of Arwad/Ruad, a delightful speck in the Mediterranean of no possible strategic value.[3]

The Templars were to succumb to the envy, greed and ruthlessness of the French Crown. In 1307 King Philip ordered the arrest of all the Templar brothers in France. Arrest led to torture, torture to confessions and confessions to executions – on a grand scale. The weakened papacy under Clement V gave in to political pressure and the Templars were hounded, persecuted and eventually suppressed at the Council of Vienne in 1312. Their property was transferred in principle to the Hospitallers, although in practice it seems to have remained often in secular hands. The most serious long-term consequence was the development of an obsessive interest in the Templars and their 'treasure', leading to the Templar Myth. This was an eighteenth-century German invention that has cluttered bookshops, TV screens and magazine racks with reams of nonsense, up to and including the present day!

2 The Austrian Infantry Regiment 'Hoch und Deutchmeister', which still exists, claims descent from the Teutonic Knights. During the eighteenth and nineteenth centuries the Regiment was considered the elite Regiment of the Austrian Army and was kept in the German order of battle even after Austria was united with Germany by the Anschluss of 1936. I am grateful to Stephen Ede-Borrett for pointing out this surprising survival.

3 Used in 1978 for dummy rocket attacks by the Syrian Air Force Sukhoi 7s.

The Road to Rhodes, 129 –1476

Only seven knights had escaped alive from the disaster at Acre and there seemed little, if any, hope of reviving the Order. Cyprus was the obvious first resting place for the Hospitallers. It was a possible base for military operations but it seemed very far from the East and it would not have permitted them freedom from political interference by the Lusignans who governed there. If the Order was to survive and flourish it, had to remain an outpost of Christendom confronting the power of Islam. William de Villaret the Grand Master sought to reinvent the Order as a maritime power and chose Rhodes as a likely base. From there raids could be launched against the trade routes passing from Mameluke Egypt along the Eastern Mediterranean coast. Rhodes was ostensibly Byzantine and therefore Christian territory, although its loyalty to Emperor Andronicus II was nominal, and Orthodox Christianity was schismatic as far as Latin Christians were concerned. Under William's brother, Fulk de Villaret, an arrangement was made with a Genoese pirate, Vignolo dei Vignoli, to seize and share the island. The operation began in July 1307 with little initial success, while Pope Clement V confirmed the Hospitallers right to a territory that they had not yet conquered and over which he had no real authority. To complete the conquest the Order mortgaged its revenues in Christendom for the next 20 years to a Florentine banker. Despite stiff resistance from the Rhodian population the city of Rhodes surrendered in 1309. Once established on the island the Hospitallers became a Sovereign Order operating under their own authority as the Knights of Rhodes. This enabled them to mint their own coins for the first time – a statement of their authority and a testimony to their wealth and ambition.

With the island of Kos and the Castle of St Peter at Bodrum and the other islands, the Order patrolled the principal gulfs, channels and approaches on the routes from Constantinople to Alexandria. They controlled what was one of the main trade routes in timber and spices, as well as valuable local trade in foodstuffs and drink. The wealth that this would bring would also bring the hostility of those who sought to promote another Crusade and those, including the papacy, envious of the Order's wealth. In practice the Order had been impoverished by the Florentine loan and then the economic consequences of the Black Death (1348–1349) which led to a massive reduction in its revenues from its western estates. The income and resources from the Priories and Commanderies, ostensibly at their disposal, were also often tied down by national duties and obligations. Even so the Order was able to establish its position on the island, unchallenged by the Ottomans, the Mamelukes or the Byzantines – all of whom lacked both the means and the will to do so.

Throughout the fourteenth century the Order participated in raids, both alone and as a part of a larger alliance against targets across the region. The disastrous defeat of the Crusader Army at Nicopolis in 1396 was a dreadful shock to Christendom but did not damage the position of the Order. The arrival of the Timurid Mongols in 1402 destabilised Ottoman rule and

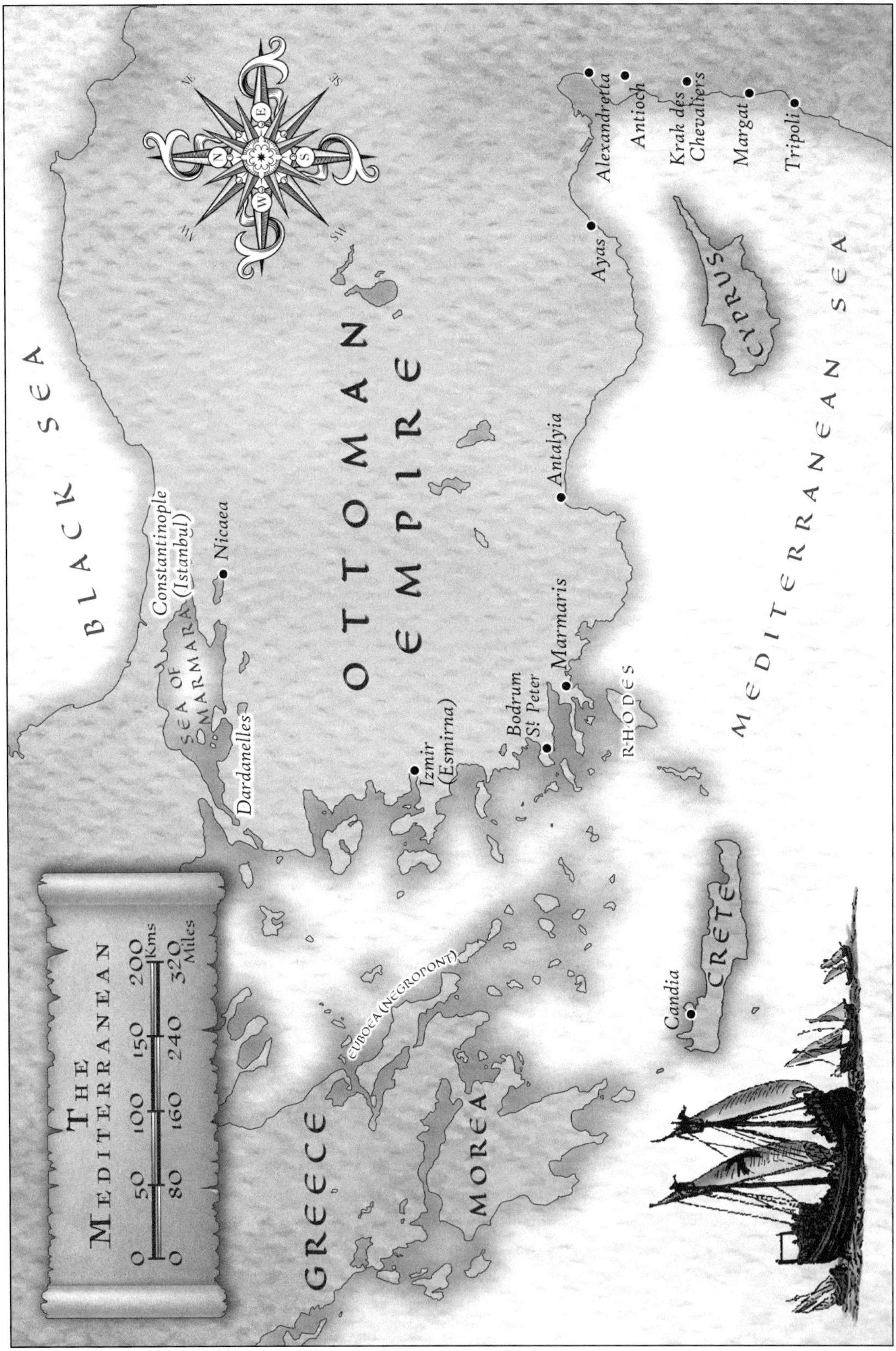
The Mediterranean
0 50 100 150 200 Kms
0 80 160 240 320 Miles
BLACK SEA
SEA OF MARMARA
Constantinople (Istanbul)
Nicaea
Dardanelles
OTTOMAN EMPIRE
Izmir (Esmirna)
Bodrum St Peter
Marmaris
Antalyia
Ayas
Alexandretta
Antioch
Krak des Chevaliers
Margat
Tripoli
RHODES
CYPRUS
CRETE
Candia
MEDITERRANEAN SEA
GREECE
MOREA
EUBOEA (NEGROPONT)

diminished the threat they posed, as the Mongol victory at Ankara was succeeded by a long and bloody succession dispute amongst the Sultan's sons. In 1403, in recognition of their status as a significant regional power, the Mameluke government allowed the Hospitallers to operate consulates in its territory and to re-establish a hospital in Jerusalem. In the same year that they had reached a rapprochement with the Mamelukes they assisted *Maréchal* Boucicaut of France in his raids against the Ottoman controlled coastline. Boucicaut's fleet was shadowed by a Venetian squadron concerned that his objective might have been Venetian controlled Crete – there was little trust to be found between Christians!

By the 1440s this honeymoon period was over, with a Mameluke attack on Rhodes itself, now under the Grand Mastership of Jean de Lastic, in 1444. A fleet of 75 or 85 ships landed a Mameluke army on 10 August but

Left. A large bronze medallion of Sultan Mehmed II by Costanzo da Ferrara in 1481. (Metropolitan Museum of Art, Open Access)
Right. A portrait medal of *Sultan Mehmed II* (reverse); a *Triumphal Chariot* by Bertoldo di Giovanni, Italian from 1480, an aftercast (that is a cast taken from an original casting). (Metropolitan Museum of Art, Open Access)
Costanza da Ferrara was sent to Istanbul by Ferdinand I of Naples at the behest of the Sultan to paint his portrait, probably between 1475 and 1478. Ferrara seems to have remained at the Ottoman court until 1481 when the Sultan died. The legend on the medallion gives him the title of Byzantine Emperor by virtue of his conquest. Another medal of the Sultan was commissioned by Lorenzo de Medici who was fascinated by the Sultan, who had recently attacked Negroponte (the island of Euboea). Lorenzo sent Mehmed another medal he had himself commissioned from Beroldo di Giovanni. This had on the reverse an image of the Sultan riding a triumphal chariot holding in his hands a rope tying three crowned female figures, representing the territories he controlled: Asia, Greece and Trebizond.[4] There was no sense of western or Christian superiority in Lorenzo's gift coming from *il Magnifico* to the *Conqueror*. Mehmed saw himself as the successor to the ancient Emperor of Byzantium and Rome by right not just by conquest. The assumption that the powers Christendom and Islam were at daggers drawn on all occasions is clearly wrong.

4 The Kingdom of Trebizond on the North-East coast of Turkey was the last remnant of the Byzantine Empire and fell to the Ottomans in 1461.

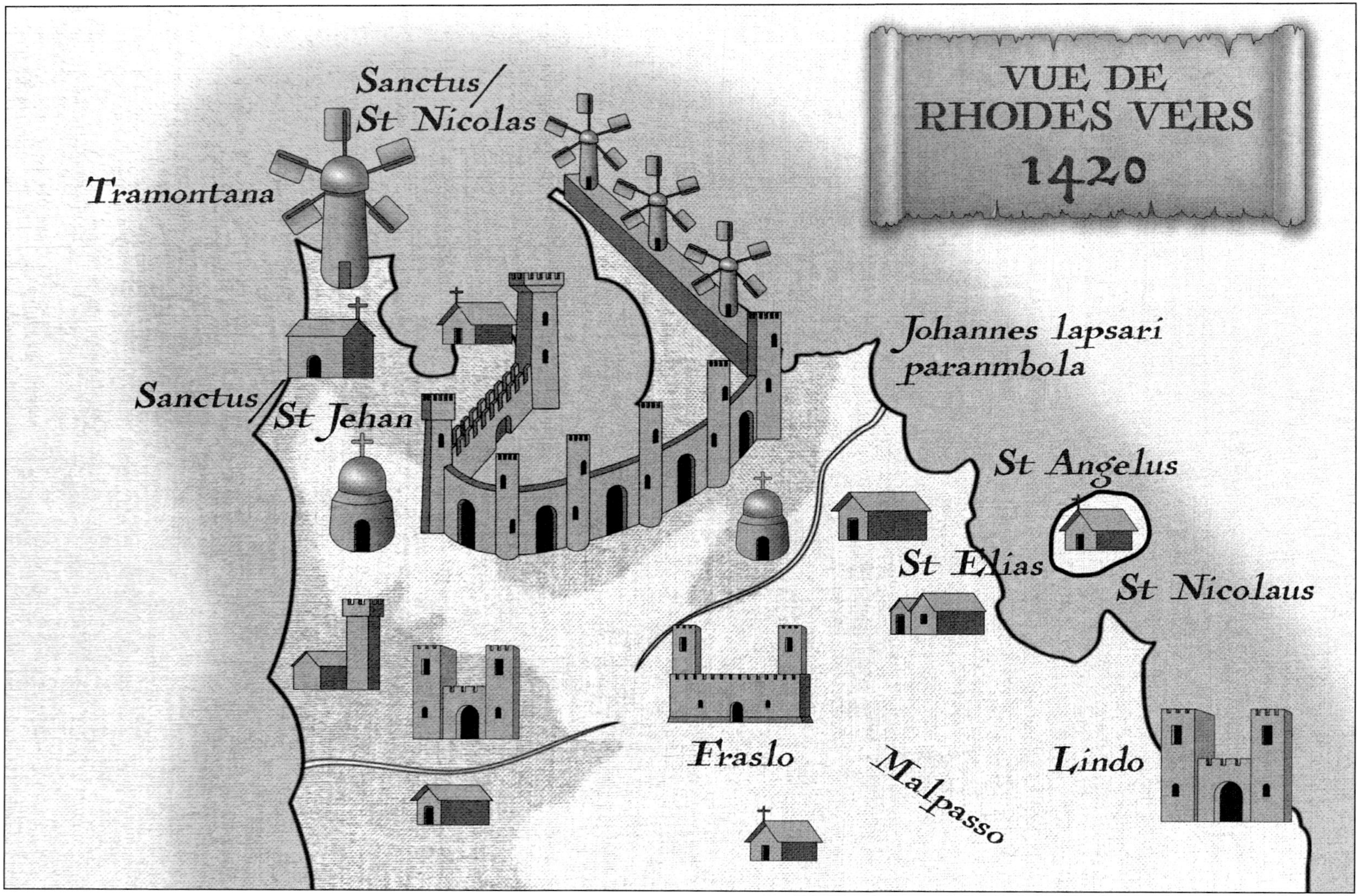

One of the earliest views of the city of Rhodes from around 1420. Taken from a miniature in the *Liber Insularum* of Cristoforo Buondelmonti. (*La Cité de Rhodes*, Albert Gabriel)

after some skirmishing and a poorly prosecuted siege they withdrew on 18 September. The Mamelukes misjudged how long it would take to subject the Hospitallers and were forced to retreat as the customary October storms threatened. The main consequence of the siege was the realisation by the Grand Master that Rhodes, which had not been directly involved in the bloody struggles in the region, was in fact desperately unprepared for a serious siege conducted by a major power.

The real threat was eventually not to come from the Mamelukes but from the Ottoman Turks. Under Sultan Murad II (1421–1451) the Ottomans began to restore and then expand their territory, defeating the Crusading Army at Varna in 1441 and the Hungarians under Hunyadi at the second battle of Kosovo in 1448, threatening south-eastern Europe. Mehmet II, son of Sultan Murad, succeeded to the throne in 1451, with the capture of Constantinople as his first objective. The resources that he had at his disposal were immense. The Ottoman Army was estimated by some as being 200,000 strong, although probably its true strength was only half that. What was incontrovertible was the extraordinary battery of heavy artillery that he had at his disposal, some at least cast primarily, if not solely, for the siege. The original defences built between 408 and 413 CE were enormously impressive and had withstood many sieges. Although they remained strong, the great city had lost its empire and therefore lacked the soldiers and resources to man the walls of Constantinople. The Ottoman bombardment lasted 55 days, with 120 rounds fired from the large bombards, the principal armament of the Turkish attackers. Without reinforcement, successive assaults finally overwhelmed the defenders on 28 May. It was another disgrace and humiliation for the West and especially for the papacy, which had tried and failed to rally support for the Byzantine Emperor.

Mehmet did not turn next to a full invasion of Rhodes, instead he launched attacks on Belgrade in 1454 and Trebizond in 1461. Raids between the Hospitallers and Turks continued while Grand Master de Milly (1454–1461) attempted to negotiate a truce with Mehmet. In 1457 a raid on the island and its inhabitants proved particularly damaging to the Rhodian economy. Having been defeated at the siege of Belgrade, the Turks needed to restore their forces and morale. They were in no position, after successive expensive and punishing campaigns, to launch a major seaborne assault.

The Hospitallers continued to support, and participate in, papal and other Christian raids while at the same time attempting to reach a modus vivendi with the Ottomans. This was impossible while the Grand Master refused to give tribute to the Sultan, an act that would have recognised his supremacy. This unstable and unsatisfactory situation could not be allowed to continue, and by1476 it was clear to the new Grand Master, Pierre d'Aubusson, that the Sultan would inevitably launch an attack on Rhodes. d'Aubusson's predecessors had begun a massive rolling programme of refortification which he accelerated, while at the same time he called upon all of the Order's Convents and Commanderies to send men, weapons and money to reinforce the city and the other fortifications for which it was responsible.

Christendom, the Crusades and Rhodes

The concept of Christendom may seem absurd to modern secular eyes but in the late Middle Ages it most certainly did not. Within Christendom, Holy Mother Church reigned supreme. If Jerusalem was at the centre of their physical world, Rome was the real centre of the Catholic World. The papacy had admittedly faced the crisis of the schism between rival Popes in Rome and Avignon (1309–1377) but that had eventually been resolved. The Pope, throughout this period, possessed immense moral authority and real material power. The Church was the only major universal institution and although its relations with Christendom's secular powers were not always easy, it was in the interests of both to ensure comparative harmony. The collapse of the Latin States and the capture of Acre in 1291 was a dreadful blow to the Church and to Christendom as a whole. The attempt to counter the advance of Islam by a Christian force, drawn from across Europe, came to a dramatic and disastrous end at the battle of Nicopolis in 1396. Christendom was on the defensive in the East but on the offensive in the West where in Spain there was a slow but steady ascendancy of the Christian kingdoms over Moslem Granada.

The major powers in Western Europe were busily engaged in their own disputes. France and England, who had once led the Crusading movement, were engaged in what would become known as The Hundred Years' War and which lasted from 1340–1453. England subsequently engaged in its own fratricidal conflict – the Wars of the Roses, off and on from 1455–1487. England, France and the Empire continued to needle one another whenever feasible, while the growing power of a semi-independent Burgundy challenged that of the Kings of France. This was a conflict that would only conclude with the defeat of Burgundy in 1477 at the battle of Nancy. The final disaster that overtook Europe was the expedition that Charles VIII of France led through Italy in 1494 to lay claim to the Kingdom of Naples. Massively destructive and strategically senseless, it began a series of wars between France, Spain and The Empire that would continue on sporadically until 1559, when all sides were exhausted. There had been a western counter-attack to Islam, led by Hunyadi in the Varna Crusade of 1444, involving an impressive coalition of forces from Hungary, Poland, the Balkan states, Burgundy, the Greek Emperor and Venice and Genoa, but Hunyadi was defeated, first at Varna in 1444 and then decisively at Kosovo in 1448. The loss of Constantinople in 1453 was a symbolic rather than a real challenge to Christendom.

If Christendom was united in one religion, it was clear that it was profoundly divided politically. It was therefore inevitable that despite the best efforts of the papacy to unite the Christian powers in the defence of Christendom that there was little hope of mobilising the forces that had seen western sovereigns leading armies to the East in previous eras. In 1460 Pope Pius II attempted to mobilise the forces of Christendom against the Turk as had been done in 1444. Pope Pius declared:

> We are now free to turn our arms against the Turks.... We.... will lay down our life for our flock in no other way can we save the Christian religion from being trampled by the forces of the Turk. We will equip a fleet as large as the resources of the Church will permit. We will embark, old as we are and racked with wickedness. We will set our sails and voyage to Greece and Asia.[5]

Pope Pius II. A bronze medallion of 1460, attributed to Andrea Guazzalotti (1435-1495), diameter: 56mm. Pius was from very humble beginnings. He was born near Siena the son of a simple soldier. He flourished as an administrator and diplomat in the Church, travelling in its service as far north as Scotland, where he complained of the cold and damp. Despite the discomfort he received some solace and fathered a child, who later died. He continued working as a capable 'fixer' for the Church in warmer, and more civilised climes, while at the same time pursuing numerous amorous conquests. He was the author of the erotic novel, *Tale of two Lovers*, of some literary merit but still scandalous considering his calling. He proved eminently successful in both Papal and Imperial service, rising through the ranks to become Bishop of Trieste. He was elected Pope in 1458, through his ability to be everyone's friend, thereby gaining a majority in the College of Cardinals. Intelligent, educated in the humanist tradition and notably dissolute in his lifestyle, he was transformed by the Papal tiara into an enthusiastic crusader. He called for Christendom to unite and smite the Turk. His diplomatic efforts to secure peace within Christendom failed and he died attempting to revitalise the Crusade. There are no miracles ascribed to Pius II. (Metropolitan Museum of Art, Open Access)

He was realistic about what the English could offer, mired as they were in civil war. The Nordic countries could also contribute little as they were: 'too far away to be able to send soldiers and they have no money to contribute, as they are content with fish alone.'[6] The French, Castilians and Portuguese, the (reluctant) Venetians as well as the Burgundians, Germans and Hungarians, would provide an army that he calculated would number 88,000. To this would be added the Albanians led by the legendary Skanderberg, while the Christian Armenians would attack the Turk from the rear. It was a vision of a united Catholic Christendom, but it was only a vision and the Pope died in 1464 on his way to Ancona, while those few who had assembled there deserted from the ships intended to carry them to glory. Only Venice and the Hospitallers answered the call and Venice lost Dalmatia, Lemnos and Morea, which was a heavy blow.

5 Eric Brockman, *The Two Sieges* (London: John Murray, 1969), p.5. Aeneas Silvius Piccolomini (Florence A. Gragg trans., Leona C. Gabel ed.)., *Pius II : Memoirs of a Renaissance Pope* (London: Putnam, 1960), pp.143—150.

6 Eric Brockman, *The Two Sieges* (London: John Murray, 1969), p.5. Aeneas Silvius Piccolomini (Florence A. Gragg trans., Leona C. Gabel ed.), *Pius II : Memoirs of a Renaissance Pope* (London: Putnam, 1960), pp.143—150.

1

The Art of Attack and Defence

Early Firearms: Misconceptions and Reality

It is very difficult to escape from the misconceptions about early firearms and those about artillery in particular – that they were at best unreliable and inaccurate and at worst as dangerous to their users as their enemies. Garret Mattingly in his magisterial work on the Spanish Armada of 1588 wrote some very silly things.

> The most experienced gunner might hesitate to predict whether when he next fired it his gun would send its shot directly to the target, drop it with a sort of discouraged burp a few hundred feet ahead, or blow up at the breech, probably killing him and his crew.[1]

In 2017 Martin Smith in his otherwise excellent study of battlefield trauma *'Mortal Wounds'* assumed pretty much the same thing. He wrote of hand-held firearms:

> There is a common perception that pre-modern firearms were rather ineffective, and in several regards such opinions are well based in fact. The earlier handguns had a tendency to explode and injure the person using them, match-lock guns carried the inherent health and safety risk of trying to manipulate a container of gunpowder in one hand and a piece of burning string in the other.[2]

1 Garret Mattingly, *The Defeat of the Spanish Armada* (London, Jonathan Cape, 1960), p.105.
2 Martin Smith, *Mortal Wounds* (Barnsley: Pen & Sword Books, 2017), pp.223–224.

There is no doubt that early firearms were dangerous to their users, archaeological, pictorial and written evidence all provide examples of catastrophic failure of artillery pieces. It is absurd on the other hand to consider that such weapons would be employed by those using them if they felt they were at such great risk. Everything about the design of weapons and their use would suggest that those who made and used them were well aware of the dangers and took great care to minimise those dangers. The unfortunate demise of the Scottish King, James II, in 1460 when an artillery piece exploded, is usually cited by the detractors of artillery but the premature demise of one monarch did not stop others acquiring and employing large numbers of similar bigger and hopefully better cannons.

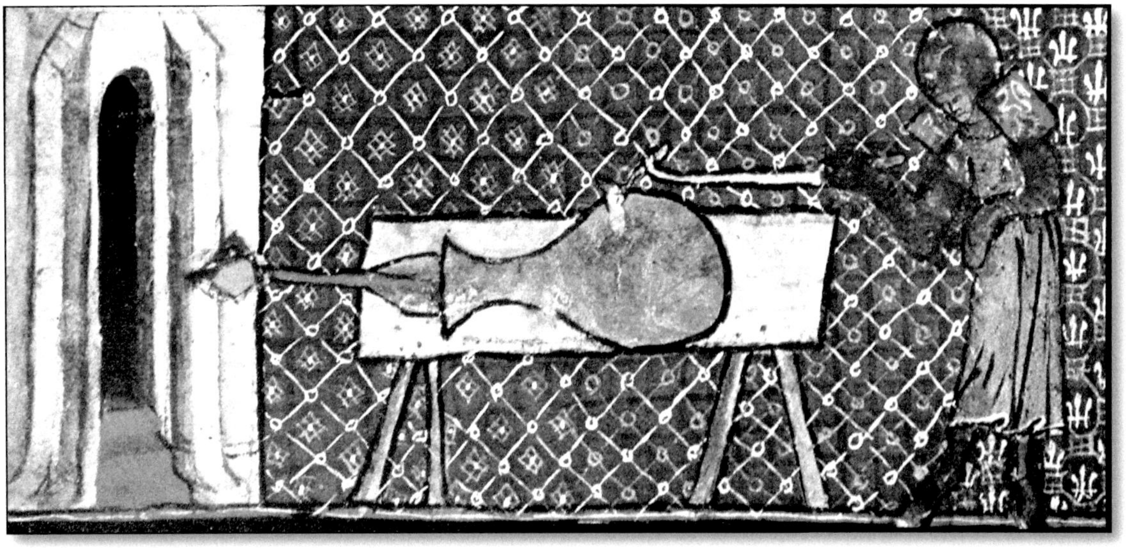

There has been much debate about this illustration and whether it shows an actual example of a real piece or whether the image of the cannon was exaggerated in order to show it in detail. A full-scale reconstruction by the Royal Armouries firing what was in effect a short spear, weighed 800kg! The use of gun arrows or 'garros' was sensible and practical, as the fine examples of this type of projectile from the Castle of Burg Eltz have shown. ('De Nobilitatibus Sapientii Et Prudentiis Regum Manuscript', Christ Church Ms 92 fol. 70v. Illustration via Wikimedia Creative Commons World Imaging)

The first incontestable depictions of gunpowder weapons are to be found in the Holkham and Milemete manuscripts dated to 1326–1327. The weapon depicted is a large vase-shaped bronze cast piece, shooting a *garros* or gun arrow.[3] There is much debate as to the actual scale and internal architecture of the weapon, what is not in doubt is that it was a viable weapon. The small Loshult cannon, the earliest firearm discovered in the West and probably dateable to about 1340, weighed only about 10 kilograms and was 30cm, or about 12in, in length. During the trials conducted at the

3 'De Nobilitatibus Sapientii Et Prudentiis Regum', Christ Church Manuscript 92, fol. 70v.

Danish Middle Ages Centre, it proved a most reliable and effective weapon, shooting arrows, lead balls and iron dice-shot.

The first reference to a gun being used in battle is at Crecy in 1346, the battle that incidentally saw the triumph of the longbow. The transformation of the gun from a noisy novelty to an essential aspect of medieval armament was the result of two technological innovations. The first was the development of saltpetre plantations and the second was the increased availability of cheap iron. Saltpetre was the principal ingredient of gunpowder, providing the oxygen required for the charcoal to burn. It was very expensive as it had to be imported from the East, probably from India. The mass production of saltpetre led to a rapid reduction in cost. In Frankfurt the price fell from 41 florins per hundredweight in 1381 to 16 florins per hundredweight in 1410, while between 1385 and 1417 the price fell by more than three-quarters in England. Cheaper powder meant that larger quantities and therefore more, and bigger, guns could be used.

The introduction of the Catalonian furnace allowed much larger blooms of iron to be made at a much lower cost. The application of water power to the iron industry led to the development of the blast furnace and water-powered hammers. The consequences of these developments were the increased production and lower cost of iron. Wrought iron was ideal for the manufacture of guns of all sizes, because of the special quality of the material. Wrought iron has a very low carbon content of less than 0.1 percent, fibrous slag inclusions which make up about 2 percent of the mass give it a "grain" and assist the process of heat welding and resists corrosion. Wrought iron can also be heated again and again and reworked. The material is ductile with a high tensile strength making it an ideal material for the manufacture of artillery as it is easily worked and strong. If the metal is brought into the range 1,150–1,350 degrees centigrade then by hammering it can produce almost perfect welds as the slag inclusion melts and covers the join, which stops the oxidation process which would make the weld fail.[4]

The preferred material for the manufacture of guns remained bronze, an alloy of copper and tin, which could be cast in moulds. This was because it was exceptionally strong, would provide an indication of weakness before failing and could be recycled by melting down to make another piece. It cost many times more than the equivalent weight of iron, even so it is surprising to see the great number of bronze pieces in contemporary illustrations. As so often in matters relating to war, expense was often no object.

With larger guns, using bigger charges of powder, the role of gunpowder weapons was transformed not so much on the battlefield but in the siege. The predominant heavy siege machine of the pre-gunpowder era was the trebuchet, using a fixed or swinging counterweight. It used gravitational force to transform potential into kinetic energy. The key feature that made the weapon so effective was the sling that greatly increased the velocity of the projectile. In 1998 Nova built two full-scale trebuchets, one with a fixed

4 Jonathan Davies., *The Medieval Cannon* (Oxford: Osprey, 2019)

and one with a swinging counterweight.[5] They were sited at Castle Urqhart next to Loch Ness, where they were shot against a reconstructed medieval wall 200 yards away. They used round stone balls weighing between 250 and 300 pounds travelling at 120mph (176 fps or 54 ms), achieving hits with both machines. The impact on the walls was like a slow-motion car crash rather than an explosion. The damage was caused by the shock wave travelling through the wall rather than by mechanical injury to the face of the wall.

Although very impressive, large trebuchets presented major problems as well as advantages. Like all timber frame structures, it could be disassembled, transported and reassembled if necessary but to be of any use, trebuchets also had to be very large. One of the trebuchets used at the siege of Acre in 1191 required 100 carts to transport it, while the single engine on the Tower of St Pauls at Orleans was carried in 26 carts. When they were assembled the weight and rigidity of their structure meant that they could only hit what was directly in front of them. The wood and ropework were also subject to natural decay and required careful handling. They were additionally very large and vulnerable targets for counter-battery fire. It is often said that they could only use a high angle trajectory, however this is not the case as they can 'flat shoot' if the sling rope is lengthened or the projectile is lighter, making for a later loose. This makes it much easier to hit a wall, as a steeply curving trajectory makes hitting a narrow target difficult.[6]

The heroic author (in white) undergoing instruction, in order to captain this full-size trebuchet at the Middelealdercentret, Denmark. At this point I am trying to avoid making a 'mouse nest mess' of the ropework. This is a wonderful machine, incredibly accurate, very powerful but also a very large target. A large castle or city would be defended by its own trebuchets, mounted on towers and within their walls. It is important to remember the soldier's adage, 'if the enemy are within range, so are you.' (Author's photograph)

5 *Nova Secret of Lost Empires Medieval Siege* https://www.youtube.com/watch?v=QVO8VznqMeQ

6 Based on my experience over many years of shooting cabbages into and out of English Heritage castles!

The Bombard

Iron and bronze cannon both had major advantages over trebuchets in terms of size, weight and longevity. Although heavy they were considerably lighter and also made smaller targets for enemy counter-battery fire. Above all they produced a higher velocity projectile, still of stone but now with far more energy. They were also almost indestructible and were a valuable display of wealth and power when not in use. To increase the effectiveness of a cannon either the velocity or weight of the projectile might be increased or preferably both. In practice the nature of the powder and the strength of the available materials meant that the pressure that could be generated in the breech and barrel was limited. The only alternative was to make the projectile heavier, while the ratio of powder to shot remained roughly the same for all sizes of gun.

The gun could not be a tube of a constant diameter as it would be unable to withstand the pressure of the expanding gases. Therefore, the breech portion of the gun, where the combustion of the powder took place, was reinforced or thickened. This was then attached to the larger diameter barrel whose job it was to simply direct the projectile. The breech was where the high pressures would be generated, in the barrel the propellant gases entered a larger space, which would result in a much lower pressure. The gun that was the result of this is generally referred to as the bombard, the medieval 'supergun'. Until the radical transformation of artillery design in the last decades of the fifteenth century, the bombard was the wall smasher that dominated siege warfare. Manufactured from wrought iron, cast from bronze or, exceptionally, cast in iron, it was a brilliant but clumsy creation

The reproduction of historical artillery over the past 40 years has led to some very impressive results which give the lie to many of the earlier assumptions as to the utility and safety of early gunpowder weapons. The most recent tests of a late medieval bronze cannon or *pesterau* were organised by the HO Group (a team of international scholars), at the Medieval Centre in Denmark.[7] They set themselves the task of designing, casting and test firing a fifteenth century bronze cannon. The Group chose an example from Historische Museum, Berlin (Steinbüchse W 437) which weighs approximately 120kg. The balls, weighing about 3.75kg, flew at a very respectable 130 metres per second – almost two and half times as fast as a trebuchet ball.[8] As kinetic energy is calculated by the formula Ke = half Mass X Velocity squared, the impact of the 3.75kg ball from the cannon

7 A short-barrel, muzzle loaded weapon like a mortar, usually of wrought or cast iron from the very late fifteenth century, described in DeVries, Kelly and Smith, Robert Douglas., *The Artillery of the Dukes of Burgundy* (Woodbridge: The Boydell Press, 2005), pp.225–226.

8 For a full account of these and other trials of recreated artillery see Jonathan Davies, *The Art of Shooting Great Ordnance*, Retinue to Regiment no.22, (Warwick: Helion & Co, 2022), Chapter 9.

was equivalent to an 11kg projectile from a trebuchet. Although figures in the trial varied in general the breech pressures were roughly three times those found in the barrel demonstrating the effectiveness of the high/low pressure system.[9]

The HO Group trials provided key information concerning the correct loading of such a piece. It was essential that the ball was placed at the face of the chamber and that it was carefully wedged into position to ensure that it was central. The use of the tampion, a wooden plug hammered into the mouth of the chamber, was crucial to produce consistently high chamber pressures and velocities. Where no tampion was used the results were very wayward and disappointing; the chamber pressures were much lower as were muzzle velocities, which produced considerable variation between shots. The wedges were for centring the ball and to hold it firmly in place. This loading procedure led to significant pressure increases in the barrel. If breech pressures in large bombards were to remain within safe limits, the quantity of powder was limited. There was a ratio of seven or eight to one, of projectile to powder weight, for the largest examples (3–400lb shot), the smaller cannons had a slightly higher ratio of powder to shot.

Dulle Griet (*Mad Margaret*) was the 'bigger sister' of *Mons Meg*. They were both built in the workshop of Jean Cambier for the Duke of Burgundy and represented different sizes of the same basic design. It consists of a large diameter barrel and a smaller diameter reinforced breech. The barrels *Dulle Griet* and *Mons Meg* are both seven tenths of the total length, and the internal length of the barrel is five to five and a half times the bore. The Ottomans preferred to cast their bombards from bronze, in two pieces. Bombards were not the absurd aberrations once thought but impressive and effective contributions to the siege train of any medieval autocrat. (Public domain via Wikimedia Commons)

9 A principle also successfully employed in the ammunition developed for the M79 grenade launcher.

What could negate the advantage of the cannon was the material and velocity of the stone. If the stone projectile was less hard than the wall it was being shot at then at high velocity it would simply disintegrate into a mass of powdered stone. This happened to a limestone ball fired from 338m against a stone wall during the test of a *Mary Rose* port piece, a large wrought iron chambered gun. The famous Italian gunfounder and expert on all things metallurgical, Biringuccio, when considering the use of stone-firing weapons declared that: 'These are not good for breaching walls and serve only for shooting at infantry or cavalry and at armed ships at sea.'[10]

The term bombard is supposedly derived from the Greek word *bombos*, which means a buzzing sound, and was a term at first applied to any gunpowder weapon. As the heavier siege weapon became a distinctive type, the term bombard came to be employed exclusively for a weapon of large bore suited only to such operations. The Ottoman bombards appear to have been manufactured primarily from cast bronze, which, although safer, was also more expensive and heavier. This led them to be constructed in two parts with the powder chamber separate from the barrel, which was to enable easier manufacture and transport. The two parts could then be screwed together on site, using the windlass sockets fitted on the breech and barrel. It is most unlikely that the breech was unscrewed, loaded and then re-attached after each shot as this would have required the destruction of the carefully constructed emplacement.

The junction between breech and barrel in the Dardanelles Gun, in the Fort Nelson collection of the Royal Armouries. It is easy to see how the windlass sockets would have made the 'mating' of the two parts relatively straightforward. The gun would then be mounted on a large wooden bed with a substantial recoil system consisting of baulks of timber, held in place by ground anchors. As with the trebuchet, once in position it would be difficult to move, although ranges could be adjusted by altering the powder loading. (Author's photograph)

10 Vannoccio Biringuccio, *The Pirotechnia* (New York, Dover Publications inc., 1990), p.225.

One pair of Ottoman guns employed at the siege of Constantinople had barrels three feet in diameter, pulled into position by 70 oxen and 1,000 men. They fired projectiles weighing 875lbs up to 1¼ miles. Perhaps unsurprisingly one gun burst on firing – which was attributed to Christian sabotage. One of the most famous examples still in existence is the Dardanelles Gun which was manufactured in 1464 for Sultan Mehmet Khan, as part of a battery of 42 cast bronze weapons. It weighed 18 tons and fired a ball of 6cwt from a 25 inch diameter barrel. In 1807 this type of gun was used against an English squadron attempting to breach the Dardanelles; one shot from the battery killed and wounded 60 men and left a gaping two-foot wide hole in the hull of the unfortunate ship it struck.

Preparing such massive weapons must have been time-consuming. The best contemporary record of the loading and firing of a bombard is by Kritovoulos, a Greek author writing in 1467, describing the cast bronze bombards of Mehmet II.

> First they put into it that which is called powder, filling the chamber behind completely up to the mouth of the enlarged part of the bore, which is intended for the stone shot. Then they introduced a great stopper, a very strong plug of wood [tampion], which they batter down with iron rammers so that it shall closely confine the powder in such a way that only the force of the ignited powder can discharge it; then they placed the stone shot upon it, ramming this down forcefully so as to make it enter into the wooden plug and make a round cavity [the plug was concave in shape so as to accept the shot]. After this, having turned the cannon towards the target, and given it an angle of elevation according to the rules of their art and experience, they brought great beams of wood which they laid under it, and on top and on all sides, so that it might not be disturbed and strike wide of the mark as a result of the shock and the recoil. After all this, they applied the fire to the little orifice behind[11]

Kritovoulos, using information from those who were present, describes the gun as being 30 feet long and a single casting.

The discharge of the weapon would have produced considerable fouling of the chamber that would have to be cleaned, and the recoil of the weapon must have caused damage to the mounting, with the gun needing to be re-laid after each shot. The experience of the crew, the number of labourers available, the availability of powder and shot, and the urgency of the siege all affected the rate of fire. At a siege of Metz in 1437 one gunner achieved the apparently remarkable rate of three rounds in a single day. The only explanation was that he had employed the assistance of the Devil and he was sent to Rome on a penitential pilgrimage. In 1513, at the siege of

11 https://www.worldhistory.biz/middle-ages/21929-artillery.html

Therouanne, it was recorded that an English bombard was shot five times in a day, throwing an iron ball weighing 260lbs. In 1453 the great bombards fired at the city walls of Constantinople seven times a day. The low rate of fire and expense in the weight of powder and shot meant that every effort had to be made to make each round count. Capsali reported that at the siege of Constantinople the Ottomans placed a smaller gun alongside the bombard which they used as a ranging weapon. This was the system later used by the British 120mm recoilless rifles, which were fitted with a 12.7mm ranging rifle to conserve ammunition and to avoid immediate retaliation by an enemy spotting the massive back blast from the main gun. This system would, of course, only work if the projectiles from both weapons shared the same ballistic profile which in the case of the bombard combo seems unlikely.

The emplacement of a bombard was a considerable challenge. Large baulks of timber or an oak or elm bed could support the gun. It could be elevated by simply raising the muzzle on trestles, or by raising that on an earthen ramp. The recoil was dampened by the use of a lead 'pillow', held in place with solid timber reinforcements and an earth bank or, in the case of the Dardanelles Gun, a reinforced wall. Caoursin describes how the great bombards were emplaced:

> And also for to show and declare the marvellous greatness of the said bombards and guns: the great piles and posts strong and mighty that were sticked in the ground behind at tail of the foresaid great bombard gave such great and mighty shaking that the houses of Rhodes other whiles shaked in such a wise like if it had been an earth quake.[12]

The weight of the guns and the additional weight of the means to emplace and protect them added to the weight of shot and powder meant that once a gun was laid upon the target further movement and the engagement of other targets was impossible unless there was a major change in strategy that desperately required it.

At the first siege of Rhodes, it was to be the bombard that would predominate in the main features of the story although other gunpowder weapons such as the 'sling' are mentioned. Robert Smith and Kelly de Vries in their monumental effort recording and analysing the gunpowder weapons of the Dukes of Burgundy have highlighted the difficulties in associating a specific name with a particular type of weapon.[13] This is hardly surprising but somewhat frustrating as it is impossible to establish

12 Guillaume Caoursin, *The Siege of Rhodes* (London: *c.*1482), unpaginated.

13 Kelly DeVries and Robert Douglas Smith, *The Artillery of the Dukes of Burgundy* (Woodbridge: The Boydell Press, 2005).

the calibre, length and capability of any weapon even if the author himself understood it.

We are fortunate in having both Ottoman and Western bombards available for study. The closest example to the types described by contemporaries has a length of 3.64 meters. Smith and De Vries list four large Ottoman bombards averaging about 4.25m in length and with a bore averaging 66cm. These could shoot a ball averaging 350lb, with a rate of fire of six to seven rounds a day. The distance from the Church of St Anthony, where the bombards were emplaced in the first siege, to the Tower of St Nicholas was 230 metres (250 yards).

The large diameter wrought iron and cast bronze artillery piece had by the end of the fourteenth century become the essential participant in any siege. In only one respect it had not replaced the trebuchet, and that was in its ability to shoot a variety of projectiles over the walls of a city or castle. Even the large diameter bombard-mortar could only shoot stone projectiles. The trebuchet could shoot barrels of ordure, bee skeps, enemy heads or any other unpleasantness that could be placed in its sling. It is perhaps unsurprising to note that although firearms predominated in the list of essential equipment provided by Christine de Pisan (1410) and Jean de Bueil (1466) they also included trebuchets. In the siege of Rhodes in 1480 both sides constructed and successfully employed trebuchets.

The Defences of Rhodes 1309–1480

When Rhodes was conquered by the Order in 1309 there was little of the former Byzantine defences left, yet there was no need initially to build new walls. The Order's galleys would be defence enough, as no power that had substantial naval strength was interested in attacking Rhodes and those that were potentially interested, lacked the ships.

The town that the Hospitallers now possessed was divided into three distinct enclaves. The first was the *Acropolis* which would become the site of the Grand Master's Palace. The second was the *Collachio* or castle and the third the *Burgus* or lower town. There was a defensive line between the *Burgus* and *Collachio* consisting of a wall, towers and a *fausse braye*. The remainder of the lower town would have had some form of curtain wall. Much of these early fortifications has been lost or incorporated into the later defences.

It seems probable that initially the only significant building programme that took place was the rebuilding of the Byzantine wall around the *Collachio* (the Northern portion of the city). This project did not encompass the growth of the developing new town or harbour. Progress in the development of the city's fortifications was slow. Grand Master Fenandez de Heredia (Grand Master 1376–1396) completed some work on the north side, including square towers to the West of St Paul's Gate. Philibert de Naillac (Grand Master 1396–1421) built the tower named after him. Grand Master Anton Fluvian (1421–1437) extended the defences on the landward side, making the old Byzantine defensive line irrelevant. The defences consisted of a curtain wall with tall rectangular towers, a *fausse braye* and beyond that a dry ditch.

It was the short and weakly pursued Mameluke siege of 1444 that prompted the Order to take serious action. It is very fortunate that each Grand Master identified his contribution to the new defences by placing his Coat of Arms in stone in situ. Grand Master Jean de Lastic (Grand Master 1437–1454) seems to have been particularly busy and his work was completed by successive Grand Masters. Giovanni Batista Orsini (Grand Master 1467–1476) seems to have concentrated his efforts on the walls surrounding the harbour. The harbour was further protected by a tower at the end of the Windmill Mole, which was where an iron chain from the Naillac Tower could be raised to control entrance to the harbour. What turned out to be the critical fortification in 1480 was the Tower of St Nicholas. It was built between 1464–1467 at a cost of 12,000 gold solidi, a gift from the Duke of Burgundy (Philip the Good) and bore his Coat of Arms. It was placed on the mole to the north of the city protecting the galley port.

Even with considerable expenditure, the improvements of the defences although extensive were unimpressive. They consisted, in practice, of the traditional high, relatively thin, external walls provided with narrow wall walks. A further lower wall with a wall walk was built in front with a 10 to 12 feet gap between the two walls. This was the *fausse braye* which was a common feature of medieval fortifications, one for example was provided for the defence of Boulogne and proved very effective. Defending the walls were a series of detached rectangular towers that were joined to the curtain wall by an easily removable wooden bridge. Gateways were protected by round towers, with drawbridges and portcullis. Machicolations and hoardings were still to be found on the walls, from which hot sand, quick lime and oil could be poured on attackers. Rhodes was in fact protected by the sort of city wall that could be found almost anywhere across Europe. It could hardly be expected to match the majesty and proportions of the fortifications of Constantinople but it had to face an equally well-armed and determined enemy in 1480.

There was little special provision for the use of gunpowder weapons and even less for defence against them. As most of the work had been completed by the middle of the fifteenth century, it is difficult to criticise the Grand Masters and their advisers for having built what were essentially pre-gunpowder defences in principle, relying on height and concentricity. Firearms were, however, incorporated in these defences with gun ports allowing small artillery pieces mounted in frames on battlements and towers to be used. The *pesterau* or small bombard used by the HO Group, and based on a mid-fifteenth century example, is only a little more than two feet in length. It could fire far enough to discommode any enemy bombardier, easily smashing the timber hoarding protecting his gun. If instead of a single stone ball it was to shoot scraps of iron and shards of stone at a mass of Janissaries, at a few tens of yards, it would also prove very effective. It is also worth considering that the large calibre stone shot from a bombard would achieve its effect by shock wave damage to the structure rather than mechanical damage to the exterior. This was especially evident during the *Nova* trials of full-scale trebuchets.[14]

14 https://www.youtube.com/watch?v=QVO8VznqMeQ&t=2645s

2

Prelude to the First Siege

The Organisation of the Order

The Order was a major international organisation which reflected the prevailing social structure of Christendom. It was dominated by an aristocratic elite but its structures, processes and procedures were meant to ensure that the Order remained well-governed and free from excessive interference or influence, whether personal, familial or national. It was this that enabled it to establish itself, flourish and survive the collapse of the Latin East, and then to re-establishment in Rhodes. As an aside it is worth mentioning that the first non-European, non-aristocrat was only elected as Grand Master in 2023!

The Knights of Justice were the fighting strength of the Order. They were required to prove a long aristocratic descent, up to 16 quarterings of arms in the case of German knights. They had to serve a year in the Convent in Rhodes and another year in a 'caravan' on patrol duties. This now involved service aboard the Order's galleys, rather than in defence of pilgrim 'caravans' in the Latin East. After this they could continue military service in Rhodes, or pursue administrative or diplomatic service in any of the national Priories or Commanderies. These were the elite of the Order and controlled all of the major administrative posts and military offices. The next group were the Chaplains of Obedience, of which there were three grades: clerics, chaplains and priors. Their role was primarily religious but they could *in extremis* bear arms. They were expected to serve as military chaplains on operations. The next class were Serving Brothers or Servants-at-Arms, who were at the very least gentlemen and provided additional fighting power. One group that ranked 'with but after' the Knights of Justice, were the Knights of Grace who were secular individuals appointed because of their merits, irrespective of any lack of noble birth.

The Order was organised according to the 'Langue' (tongue, language) of their members. By 1480 the Langues by order of seniority were: Provence, Auvergne, France, Italy Aragon, England, Germany, Castile

The Street of the Knights. The principal Langues were to be found on the street; the Grand Master's Palace and the Hospital were both adjacent as was the Order's Church. The English Langue was in a nearby building – today a tourist shop. Much work was done to restore the street using the architectural drawings made by the French architect Albert Gabriel, who provided the first and up to this date the only detailed record of the civil and military architecture of the city in his two monumental works published in 1921 and 1923. (Author's photograph)

and Portugal. The Langue could be subdivided into priories, thus France was subdivided into France, Aquitaine and Champagne. The English Langue included those Knights from Ireland and Scotland (which was a separate Commandery) – this was not a popular combination with its naturally obstreperous membership.

The Order was governed by the Grand Master and the Council. This consisted of the local Bishop, the Prior of the Conventual Church, the *piliers* (leaders) of each Langue and all Knights Grand Cross (most senior knights) who were present. Lawmaking was in the hands of the Chapter General. The Council elected two representatives from each of the Langues who would form a lawmaking commission.

The Grand Master's election was also subject to a complex process. The Langues would choose 24 electors forming the Conclave. The Conclave would choose three electors, a Knight, a Brother and a Chaplain. This triumvirate elected a fourth member. The fourth chose a fifth and the fifth chose a sixth until sixteen were chosen. These then chose the Grand Master. It was a complex process designed to avoid the problems of bribery or undue influence. Of the 11 Grand Masters chosen between 1305 and 1522 eight were French, which reflected the preponderance of the French in the Order but does not seem to have resulted in a pro-French foreign policy. At worst it was a system that produced capable compromise candidates but at critical times it provided outstanding leaders such as d'Aubusson and de l'Isle Adam.

The eight major offices were distributed among the *piliers* of the Langues. The Grand Commander (Provence) was the Grand Master's deputy and had overall management of the finance and resources of the Order. In this he was assisted by the sub-commander and the granary inspector. The Marshal (Auvergne) was responsible for providing the land and naval forces with the wherewithal to conduct operations. He was assisted by the Grand Groom and the Constable, responsible between them for the cavalry. The Grand Hospitaller (France) was as his name suggests responsible for the hospital and its extensive staff, including the infirmarer, physicians and pharmacists. Close supervision of the hospital was conducted by the Grand Master as well as representatives of the Langues. When present, the Grand Master might be expected to personally tend to the sick in his daily visits.

The Auberge d'Auvergne which is in a remarkable state of preservation and is currently the Museum of Modern Art (sadly, it was closed when I last visited in 2023. It is remarkable how so many of the original buildings and their features remain. I would recommend travelling before the Greek National Holiday after which the tourist season begins.) (Albert Gabriel, *La Cité de Rhodes*)

The Admiral (Italy) was responsible for the conduct of all military operations involving the small fleet of galleys and larger vessels placed at his disposal. The Draper (Aragon) was responsible for the provision of all clothing for the Order, an indication of the importance with which such matters were considered. The Grand Turcopolier (England) was responsible for the Turcopoles or light cavalry.[1] The Treasurer or Grand Bailli (Germany) oversaw the victuallers, store keepers and the provision of all livestock. The last office was that of the Grand Chancellor, who supervised the Grand Master's secretariat and was therefore an influential figure in day-to-day affairs, as well as great matters of state.

The Order established on the Island of Rhodes and on its other possessions a signalling system that would advertise the arrival of enemy vessels. The Hospitallers had used carrier pigeons in the Latin East and in the fourteenth century there is a reference to the use of signal mirrors. The system in the late fifteenth century seemed to rely on signal fires producing smoke in the daytime and firelight at night. To ensure rapid communication there was considerable visibility between towers and castles across Rhodes and her possessions, as far as Cos. A code dated to November 1449 explained the duties and penalties for those responsible. On seeing an enemy vessel, the appointed guard should light a signal fire. If no signal fire was lit in reply by the next in the chain, on the next night a second fire set alongside the first should be lit and so on until the first fire was acknowledged. When it was, the original signaller should indicate the number of enemy ships by lighting the appropriate number of fires. This would suggest that they were preparing for a small raiding party rather than an enemy fleet. If a signaller was derelict in his duty, he would have his beard and hair cut off and 'have twenty-five [lashes] in the pillory.'[2] The system was not necessarily all that effective in either warning of an attack or eliciting a suitable response. In 1508, when an attack on Leros took place, four days elapsed before the Grand Master was informed and by the time the relief force arrived the raiders had gone.

Justice was administered in Rhodes by the Bailli, appointed by the Grand Master. There was also an independent mercantile court, which was essential if Rhodes was to operate as a thriving centre of commerce. As a

1 A somewhat notional office for what was primarily a maritime force.

2 Anthony Luttrell, 'Smoke and fire signals at Rhodes 1449' in *The Military Orders Vol.5* Peter W. Edbury (ed.), (Farnham: Ashgate publishing Ltd, 2012), p.129.

sovereign state, for both practical and status reasons the Order struck its own coinage, this was based on the *denier tournois* of the Abbey of St Martin of Tours which was one of the main recognised coinages of France.[3] The Greek population of Rhodes seem to have had their own system of administration and legal process, which only rarely involved the Order. There is no doubt that the Order 'ruled the roost' and that the native population was not involved in its affairs. The rural population became, in practice, serfs to the Order, which operated as any western feudal society did at the time. The Greek Orthodox faith was seen as schismatic by those of the Latin faith, after the Great Schism of 1051 had formalised the division. This added to the tensions between the Order and the Rhodians but their opinions could not be ignored, as events in both sieges proved.

In addition to the native Greek population there were residents and settlers from the West engaged in the lucrative trade of the region, especially

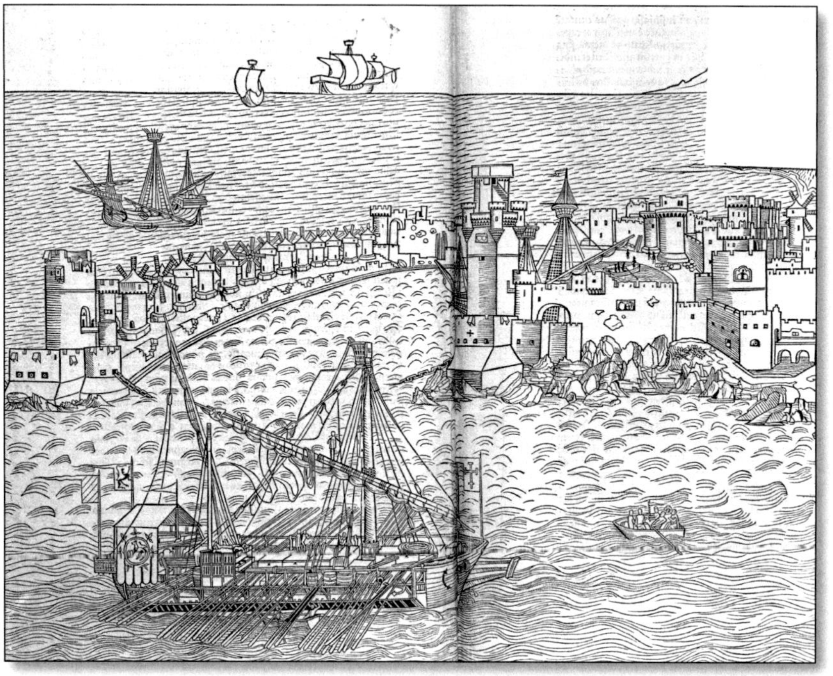

The entrance to the commercial harbour at Rhodes, Bernhard von Breydenbach's *Peregrinatio in Terram Sanctam* (Gernsheim Peter Schoffer the Elder, 1425–1503 Mainz, illustrated by Erhard Reuwich of Utrecht 1496)
This illustration shows the Windmill Mole to advantage as well as the iron chain that controlled access to the harbour between the Windmill Tower and the Naillac's Tower. The reconstruction by Albert of Naillac's Tower relied heavily on such rare illustrations. The defences show some sign of damage but were clearly still formidable. There is a sailing vessel in harbour but outside there is an excellent illustration of a large commercial galley awaiting entry. It is the type of ship used for pilgrim traffic and valuable commercial cargoes. (Metropolitan Museum of Art, public domain)

3 NB if you want to acquire a Hospitaller denier beware, there are apparently many forgeries around!

Genoese merchants whose position was somewhat ambivalent to the Order and invariably hostile to the Venetians their great rivals. Within Rhodes there was also a small Jewish population, which was subject to persecution and harassment as it was across Christendom. The Jewish women were skilled weavers and their work was purchased by the Order. In 1502 it was ordered that all adult Jews should be baptised within 40 days or be forced to abjure the Island. How successful this was it is difficult to say as there were certainly Jews in Rhodes at the time of the second siege.[4]

The Icon of Philermos (nineteenth century copy). The Icon of Philermos was one of the most important sources of inspiration to the Knights and the Rhodians in both sieges. Ostensibly it was the work of the Evangelist Luke and painted in 46 BCE, although it seems more likely to be of Byzantine origin and dating from the eleventh or twelfth centuries. It was an object of devotion and even adoration for the Orthodox and the Catholic alike and was paraded through the streets in moments of crisis. On the departure of the Knights in 1523 it was attached to the mainmast of the Grand Master's ship and afterwards continued to be an important possession of the Order until its demise in 1798. After many further seemingly implausible peregrinations it is now to be found in the National Museum of Art of Montenegro in Cetinje. The original is so blackened as to make it impossible to distinguish any features. (Public domain via Wikimedia Commons)

Relics, that is physical items associated with religious figures, were of profound importance to the Order, to the Rhodians, and to Christianity as a whole. They were imbued with the power of the individual with which they were associated and possessed an extraordinary ability to mobilise and motivate their worshippers. They could be associated with particular properties, the ability to cure specific diseases or assist in conception and childbirth for example. They were also immensely valuable as potential sources of revenue from those pilgrims who travelled to see them and experience their benefits, both spiritual and material. They could act as talismans that would unite and inspire, such as the 'True Cross' that led the armies of Jerusalem.

The Order possessed a great number of very powerful relics which they had originally acquired during their service in the Latin East. The German priest Ludolf von Südheim, who as a pilgrim visited Rhodes in 1336–1341, referred to some of the Order's relics, including the bronze cross which was supposedly made from the basin which Christ had used when he washed the feet of his disciples. This had been inherited from the Templars on their demise and although apparently a humble object, highlighted the principal purpose of the Hospitallers, which was to serve others.

4 The Jewish population continued to live in Rhodes throughout the Ottoman occupation and into that of the Italians after 1912. The remaining 1,700 Jews of Rhodes were rounded up by the German occupiers in 1944 with only 161 surviving the extermination camps.

Bernhard von Breydenbach wrote a guide for pilgrims to the Holy Land in 1486 – his *Peregrinatio in Terram Sanctam* was the world's first illustrated travel book.

He included a description of Rhodes and an account of its famous siege in what might be described as the first battlefield tourist guide. He added to his account a list of some of the relics in Rhodes including the heads of Saints Philomean, Eufemia and Polycarp as well as the hands of Saints Claire and Anne and finally portions of the arms of Saints, Stephen, George, Thomas, Katherine and Leodgard. Perhaps the strangest relic was one of the 30 pieces of silver paid to Judas for betraying Christ. The most important relic was the hand and arm of St John the Baptist, more of which later.

The Island of Rhodes

The island of Rhodes is the principal island of the Dodecanese and is exquisitely beautiful. The highest point is Mount Ataviros at about 4,000 feet. The hills and mountains are well wooded and watered, while the flatter land produced wheat as well as a fine crop of citrus fruits, figs and pomegranates. It could be both a haven and paradise. It has a delightful climate for most of the year, even though from June to August there is virtually no rainfall. From November to January, it is subject to hail, rain storms and frosts. The climate and the seasons would be an important factor for those besieging and those besieged. In the campaigning season the greatest problem would be the heat and shortage of potable winter. If the siege extended into winter, as it did in 1522, it would be the cold and mud that would make the lives of the besiegers miserable.

The only important town was the city of Rhodes although there were numerous villages and 17 small castles and watch-towers placed along the shore, but these had little chance of sustaining a prolonged siege once the capital was captured. The fortification on Lindos for example was virtually impregnable but it could not hope to withstand a prolonged siege without the hope of relief. The Order controlled eight smaller islands upon each of which a fortress had been constructed. On the Turkish coast itself they had acquired the Castle of St Peters in Budrun (Bodrum), the ancient town of Halicarnassus.

The Island is only seven miles from the Turkish coast at its closest point. It is 300 miles from Famagusta in Cyprus, 360 from Alexandria, 600 miles from Constantinople, and 1,400 from Marseilles. The nearest enemy port was 18 miles away at Marmaris, as little as only four hours sailing away. This short Ottoman supply line made it possible for the siege of 1522 to be prolonged, well after the end of the normal sailing season. It also meant that it was unnecessary to capture a safe anchorage, which was considered a necessity during the later siege of Malta, a factor which had a profound impact on the strategy and was one of the reasons for the failure of that siege. A well-handled vessel of the time could make about 100 to150 miles a day, although the greater the distance the greater the chance of ill-luck.

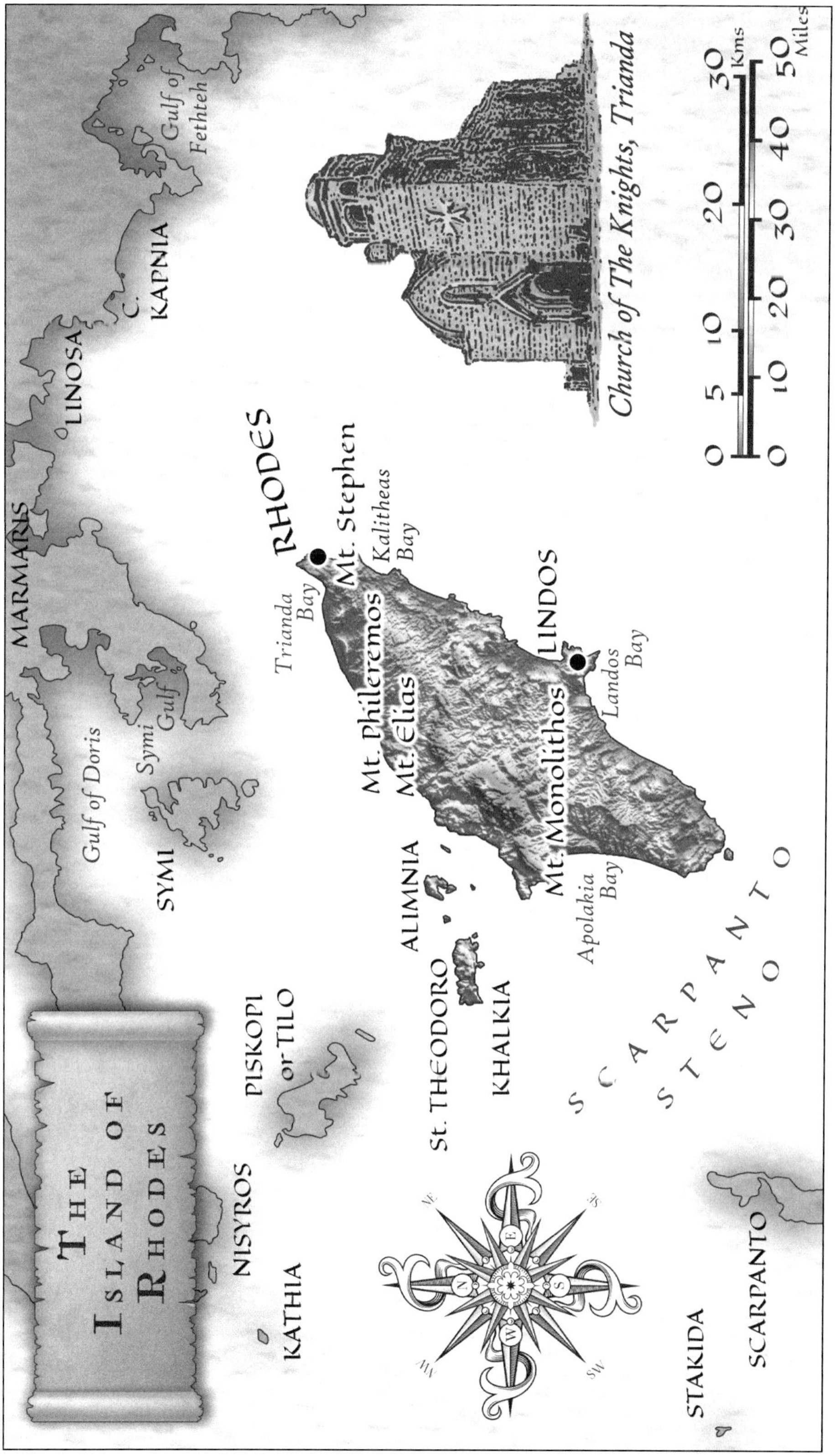
THE ISLAND OF RHODES
NISYROS
KATHIA
PISKOPI or TILO
SYMI
Gulf of Doris
Symi Gulf
MARMARIS
LINOSA
C. KAPNIA
Gulf of Fethteh
RHODES
Mt. Stephen
Kalitheas Bay
Trianda Bay
Mt. Phileremos
Mt. Elias
LINDOS
Landos Bay
Mt. Monolithos
Apolakia Bay
ALIMNIA
St. THEODORO
KHALKIA
SCARPANTO STENO
STAKIDA
SCARPANTO
Church of The Knights, Trianda
0 5 10 20 30 Kms
0 10 20 30 40 50 Miles
N E S W

The potential friends of the Order were a far greater distance away than their enemies. This did not stop individual vessels risking the Ottoman blockades and making their way safely into harbour, causing humiliation and frustration for the Ottoman admirals.

The local vessels would use wind and oar for propulsion. Large vessels from the West carrying goods and reinforcements tended to use their sails alone. Sailing vessels could only rely on a fair wind in July and August, when the Etesian winds blow from the North-West, stronger in the morning but declining in the evening. May and June produced light variable winds and for the rest of the year the island suffered from South-Easterly gales in January and February and North-Easterlies in November and December. These would make navigation in Rhodian waters dangerous, even for those well acquainted with the region. In the summer it was recommended to anchor off the South-East coast; in the winter it was best to look for a safe harbour. The prevailing winds and weather were important whether you were a Hospitaller hoping for reinforcement, or an enemy seeking to land and sustain a siege. Landing was possible at Trianda Bay which had a shingle beach and where there were fresh water streams to be found flowing from Mount Stephen. The South-East of the island has small bays and anchorages. The city of Rhodes lies north of the Bay of Acandia while the surrounding bays also allow landings, especially in the summer months.

Grand Master d'Aubusson and the Road to War

Although no portrait or detailed description of Grand Master Pierre d'Aubusson survives, this powerful character dominated the events surrounding the siege of 1480. In 1480 d'Aubusson was 57 years old, having been born in La Marche, the second son of Renaud, Lord of Monteil and Vicomte de La Marche and Lady Marguerite Chambon. The extensive lands the family controlled had been theirs for almost 500 years by the time Pierre was born. He was from an ancient house and was an inheritor of a chivalric tradition that still held sway in the hearts of many. Caoursin sums up the man well:

> Master Peter Daubusson: a man of high prudence and of the noble blood and house of France.[5]
>
> He receiv'd from nature together with a Noble Birth, a strong and proportionable body, fit for great undertakings; a quick wit, and vertuous inclinations.[6]

5 Guillaume Caoursin, *The Siege of Rhodes* (London: *c.*1482), unpaginated.

6 Dominique Bouhours, *The Life of the Renowned Peter D'Aubusson…* (London: Geo. Wells, 1679), p.2.

His upbringing and education were as one might expect, a preparation for service at Court and on the field of honour. He was brought up for a time in the household of Emperor Sigismund, although he served in his first campaign, against the intractable Swiss, on this occasion in the service of the French Dauphin in 1444. He later served under King Charles VII, who provided him with the recommendation that he needed to gain a place amongst the Knights at Rhodes. He was admitted to the Langue of Auvergne and was rapidly promoted to a Commandery of Salins in the Auvergne, a post in the personal gift of the Grand Master. He was the ideal choice to be sent to the West in 1454 by Grand Master de Lastic. He went to raise funds and increase the profile of the Order, as it prepared for what they considered the inevitable Ottoman onslaught. He also served at sea, commanding the Order's galleys in a combined effort with the Venetians to hold Euboea, which failed due to the craven desertion of his allies.

His service on land was also notable. He had fought in the defence of Cos in 1456 and the failed campaign on Cyprus in 1459. He also advised the building of Fort St Nicholas, with the Burgundian money, a decision which would later be seen to be decisive in the successful defence of the island. Under Grand Master Orsini he was promoted to Captain General of Rhodes and was thus responsible for the completion of its defences. His contribution was to build a stronger wall facing the seaward approach as well as the widening and deepening of the ditch surrounding the walls. When Orsini died, the election of d'Aubusson on 17 June 1476, was a formal recognition of the role that he had already played on the island for some years. D'Aubusson as Grand Master continued to strengthen the defences with three new towers and a massive wood and iron boom to defend the commercial harbour. In October he summoned all Hospitallers across Christendom to Rhodes in defence of the Order and in July 1477 called a General Chapter, to plan for the defence of the Island. In the years before the siege, he spent his time collecting stores and money from wherever the order possessed resources and credit.

Grand Master Pierre d'Aubusson, an imaginative engraving from Abbé Vertot's history of the Knights of St John. The French felt a strong association with the Crusades and the Latin States. Their control of Syria as a Mandated Territory after the First World War was accompanied by a massive archaeological programme. This was undertaken by the French authorities with the archaeologist Paul Deschamps, on what was seen as their Crusader heritage. Francis I of France, despite the Order's close association with his Kingdom, was not as one might expect distraught at the loss of Rhodes and was happy to seek the support of Suleiman in the continued conflict with The Empire. He began to seek support from Suleiman after 1525 and this was transformed into a long-lasting treaty in 1536. (Metropolitan Museum of Art, public domain)

In May 1480 d'Aubusson hired the services of Johannis Berger de Nördlingen, a mercenary gunner, to share his expertise concerning the future defences of the city. It was the extent and success of these preparations which would make the successful defence of the city possible. The powers in Christendom seemed to have been uninterested in the impending siege and did not look to send men or money, except for small sums sent by Louis XI and Pope Sixtus IV. D'Aubusson might well have addressed his 'band of brothers' as Henry V had and with greater justification:

> We few, we happy few, we band of brothers;
> For he today that sheds his blood with me
> Shall be my brothers

The Ottoman Foe

During d'Aubusson's career, relations with the Ottomans and perhaps surprisingly the Venetians had gone from bad to worse. The Ottomans having been refused tribute by successive Grand Masters, took to raiding the smaller islands under the Order's control. The Venetians, whose only loyalty was to their own self-interest, fell out with the Order over the issue of the succession to the throne of Cyprus that concluded with a Venetian raid on the island of Rhodes itself in 1462. In the face of Ottoman aggressiveness and without any real hope of support from the principal Western naval power in the region, the Order sought to protect its rear by reaching trade agreements with the Sultans of Egypt and Tunis.

If the Venetian Council of Ten were no friends to Rhodes the real foe was Mehmet II the Conqueror of Constantinople. In the light of his triumphs, it is surprising to note that his succession to the throne was not an easy one. His father Murad had abdicated in 1444 in favour of Mehmet who was then only 12 years old. Unsuited to power at such a young age, and childishly intent on war and conquest, his reign was suspended as Murad was forced to return until his death in 1451, when an older and wiser Mehmet succeeded. To ensure that there was no possible challenge, Mehmet had the young son of his father's widow drowned in his bath, at the same time as the child's mother offered him congratulations on his succession. Mehmet's principal objective was to conquer Constantinople, which was by now a capital without an empire, impoverished and with few friends in Catholic Christendom but some enemies. Its fall in 1453 was certainly a triumph but it was more a matter of toppling an ancient and unstable edifice than a great achievement of arms.

Mehmet II 'The Conqueror', saw Rhodes as a minor irritant rather than a serious threat to his already great conquest. He had defeated Hunyadi's Crusade, captured Constantinople, conquered Serbia, besieged Belgrade, conquered the Morea and Trebizond, forced the submission of Wallachia, conquered Anatolia and then engaged in a prolonged war with his principal Christian rival, Venice, from 1463 to 1479. Rhodes and its warrior knights were a paltry threat and not an important strategic or tactical objective. The Order was a potential irritant but an accommodation could be made if it ceased to interfere with Ottoman vessels and interests. Mehmet hoped that the Grand Master could somehow bring himself to present a tribute to him as recognition of Ottoman suzerainty, something which would have been quite impossible for the Order. Even so, in 1476 such a request was sent by Mehmet in the hands of Demetrios Sophianos a Greek collaborator. To win time d'Aubusson offered to send the request to the Holy Father in Rome for his opinion, knowing quite well what the answer would be.

Demetrios returned with Antonio Melagalo, a Rhodian of good family but of evil reputation. He presented an apparently well informed assessment of the weakness of the defences and divisions between the Langues, and also between the Order and the Rhodians. Caoursin provided a colourful picture of the foremost plotter of the Order's downfall:

> Antony Melagolo a man unkind to god & to man. He was noble of birth & evil of conditions & living the which by fore times thorough evil guiding & unthriftinesse [self-indulgence] had brought him self to poverty.[7]

These two were joined by George Frapan or 'Master George', a German engineer and artillerist, who provided technical advice for the venture. He was, according to Caoursin, '[a] renegade man of subtle wit that dwelled in Constantinople and there had wife & children. And known for his subtle wit & great cunning in making of such instruments of war.'[8] The final addition to the plotters was Misac Palaeologos Pasha, a very distant relative to the Byzantine royal family who added a touch of class to a polyglot plot. A vizier of the Sultan, he had accompanied the Ottoman Army on its conquests and had gained considerable military experience.

The Sultan's advisers were less sanguine about the prospects of conquest. Caoursin's account stressed disagreements in the Ottoman ranks as to the wisdom of attacking such a strongly defended island held by the illustrious Order. They were aware of the strengthened defences, the well-filled granaries, store rooms and magazines. They were also afraid that Christendom would rally to the Knights' aid and that the Sultan's eastern enemies would take the opportunity to unite against him. This report of Ottoman indecision might be Christian propaganda after the event, rather than a real account of the debate within the Ottoman ranks. The encouragement of the plotters led finally in 1479 to a series of exploratory raids along the coast of the island of Rhodes, led by Misac. Villages were burnt and the strength and resolve of the defenders tested. The Order was prepared, the villages were empty and their people and their food and animals were safe, unlike the raiders who were ambushed and repelled, fleeing first to the island of Tilos and then the safe nearby anchorage at Marmaris (then Physcos). The death of Melagolo was now reported with glee as a propitious prelude to the siege:

7 Guillaume Caoursin, *The Siege of Rhodes* (London: *c.*1482), unpaginated.
8 Guillaume Caoursin, *The Siege of Rhodes* (London: *c.*1482), unpaginated.

> His body was all over nothing but corruption; and besides the insupportable stench of his Corps, the Worms which eat him alive, rendered him a miserable spectacle to all the world; the sight of which was dreadful to behold. After he had endured the utmost extremities of Torment, and in vain implored relief from Heaven, he died blaspheming God, and cursing men, almost in view of Rhodes.[9]

9 Dominique Bouhours, *The Life of the Renowned Peter D'Aubusson…* (London: Geo. Wells, 1679), pp.127–128.

3

The Siege of 1480

As always it is impossible to rely upon contemporary accounts relating to numbers of combatants, which swell or dwindle according to the loyalties and purpose of the author. The Ottoman soldiers were assembled at Constantinople and then marched to Marmaris, while the stores and equipment, especially the weighty artillery pieces, travelled by sea. Misac sailed from Constantinople and was safely over-wintered in the anchorage at Marmaris where he waited for the arrival of the army that would conduct the siege. He conducted a series of unsuccessful landings against the castle at Fano and on the Island of Tilos.

Rumours that the objective was Mameluke Alexandria, or that the Sultan was dead and that troop movements were to ensure internal peace were widely disregarded by the Order. The operation was still arguably something of an afterthought by Mehmet. He was also involved in operations in the Otranto region of Italy, at Belgrade in the Lower Danube as well as on the Persian frontier. Any attempt of Ottoman dissimulation, as to the purpose of the expedition, was however useless in the face of a Rhodian intelligence gathering system that was certainly as good as that of the Ottomans. This was provided by a network of merchants travelling in the East, in return for trading rights granted by the Order and freedom from the depredations of the Knights' navy.

The main Turkish fleet first made its way from Constantinople to Marmaris to rendezvous with Misac's ships before descending on Rhodes, anchoring in the bay of Trianda, which provided a safe anchorage, an easy landing for troops and equipment as well as a supply of fresh water. The long-expected invasion fleet was first sighted from the top of Mount Stephen on 23 May. Grand Master d'Aubusson had already ordered the inhabitants of the countryside to take refuge in Lindos, Pharaklos, Monolithos, Niokastro (Kastellos) and Kattavia castles, while inhabitants of the islands of Nisyros, Chalki and Tilos took shelter in Rhodes town. The appearance of the Ottoman fleet was truly magnificent, enough even to make d'Aubusson now fear the consequences of facing the might of the Great Turk Mehmet.

As with all such operations the defenders were faced with the question whether they should 'fight them on the beaches' or retire within the walls.

The arrival of the Ottoman fleet from *De Casu Regis Zyzymy* (The Case of Sultan Djem) printed in Ulm by Ioannem Reger in William Caoursin's *Obsidionis Rhodiae Urbis Descriptio* 1496. As with the Spanish Armada of a century later the transport vessels of the Ottoman fleet were in the centre and the fighting vessels on the flanks protecting them in the crescent formation. The Order had only three fighting galleys available and these would have been swamped by enemy vessels if they had attempted to intervene. Their crews were of more value serving on the city's battlements rather than their ships' decks.

The Viscount of Monteil with more bravery than judgement led a mounted attack on the invaders, which achieved little other than the death of de Murat, a knight of the Auvergne Langue. This man was decapitated and his head was mounted on a spike but his brother knights recovered his body and on the orders of the Grand Master it was buried with full honours in the Order's principal church. The walls were manned and the Icon of Our Lady St Philermos brought out to the people to comfort them and stiffen their resolve.

The enemy land forces numbered, according to d'Aubusson, about 70,000 and outnumbered those of the Order by 30 to 1.[1] There were about 600 Knights and Servants-at-Arms and 1,500 mercenaries and militia in the garrison.[2] These were hardly enough to man walls that stretched some 2,460 yards around the city, excluding the numerous towers and gates. There had been a trickle of reinforcements, including d'Aubusson's nephew, Antoine Comte de Monteil, together with six other knights of note and worth and their retinues. Antoine, despite being married was appointed as Captain General of the city, more to raise morale than a change of command, which at all times lay with his uncle.

D'Aubusson had done well. The city walls were in the best state they had ever been and could have been, considering the resources available and the state of military engineering of the time. The land in front of the walls had been cleared of anything that could have provided cover or material for an enemy. The two churches of St Anthony and Notre Dame of Philerme were demolished,

1 Caoursin gives a figure of 100,000 and Master George on his defection provided a figure of 170,000. NB all figures given by contemporaries ought to be treated with distrust if not disdain.

2 Nicholson gives the figures as '250 warriors of the Hospital in Rhodes, with a militia of around 2,000 from the town and mercenaries, perhaps 3,500 defenders in all.' Helen Nicholson, *The Knights Hospitaller* (Boydell Press, 2001), p.61.

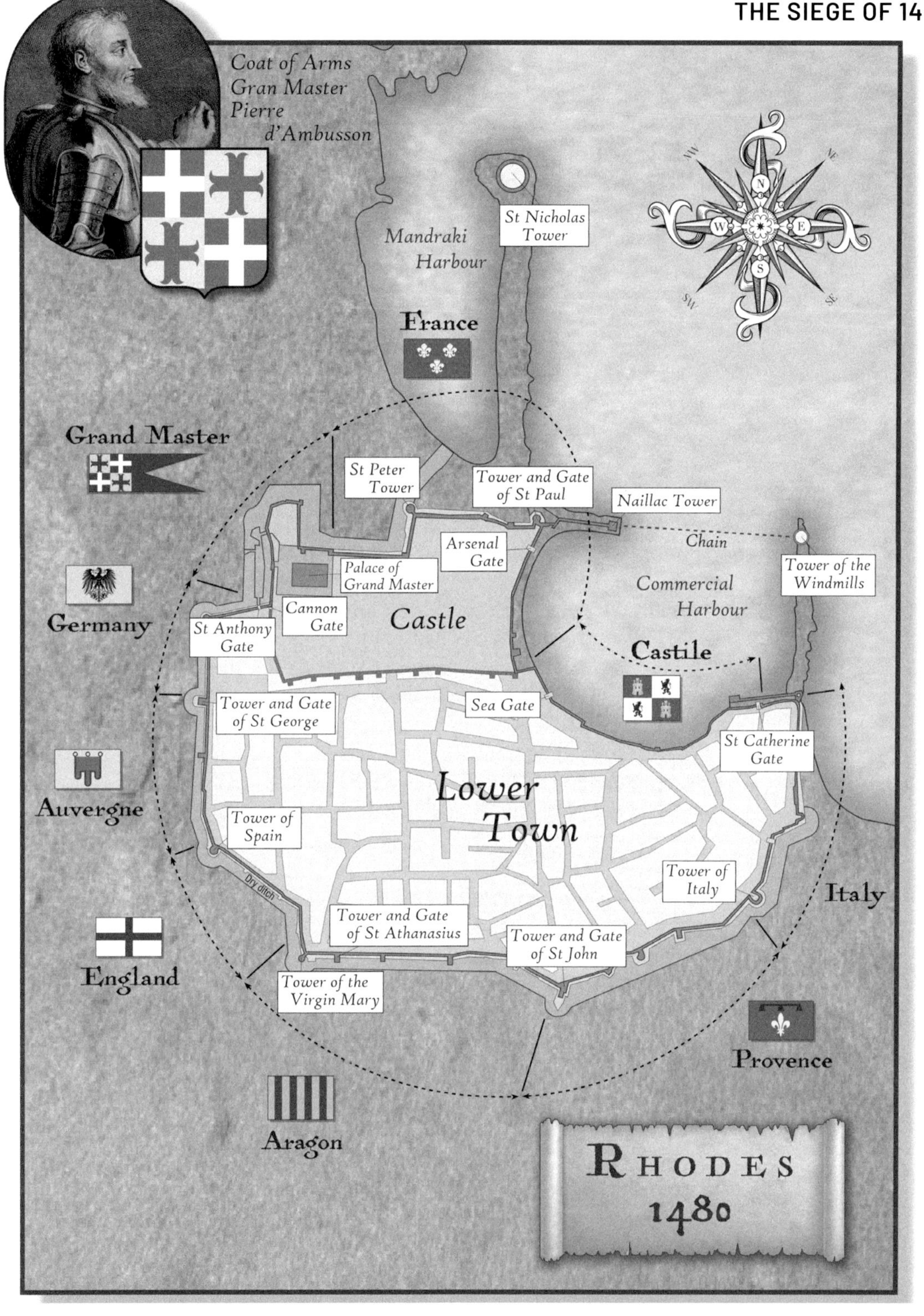

The defences were fairly well divided between the Langues. The French held three sectors (France, Provence and Auvergne) a recognition of the much larger number of French knights in the Order. It is clear that the defences were extensive but fundamentally late medieval in style, with little or no account made of the developments in artillery. The walls were tall and thin and the towers, sparse, square and unimposing. It must have looked a relatively easy task to capture it, from the perspective of the conqueror of Constantinople with its monumental Byzantine walls.

after of course the famous icon had been removed from the latter. There were two years of provisions in store and above all the Order was united under a leader whose qualities were universally recognised as outstanding. Father de Curti recorded the state of preparedness in the city, in a letter to his brother in Venice:

> The city is well provided with grain, wine, oil, cheeses, salted meat and other foodstuffs .... many crossbows and both heavy and light guns and earthenware firepots full of pitch lashed together .... and there is a continuous watch by day and night of select companies of crossbowmen and hand-gunners and one hundred cavalry.[3]

The Ottoman Army had by 24 May found itself comfortably settled on the slopes of Mount Saint Stephen, where Misac pitched his no doubt very large and very impressive red silk tent. The strategy he now proposed was to concentrate the Ottoman efforts against St Nicholas Tower, a plan originally suggested by a renegade Dutch engineer. If the tower was captured, the control of the mole gave access to the harbour which would permit an assault on the North wall at the St Paul Gate. D'Aubusson had realised the risk, which is why he had insisted on building the tower and re-fortifying the sea wall. The Turks were soon committed to an assault that would become in turns an ambush and then a massacre.

Against the Tower was placed a battery of 'three great bronze basilisks of an incredible size and power, capable of firing balls of nine palms (7ft) in circumference (26.74ft in diameter).'[4] A basilisk in the west was a term later applied to a very long-barrelled narrow-diameter piece shooting iron balls, but these guns must have been large diameter stone-firing bombards. The Ottoman basilisk, variously known as the *baciliska*, *bacaluçka*, *badaluçka*, and *badoluçka*, was of wrought iron and hooped construction. One basilisk that was sent to the Istanbul foundry for re-casting in the early 1520s weighed 11.34 tons, although the average weight of basilisks cast between 1522 and 1526 was 4,193 tons.[5] To counter this bombardment, the Order placed three of their own heavy pieces in the garden of the Palace of the Auvergne, able to bear on the flank of the enemy guns. Before the opening bombardment Misac began with the usual formalities. He called upon the Knights to surrender and offered the Greek civilian population honourable and even generous terms, if they were to surrender at once. D'Aubusson disdained to give a reply for the Order, and the Rhodians had no say in the matter.

3 Eric Brockman, *The Two Sieges* (London: John Murray, 1969), p.65.

4 Eric Brockman, *The Two Sieges* (London: John Murray, 1969), p.67; Pauli, quoting Freher, *Rerum Germanicarum Scriptores* Vol.II, p.158

5 Gábor Ágoston., 'Ottoman artillery and European Military Technology in the Fifteenth and Seventeenth centuries', *Acta Orientalia Academiae Scientiarum Hungaricae*, 1994, Vol. 47, No.1/2, p.38.

The bombardment, although concentrating on St Nicholas, struck across the city. Misac sought by damaging the civilian houses as well as the fortifications, to sway opinion in favour of surrender. To the normal stone projectiles were added fireballs and incendiary arrows and bolts. The effect of the bombardment was to seriously damage the walls and towers as well as flattening the Grand Master's Palace. The discursive Father de Curti wrote that: 'the ground trembled under his feet .... no one from any nation had ever before seen such cannon .... Had you been here, you would certainly have taken refuge in a cave.'[6]

After about 10 days the bombardment of St Nicholas finally achieved its objective, with each of the three bombards having fired at an impressive rate of 14 rounds a day.[7] The fine-looking tower was reduced to a highly defensible pile of rubble. The tower was manned by a determined garrison led by Fabrizio del Carretto, a man who would clearly go far in the Order, if he survived the siege. Not only was the Tower still held strongly but the mole itself had been turned into parts of the defences, with ditches dug and palisades added. In addition to the defences above the waterline, the seaward defences had been provided with stakes driven into the seabed, which would make the approach of even shallow draught boats difficult. This work was achieved by using not only slaves and soldiers but the citizenry, including the women, whose many roles during a siege are often neglected.

28 May was a red-letter day in the life of the garrison. This was when a message was sent by d'Aubusson ostensibly just to the Knights of the Order beyond Rhodes but in practice to the whole of Christendom. It summarised the events leading up to the siege, and then enumerated the scale of the Ottoman effort with its 109 ships and its 'great many cannon, bombards and wooden towers.' He lauded his own men and denounced his enemies for:

> We are no effeminate Asiatics. Their [Knights of the Order] fidelity is proved and we have abundant cannon and bombards and good store of munitions and victuals. We will continue to confront the enemy while we await the aid of our Brethren. Above all we are sustained by our loyalty to the Holy Religion.[8]

He hoped for reinforcements, which would be aided by the westerly winds in the 'summer and Autumn.' He was also highly critical of those who had not yet brought help to the Order:

6 Eric Brockman., *The Two Sieges* (London: John Murray, 1969), pp.67–68.

7 An impressive rate of fire considering the expected rate was less than half of this.

8 Eric Brockman, *The Two Sieges* (London: John Murray, 1969), p.71.

> We have implored your help. In answering our pleas some have proved more obdurate and more idle than we could have believed possible. We have warned you. We have sought your aid. We have been answered with words .... You would not heed our warnings. Now believe the facts...[9]

It was still not too late for the laggards to redeem themselves, 'Not one of you may excuse himself. Not the aged or the inform, nor the poor .... much less the young, the robust or the rich.'[10] It is doubtful whether he really hoped for a massive response from the Order. It was certainly a clear statement that he intended to remain and fight, come what may. Some aid did arrive: on 1 June a carrack loaded with grain and carrying some more volunteers broke the clearly inadequate Turkish blockade and entered the port of Rhodes. It would make little difference to the course of the siege but it was important for the morale of the defenders and was a public rebuke to the careless besiegers.

The second event on 28 May, that took place before the Tower of St Peter, was the defection of Master George, the chief gunner of the Ottoman Army and one of the promulgators of the siege. He claimed that he was driven to join his co-religionists out of sympathy with their faith and perilous position and because he was in bad favour with Misac as his artillery had failed to perform 'as advertised.' His arrival was recorded by Caoursin in some detail. Caoursin was the Vice-Chancellor of the Order in Rhodes and his account must be considered as an authoritative, if official, document:[11]

> George the great gunner of the which we have said afore: came soddenly as amazed man [in a distraught state of mind] to the ditch of toward the palace of the Lord master and saluted and greeted the Rhodians friendly and meekly [he] cried and prayed that he might come in to the city and so he was received. And because that he had the raiment and livery of the Turk some smote at him. But many defended him and brought him unto the Lord master of Rhodes. This George was a personable man and welbesene [well-be-seen, impressive]: of great eloquence and of great malice a German man borne.[12]

He received a very guarded welcome but the military intelligence that he provided voluntarily was apparently well informed:

9 Eric Brockman, *The Two Sieges* (London: John Murray, 1969), p.72.
10 Eric Brockman, *The Two Sieges* (London: John Murray, 1969), p.72.
11 *Obsidionis Rhodiæ Urbis Descriptio* (Description of the Siege of the City of Rhodes)
12 Guillaume Caoursin, *The Siege of Rhodes* (London: *c.*1482), unpaginated.

> …& as it seemed with truth answered to the questions and said that the turk had the number of an hundred thousand fighting men and xvi. great bombardes every each one of xxii. foot of length of the which the least casted stones every stone of ix. spans in compass about.[13]

The Abbé Vertot in his account of Master George's speech to the Master spoke of 16 great 'basilisks' cast specifically for the siege, each 18 feet long and shooting balls two to three feet in diameter. "You will feel immediately, said he, the fury of those infernal machines, against which you cannot take your precautions too soon."[14]

Was Master George a 'plant' by the Ottomans? It is difficult to fathom why Misac would have sent one of his most important commanders into the enemy camp at this point in the siege. The information he provided about the Turkish strength was discouraging but unlikely to sway the defenders, especially as it was so early in the siege. What added to the confusion were messages, shot into Rhodes ostensibly by 'friends' to the Christians, that George was in fact a traitor. Master George was provided with a 'guard' of six knights, who were to ensure that he showed no signs of disloyalty. The Grand Master meanwhile sent a visible message to the Turks of his determination and disdain for his foe. He set to inspecting the Tower of St Nicholas from his own ceremonial galley and then by riding his white charger up and down the Mole, all the time dressed in his best gilded armour. This 'foolish' action did much to raise the morale of the defenders who saw that their leader did not fear the enemy and that neither should they.

Misac's siege was not progressing well. The bombardment of St Nicholas in particular had not achieved the result he had hoped for. The Tower and the Mole needed to be taken by an assault from the sea. Unfortunately, no precise date can be given for the attack as the sources either disagree with one another, or fail to give a date, and the use of different calendars at the time hardly helps provide a detailed chronology, although the order of events is clear. After a bombardment of 10 days an assault force set sail from Trianda. Several triremes had been modified by the removal of their sails and other extraneous equipment and provided with gangplanks over the bows from which to land their contingent of *sipahis*.[15] The bow and gunwales were also reinforced to absorb some of the inevitable arrows from bow and crossbow, and shot that the defenders would pour into them. The artillery on the tower itself was in no state to put up a strong defence, but

13 Guillaume Caoursin, *The Siege of Rhodes* (London: *c.*1482), unpaginated.

14 Vertot, Abbé René-Aubert., *The History of the Knights Hospitallers of St. John of Jerusalem*: (Dublin: J Christie, 1818), page unnumbered

15 These were not classical triremes with three ranks of oars but vessels with three men sitting on one bench, each pulled their own oar with a single bank of oars on both sides of the hull.

De Casu Regis Zyzymy (The Case of Sultan Djem) printed in Ulm by Joannem Reger in William Caoursin's Obsidionis Rhodiae Urbis Descriptio 1496.
This is a vivid depiction of the heavy fighting that took place in an attempt to capture the Tower of St Nicholas. Both sides displayed bravery of the highest order but the fighting itself was brutal, with no one expecting or giving quarter.

those guns in the Post of France could provide flanking fire on anyone attempting to land on the mole.

In an attempt to cow the defenders, the assault was made with all the ceremony and noise that an Ottoman Army could muster. This hardly helped them against the recently built defences. In addition to what was visible, there were 'tabelles [planks] full of nails' submerged on the seabed as a form of submarine caltrop.[16] There were also fireships of the Order filled with incendiary materials ready to be used to break up the Ottoman force. The landing barges proved inadequate and attempts to leap into the sea proved fatal for men weighed down with armour. Those few who made it to the shore were easily dispatched by the defenders. The explosion and destruction of one of the galleys then led to a general retreat. This was the first of three attempts on that day.

Caoursin reported the events in some detail but the numbers that he gives are as always somewhat suspect, although the gist of what happened, an Ottoman disaster, is clear.

> The turkes came with fifty galleys .... and they thought shortly to come a land and there they made a great cry and a great noise with trompes and taberettys [drums] & other such instruments because that they should make afeared our folk of them for their great noise. But anon after when the turks with their galleys came near the tower aforesaid: the bombards and other instruments of war which were there [employed] break with great might the arrays of the turks and put them off from the coast [drove

16 Guillaume Caoursin, *The Siege of Rhodes* (London: *c.*1482), unpaginated.

> them away] with their great mischief. And in this deed the Lord Mayster of Rhodes hym selfe came out of the walls of the said tower with his company: for to fight hand for hand with the turkes. And there were overthrown and put to death vii hundred turkes and many were wounded and many drowned.[17]

The failure of the attack and the resilience of the defenders led Misac to develop another front, this time against the posts of Italy, Provence and England, which concentrated on what had been the Jewish Quarter of the city. The principal siege battery of eight bombards was set against the curtain wall and Tower of Italy. Another bombard was set against the Tower of St Angelo and the windmills of the commercial port. The windmills were rapidly reduced to rubble, which would add to the labour of the women of Rhodes who would be dependent upon hand querns to grind their corn. What were really only medieval city walls would succumb readily to the fire from these bombards. D'Aubusson recognised the inevitable creation of a sizeable breach by preparing a second line of defence. He used the civilian population as well as those soldiers not needed for immediate defence and tore down the building on the other side of the wall, including the synagogue, and created a clear field of fire.[18] Behind this was constructed a strong rampart and palisade from which to slaughter the enemy's assault troops in what was now a 'killing ground.'

Caoursin reported the operation which was a testimony to the spirit of the defenders and the sagacity of their leader.

> Also were there made within the city of Rhodes great and mighty ditches: for the saving of the body of the city if the Turks gained the first walls and therefore they [the Rhodians] made day and [night?, although this word is not present in the original] mighty great works as walls of timber and many other things defensible to the which labour every creature in Rhodes of all manner of age both men and women of all manner [and] states put and applied them selves and their goods with great will and great devotion for Jesus sake. And in this while the bombards and great guns of the turks casted down and destroyed the walls of the city of Rhodes with so great mighty and strength and with so great wonder: that all they that were in Rhodes strangers and other olde and young of all the countries of Christendom said that they heard never strokes of bombardes so great and so horrible as these were.[19]

17 Guillaume Caoursin, *The Siege of Rhodes* (London: *c.*1482), unpaginated.

18 D'Aubusson had the synagogue rebuilt after the siege a rare and remarkable example of generosity towards the otherwise despised and persecuted Jewish population.

19 Guillaume Caoursin, *The Siege of Rhodes* (London: *c.*1482), unpaginated.

The weapons that were particularly feared, were those which with their high trajectory could bring down death throughout the city, making even the strongest outer defences irrelevant. It has been thought that these were gunpowder weapons known as bombard-mortars. The Grand Master wisely advised the people to find sanctuary in caves and beneath arches. The description by Caoursin would suggest that they were not mortars but were in fact trebuchets which he refers to as 'slynges'.

> The turks vexed also the Rhodians with many other and diverse instruments of war for they ordained rond above [round about] the foresaid city of Rhodes certain instruments of war the which been called Slynges or Engynes. And the turks with such instruments of war casted in to the air a pype [barrel] full of great stones the which fell upon the houses of Rhodes and putted them in a wretched ruin, with great murder of them of that were within for that time:
>
> The turks not understanding howe god journeyed [God worked] & kept the Rhodians free of harm ordained two grete slynges in a high place toward the west: from the which they might see all the city of Rhodes and from thence they cast great stones in the middle of the city.[20]

Later when he refers to the trebuchet constructed by the defenders, Caoursin mentions an 'engyne called Trebuke lyke a slynge.' Clearly the 'slynge' used by the Ottomans was a form of trebuchet. One feature of the trebuchet that is apparent to anyone who has seen and used one, is the vital importance of the sling in accelerating the projectile. Caoursin also refers to a 'pype' being 'cast' or thrown, whereas he refers to the 'fyre of the bombardes.' A mortar could not be used to fire large casks from its narrow barrel, whereas this was relatively easy for the sling of a trebuchet.

The Tower of Italy was now closely assailed and a siege battery brought forward and protected by earth and wood ramparts to negate counter-battery fire. In response the Grand Master organised a sortie of 50 young men led by a knight, who used scaling ladders to climb the steep side of the moat to enter the battery, where they killed those present, destroyed what they could and cast the guns into the ditch. This sally would have little effect upon the siege but was a boost to the defenders' morale and another blow to that of Misac and his men.

If little progress was being made against the walls of Rhodes, the Ottoman commander hoped that the next assault on the Tower of St Nicholas would succeed. The preparations were meticulous and a testimony to the genius of the Turkish engineers. A tall wooden tower was constructed to provide covering fire against those in the Tower of St Nicholas. At the same time a

20 Guillaume Caoursin, *The Siege of Rhodes* (London: *c.*1482), unpaginated.

floating bridge was being prepared that would allow a large force to cross the harbour. Caoursin provided a detailed description of the events:

> The turks also made a long bridge of the length of a quarter of a mile. the which reached from the bank [where] the turkes laye: vnto the banke of saint Nicholas tower. and was so large: that six men on horseback might ride a front [abreast]. and was made with voyded pypes [empty barrels] and with planks strongly nailed upon them. & purposed to being the same bridge by craft into the water. and they fastened and knotted strongly to the said bridge great and mighty ropes which had in the other end strong anchors: which anchors they fasted with a bote [boat] to the nether bank of the tower so that the bridge with the drawing of the cord and floating should have reached to the said bank.[21]

The plan was simple and audacious. With anchors having been dropped on the tower bank the pontoon bridge could be drawn across the harbour up to the base of the tower using ropes and pulleys.

All would have been well, but on the night of 17 June, when the anchors were being laid near the tower, an English sailor Roger Jervis heard the operation taking place. After the boat had left, he swam over the point where the anchor had been laid, dived down and cut the cable. For this great service he was awarded by d'Aubusson with a bag containing, according to legend, several hundred gold ducats. This generous act to a lowly sailor would have been recognised as an act of 'good lordship,' important in maintaining the morale of the defenders and the reputation of the Grand Master for liberality. The sailor's achievement did not delay the Ottoman attack, as they were probably unaware of his action.

A fleet of 30 galleys, large store ships and small craft now approached the Tower, this time silently, in the hope of achieving a surprise which had, of course, long been lost. Recognising that the bridge could not be drawn across the harbour, small boats would be used to push and pull it. Half of the galleys approached on the seaward side with the remainder inside the harbour. The bridge was manoeuvred across the harbour up to the tower loaded with Janissaries. The craft and the bridge landed before the defenders opened fire from the Post of France and the Grand Master's Palace. The defenders of the Tower could not be reinforced by a large detachment from what was already a diminished garrison, but d'Aubusson and his nephew Antoine with a small number of knights, came to the aid of del Carretto. The floating bridge was soon struck by artillery fire, many were drowned as they fell from the bridge and those left on the mole were unable to be reinforced or retreat. The Turks suffered from a rain of:

21 Guillaume Caoursin, *The Siege of Rhodes* (London: *c.*1482), unpaginated.

> great stones of bombardes and of gonnes & wild fire and arrows of bows and crossbows.'[22]

The fighting was bitter but the defeat of the assault forces was inevitable.

> And so all the night from twelve the clock to x. in the day they fought all by dark: but as the fire of the bombardes and the flames of the wildfire gave light. And so after that the turkes were put out [driven off]: with their great damage and harm. & that the men of Rhodes had the victory: a man might have seen three days following, dead men of the turks party casted and lying in the bank of the sea toward Rhodes. Which [dead] were found arrayed with gold and silver, precious clothing and part of their array [equipment] was seen floating in the sea.[23]

The Tower was not only defended by the Knights but a supernatural ally as well.

> With the coming of full daylight fugitives from the enemy camp who had been allowed to enter the city of Rhodes declared in public that from their camp two mounted horsemen had been seen rampaging wildly on the highest part of the tower and with fierce zeal forcing the enemy line to scatter. Moreover, some of the Turks told of how they had seen a certain lady, of conspicuous gravity of manner, on the edge of that very tower which we have already mentioned, and that she had been urging the Christian troops on to the fight. The Turks were extraordinarily terrified and impressed by the sheer novelty [newness] of this vision, knowing very well as they did that neither mounted men nor any woman had been present in the tower.[24]

Because of this humiliating disaster the 'Great Turk' retired to his, no doubt magnificent, tent for three days and refused to see anyone, this hardly helped the progress of the siege or the morale of his men. The losses had been great, Caoursin numbered them at 3,500 and this could possibly have been the case. The siege was not over, although further assaults on St Nicholas were now abandoned.

> And so after that the turks saw: that they could not win the tower by strength and might anon they turned their fantasy and studied

22 Guillaume Caoursin, *The Siege of Rhodes* (London: *c.*1482), unpaginated.
23 Guillaume Caoursin, *The Siege of Rhodes* (London: *c.*1482), unpaginated.
24 Michael Herzfeld, 'New Light on the 1480 Siege of Rhodes', *The British Museum Quarterly*, Autumn 1972, vol. 36, no.3/4), p.69.

> with all their virtue and might to assault the city and in especially they made great assault against the walls that were kept by the Jews: and also against the walls that the nation of Italy kept and defended.

The Turks now approached the city walls with greater care, digging and then camouflaging their trenches, from which they carried on continuous and accurate fire on the walls of Rhodes. It was reported that no man dared look out of the walls of the city. The besiegers filled the ditch with stones and timber, so that they could easily enter the breaches that the heavy artillery was creating. As d'Aubusson recounted, the defenders as well as reinforcing the defences around the breach;

> secretly made for ourselves an exit beneath the stones, and in secret brought them into the town. The Turks nearest the moat thought that the heap of stones had diminished and that their opportunity for an attack was lessening, unless they rapidly carried it out.'[25]

A vivid depiction of the attack on St Nicholas. The barrels used for the pontoon are in evidence and the depiction of the camp and artillery batteries an interesting addition. The confusion and slaughter that took place is well presented with the Order, as always, stalwart and triumphant. *De Casu Regis Zyzymy* (The Case of Sultan Djem) printed in Ulm by Ioannem Reger in William Caoursin's *Obsidionis Rhodiae Urbis Descriptio* 1496

Behind the breach the defenders had dug a semi-circular ditch atop of which were two more lines of defences constructed from rubble, soil, wood and no doubt some of the 3,500 stones 'pilfered' from the Turks. Caoursin described these defences and the confidence that they gave to the defenders:

25 Robert Smith & Kelly De Vries, *Rhodes Besieged – A New History* (Cheltenham: The History Press, 2011), p.58.

> within the walls not far from the ditch made a front of a wall with stakes and earth in the midst and with brushwood thrust strongly together and tempered it with water like as they make a mudwall: and upon this wall they put guns, culverin and wildfire full of pitch & sulfur and great heaps of stones & such things: that should let the turks to climb up so that it was a pleasure to see their besynes [business] again the beginning of the turks assault.[26]

Behind this, great stores of incendiary material including fire pots and hoops were prepared.

If up to this point the preparations made by the defenders had been conventional their next construction was a nod to the past. The field of fire from the walls and towers was not extensive and could not readily interfere with the Ottoman camp, consequently instructions were made to construct a trebuchet. D'Aubusson was fortunate in having available Juan Aniboa, a Basque sailor, who had garnered and retained knowledge of such things.[27] There is of course considerable crossover between ships and trebuchets in terms of technology and operation. *The Tribute*, as the machine was called, proved invaluable in bombarding the Turkish defences. Caoursin in his account provided a different designer for the machine but described its successful operation in some detail.

Although the trebuchet had long been out of use in the West it continued to appear in the increasing numbers of illustrated 'war books' of the late fifteenth and even early sixteenth centuries. This example by Phillip Mönch from *Kriegsbuch*, published in 1496, shows a fairly workmanlike example. The technology used for contemporary cranes was very similar to that needed for a trebuchet. The key to the success of such a machine was an understanding of the simple system of proportions that underlay them, the relationship between the length of sling and the length of the arm for example. (Universitätsbibliothek Heidelberg, Cod. Pal. germ. 126, p.73. Courtesy of the University of Heidelberg)

> And so anon after a man of Greece wise and expert in sieges counselled the lord master and the Rhodians to make and ordain an engine called Trebuke like a slynge which was great high & mighty and cast great and many stones into the host of the turks. and so by this meanes the turks were in great fear & [?] for their lodges and tents were broken and smitten to ground: with much & great damage and hurt to their guns, bombards, serpentines and all their ordonnance of war: so that in few days they received these hurts and damages without number.[28]

26 Guillaume Caoursin, *The Siege of Rhodes* (London: *c.*1482), unpaginated.

27 The name and origin of the engineer vary from source to source

28 Guillaume Caoursin, *The Siege of Rhodes* (London: *c.*1482), unpaginated – italicised words as in the text.

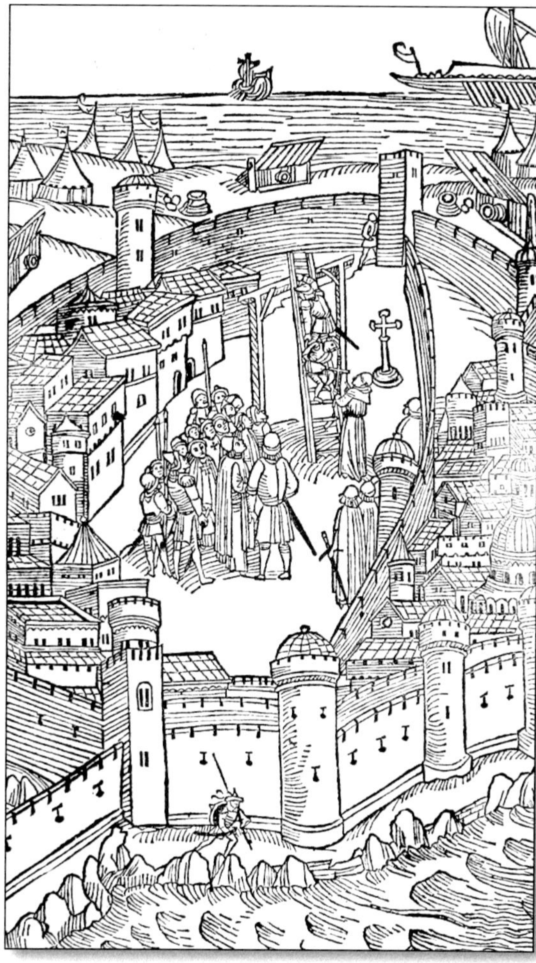

The execution was a gruesome business and in the contemporary illuminated image in Caoursin's work, the Order and especially d'Aubusson are notable for their absence. It would clearly have been a popular move with many who had always distrusted this Christian traitor. The second siege would produce another popular victim to understandable Rhodian paranoia. *De Caeu Regis Zyzymy* (The Case of Sultan Djem) printed in Ulm by Ioannem Reger in William Caoursin's *Obsidionis Rhodiae Urbis Descriptio* 1496 Fol

The presence of Master George had always been a source of disquiet. With the defenders now facing what would certainly be the decisive days of the siege they sought to resolve the conundrum of whether he was a traitor to the Turk or to the Order. He was accused of bad advice and bad faith. It was said that he had repositioned some of the batteries and that the guns he had personally laid had missed. One might have assumed that to protect himself from such an accusation he would have done his best to hit. He was arrested and questioned but gave a good account of himself, which further enraged those who sought his death. He was put to the torture and unsurprisingly confessed his many past and present treacheries and was hanged before an enthusiastic crowd.

> …and anon after every man of Rhodes returned again to keep their place with great gladness that George the false traitor of Christ's faith and he that had studied to put to death so many noble and worshipful knights: and to de-foul and ravish so many and honest women and holy virgins had at last found [an end] according to his treasons and mischievous deeds.[29]

His 'trial' and execution could be justified on the grounds that his presence remained a source of disquiet and that his death was a propaganda victory for the Order with the Rhodians. Meanwhile Misac had launched a 'charm offensive' with the citizens of the city offering them protection for their lands and goods, if they abandoned the Order to its fate. If they did not, they would share it.

The bombardment which had been regular over the past five weeks but not as yet overwhelming, reached a crescendo on 27 July, when some 300 rounds were fired preparatory to the final assault. The bellowing of guns was accompanied by the outlandish sounds of the Ottoman military bands as well as the trumpets and drums of the Order and the Rhodian defenders. It was also announced in numerous messages, shot over the battlements, that Misac had raised the black banner and that there would be no mercy shown, especially to the knights who might

29 Guillaume Caoursin, *The Siege of Rhodes* (London: c.1482), unpaginated.

expect a grisly death by impalement. It is difficult to imagine a greater encouragement to resist the impending assault. Caoursin reported with some glee the possible fate of the garrison and population:

> They that were above ten years unto twenty should have their throats cut: and all that were above that age if they were taken alive should be pierced through the fundament and through the head with a long stake. Wherefore they bore with them to the assault eight thousand stakes.[30]

After all the brouhaha, a single shot signalled the beginning of the assault at dawn on 28 July. The defenders on the walls, or rather what was left of them, were overwhelmed in the initial charge. The irregular troops clearly surprised the defenders and using ropes and grapnels captured the Tower of Italy, raising their standard above it. The intention of the Janissaries who now spearheaded the attack after the first rush, was to outflank the crescent-shaped defences of the defenders by taking the wall and infiltrating the city and taking its defenders in the rear. According to d'Aubusson 2,000 Turks had gained the walls before he organised and led the counter-attack. A further 2,000 of the enemy filled the breach and were ready to exploit any break in the defences. About 300 Turks had infiltrated the Jewish Quarter where they were met with the usual ferocity and hunted down without mercy.

Mary Dupuis records the role of the Grand Master, one he was too modest to declare himself.[31] D'Aubusson had earlier received an arrow wound in the thigh which had not healed but he still insisted on leading the counter-attack:

> The said Grand Master, who was not far away [from the Turkish assault], accompanied by many knights and other soldiers, came to one of the stairs and was the first to climb. With great courage and marvellous feats of arms he climbed to the top; but in climbing he received great and awful blows, but he gave as well as he got. And he was thrown down two or three times from the stairs [up to the wall] to the ground. But he was valiantly aided and helped by the other knights who were with him, all of whom carried themselves so well and valiantly that by force and in spite of all the Turks they climbed onto the walls, and there the Grand Master was wounded in two places.[32]

---

30 Guillaume Caoursin, *The Siege of Rhodes* (London: *c.*1482), unpaginated. (edited edition, with illustrations, 1496)

31 Dupuy or Dupuis is a French late fifteenth century account of the siege (Paris. Bibliotheque Nationale, Dupuy 255)

32 Robert D. Smith & Kelly De Vries, *Rhodes Besieged – A New History*, (Cheltenham: The History Press, 2011), p.59.

D'Aubusson had received a near fatal wound, with a thrust through his armour puncturing his right lung. This forced him to finally withdraw and seek aid but only after the attack had been repulsed.

Once the Tower of Italy had been reclaimed and the wall occupied by the defenders, many of the Turks in the breach, closely packed and without the ability to either advance or retreat or even to use their weapons, were slaughtered. Those Turks who could, turned about and fought their way back through their own side, in a desperate attempt to escape a merciless end. The defenders led by Antoine d'Aubusson together with Fabrizio del Carretto and the Admiral, Piozzasco, and as many of the knights as were still able to fight, pursued a fleeing and panicked foe. The chase took them not only into the trenches of the besiegers but into their camp. The silver and gold standard of the Sultan was captured, and the Turkish army was clearly utterly defeated.

Turkish casualties may have been the 4,000 claimed and there were certainly so many that their bodies had to be burnt, as burial would have been impracticable. Without reliable figures, Christian authors recorded up to 24,000 killed and wounded, it is probable that the Great Turk lost a sizeable proportion of his fighting strength. The Turks were unable to continue the siege, let alone mount another assault. Casualties amongst the defenders were also heavy but as always only those of high status were recorded. It was reported that 10 knights were killed in the fighting in the Jewish Quarter alone. The English Langue suffered seven killed and one seriously wounded leaving only four men able to fight but all wounded. The deaths of 231 knights were recorded, which was almost half their fighting strength; it is unlikely that the losses in the lesser ranks were

A woodcut of the key moment in the siege, not the arrival of d'Aubusson to save the day, (indicated by the presence of his banner) but the miraculous appearance of the Virgin Mary, St John and a heavenly host, which was widely reported and believed at the time. The conditions of close quarter battle are well illustrated here with only a few at the very front actually able to use their weapons, while the remainder push forward, encouraging those in the fight. Note also the early depiction of a mortar, as well as an artillery piece provided with a swinging mantlet that could be raised and lowered in front of the piece. *De Casu Regis Zyzymy* (The Case of Sultan Djem) printed in Ulm by Ioannem Reger in William Caoursin's *Obsidionis Rhodiae Urbis Descriptio* 1496, fol 51r proportionately fewer as their armour was probably less comprehensive while the risks they took were the same.

Neither side were able to conduct offensive operations and the Autumn storms had started earlier than usual, adding to Ottoman insecurity. The Turks were allowed 10 days in which to depart, embarking with their wounded and even it seems their artillery. It was recorded that the stakes meant for impaling and the ropes for tying prisoners were left behind, although this may have well have been Christian propaganda. As the Turks departed, on cue and in best Hollywood style, a carrack and a brigantine arrived flying the flags of Pope Sixtus IV and King Ferdinand of Naples. The Turks assuming that they were the precursors of the nonexistent relief armada attacked them and for a while it looked as if the brigantine would be taken but both eventually reached safety.

Misac was quite rightly blamed for the humiliating disaster and was condemned to death by the Sultan. This was not carried out as good news had reached Mehmet of the conquest of Otranto. The humiliated commander was sent to Gallipoli in disgrace but eventually wheedled his way back into royal favour and was sent by Sultan Selim the Grim to govern Egypt. Mehmet planned another assault on Rhodes, this time directly under his command but his death in May 1481 and the subsequent chaos meant that the Order had 40 years to prepare for the next assault. D'Aubusson survived what was thought to be a fatal wound and became perhaps the last great hero of an undivided Christendom. The Order gained massively in reputation and resources for its heroic efforts against what was increasingly perceived as a great threat to the whole of Christendom.

Why Were the Ottomans Defeated?

The answer that the Order and all Christians would have given was that it was the Will of God. *Deus lo Volt* (God wills it) had been the cry of the crusaders at Jerusalem in 1099 and it was God who it was thought gave them victory on that occasion. The Rhodians and the Order were sustained by their faith, which was central to the struggle. The public display of images and collective acts of worship led by the Order constantly reinforced the will of the defenders. There was even a moment when divine intervention saved the day, after the Tower of Italy was taken. Caoursin recorded what had happened to turn the tide:

> But who let them then to come down from the walls to the city: afore that the Rhodians climbed with ladders to fight with them & drive them from the walls: Certainly it was none other but God. Who was he that blinded their wit so that anon after the first assault they ordained not an other against our Christian men: which by the first assault had been piteously hurt & wounded & were all weary of fighting. it was none other but God. Who was cause of the death

> of so many of them in the space of two hours in the great & the last assault: but God & his angels that were seen in the bright air.[33]

There were several reports of divine intervention in the conflict including the battle for the Tower of St Nicholas. The most impressive sighting, apparently also reported by 'Turks' as well as by Christians took place during the height of the fighting on 28 May.

> And anon after the turks saw properly in the midst of the clean and bright air a cross all of shining gold: & also saw a bright virgin: which had in her hand against the host of the turks a spear and shield: and in that sight also appeared a man clothed in poor and vile aray: which was accompanyed with great number of fair and well-be-seen men in arms: as if they would have come down to the help of Rhodes. By the crosse of gold we may justly understand our saviour Jesus Christ. And by the virgin we may understand our lady the blessed Mary. And by the man poorly clothed we may understand the holy Saint John Baptist Patron and [?] of the order of Rhodes: which was accompanied with saints and angels of God for to help the Rhodians.[34]

If for the Christians this was a religious conflict, for the Turks it was not so vital an issue. Although their battle cry may have been *Mahumete* in response to the Rhodians *Ihesu Cryste*, many of the besieging army would have been Christians, as they had been recruited from Christian territory occupied by the Turks. The removal of the Order from the island was not a religious imperative, Rhodes had no religious significance for Moslems.

There were many reasons why the Order was successful, not least that they had been expecting and preparing for the siege for almost 40 years. The defences of the city had been completely rebuilt and the storehouses filled, so that they could feel confident about surviving a prolonged siege. What they were not prepared for was the full force of the Ottoman artillery, which could rapidly reduce and destroy the medieval fortifications that had been constructed at such expense and with such effort. The prolonged attack on the Mole and Tower of St Nicholas diverted effort, wasted time and badly affected Turkish morale. The Hospitaller preparation to receive the final assault was impeccable but could still have resulted in defeat if they had been outflanked by the assault on the Tower of Italy and the wall walk captured. This is where the decisive leadership of d'Aubusson proved vital.

D'Aubusson was the greatest asset that the Order and the Rhodians had, as he inspired confidence in both. He was always at the forefront of the defences, exposing himself quite carelessly it seems on occasion. If he had

33 Guillaume Caoursin, *The Siege of Rhodes* (London: *c.*1482), unpaginated.

34 Guillaume Caoursin, *The Siege of Rhodes* (London: *c.*1482), unpaginated.

been killed or laid low for a prolonged period the city might have been lost; as it was, he survived to play the final crucial role in its defence. His treatment of the English sailor, his appearance at whatever point was facing the greatest threat meant that his men were devoted to him. Self-effacing, brave to the point of recklessness he was the embodiment of the will of the Order and of the city to resist.

The failures on the Ottoman side were numerous. Firstly, the expedition was too small to ensure a rapid victory. Although greatly outnumbering the defenders, they were still too few to overwhelm them. Secondly a profound strategic error was made by concentrating their effort on the Mole and Tower of St Nicholas. As an exercise in military engineering their efforts were impressive but the attacks only resulted in heavy losses and damage to the morale of the assaulting troops. The change in strategy to a straightforward assault on the weak southern sector was a sound decision and could have been made at the beginning of the campaign. The final assault when it came suffered horrendous casualties, which should have been expected but which following on the failure at St Nicholas utterly crushed the spirit of the troops. It was argued that Misac's failure to confirm that the assault troops could reap their customary vengeance on the civil population made them lose heart but this explanation seems unlikely.

Konstantin Mihailović who served eight years as a Janissary before being captured by fellow Christians and freed, provided an additional explanation for the failure of successive assaults.

> There, during the battle [siege], the Janissaries urge and encourage one another to climb and fight. While this is happening a great number of arrows are fired while the muskets are reloaded and supplies replenished. During all of this, there is great noise from the drums and the cries [shouts] from the soldiers. Thus the assault lasts for an hour or two at most. If during this assault the Christians overwhelm the heathens then the Türks slowly weaken and languish while the Christians grow stronger. Thus the assault lasts until noon and it can't last any longer because the ammunition has been fired and many soldiers are killed, some wounded, and all are exhausted.
>
> They have one weakness, which they themselves do not know they have but I know it well, because I saw it well; because their infantry on the battlefield can't last long, because they don't prepare for it at all, but they think that they must always be lucky (that Allâh or Fortune are on their side).[35]

35 Memoirs of a Janissary or Türkish Chronicle by Konstantin Mihailović, 1490 (Academia edu), pp.43–44.

It appears that although the assault itself could have begun with enthusiasm it could not be sustained over a long period. Victory had to be rapid or it would swiftly turn to defeat.

The real weakness on the Ottoman side was in their commander, Misac. Although none of his decisions were bad ones, he failed to convince his men that he could lead them to victory. His response to the St Nicholas fiasco was to retire to his tent in disgrace and despair for three days. On the crucial day in the siege, when d'Aubusson was found leading his men at the very front of the battle, Misac seems again to have gone missing. Organisationally, the Ottoman force was impressive, from its landing to its final disembarkation it performed well. Victory, though, did not seem to matter to the Ottoman attackers as much as the possibility of defeat to the defenders.

1480–1522, Cold War and Cold Comfort

The siege of 1480 was an ignominious defeat for Ottoman arms. The army that had taken the almost unconquerable Byzantine capital of Constantinople, found itself frustrated by crumbling medieval walls and a few hundred Christian fanatics. Sultan Mehmet was clearly intent on clearing out this nest of vipers forthwith but his death brought this project to an end and began a long painful period of Ottoman infighting. It was almost inevitable that the Knights would eventually face a further and greater siege but they would have four decades to prepare. The account of this period can be divided into a discussion of the rapidly changing political and diplomatic position of the Order and a consideration of their military preparations as the threat and the military technology developed.

After the siege, Indulgences (remissions of the time that would be spent in purgatory for the souls of the dead) were sold on behalf of the Order, to pay for the rebuilding and improvement of the defences. The early printers provided popular accounts of the miraculous events that had assisted the defenders and terrified the Turks, which gave the Indulgences greater authority. If miraculous intervention had saved the heroes of Rhodes, then those who purchased an indulgence could surely call upon similar power. An *Army in White* had helped defend the city; golden crosses had appeared to terrify the enemy and comfort the defenders. Hospitaller priories across Christendom commissioned copies of Caoursin's account of the siege to be printed in the vernacular, thereby providing excellent publicity for the Order to the widest audience. The English copy was printed by William Caxton using the 1496 Latin text and was entitled *The Delectable News of the Glorious Victory of the Rhodians Against the Turk.*

There was to be no peace between the Mussulmans and the Order. D'Aubusson, who had miraculously been saved from death, renewed his aggressive stance towards his neighbours. He strengthened the war fleet and granted the Genoese Francisco Mego full sanction to raid Ottoman shipping, under the authority of the Order. In addition, a naval force was

The most famous relic belonging to the Order was the right arm of St John the Baptist. The hand, with outstretched finger, had pointed to the son of God and held Jesus during his baptism. The right hand was given to the Order in 1484 by Cariati Bey, who as the Ottoman ambassador in the period of peace and good relations with the Order, presented it to Grand Master d'Aubusson. Much effort was taken to authenticate the limb and it was positively identified as the one given to the Monastery of Petra by The Emperor Justinian. The relic was paraded through the streets to arouse the spirit of defence in moments of crisis. *De Casu Regis Zyzymy* (The Case of Sultan Djem) printed in Ulm by Ioannem Reger in William Caoursin's *Obsidionis Rhodiae Urbis Descriptio* 1496 fol 51r

sent to raid Mameluke territory, after the truce between them and the Order had been broken. The standing of the Order had never been higher and they could expect considerable wealth to flow, as Rhodes itself became a centre of pilgrimage for those who had wondered at the miraculous defeat of the Ottomans. Rhodes now became a popular resting point for pilgrims before they ventured to the Holy Land itself.

Although the Ottoman Empire was still enormously powerful, the death of Mehmet led to a dispute between his two sons over the succession. Rhodes was therefore in no danger from attack and in fact became the centre of a diplomatic initiative by both claimants to gain its favour. Mehmet had once had three sons: the eldest he had strangled for conducting an affair with the wife of Vizier Achmet. The second claimant, Djem, had been born after Mehmet's capture of Constantinople and claimed the ancient Byzantine title of Porphyrogenitus. The oldest surviving brother, Bajazet, was in a far stronger position than Djem, boasting the support of the Janissaries and the cuckolded Achmet. Djem was defeated in battle and forced to flee, first to Egypt and then eventually to Rhodes. He had met d'Aubusson in his father's reign and sought his aid. It was a difficult decision to accede to Djem's request for asylum but it had obvious advantages for the Order, and the possession of Djem was valuable as he was of potential use both in negotiations with the Ottomans and as a prize for Western powers.

Djem was escorted back to Rhodes in July 1482 by the Prior of Castile and welcomed with the fullest ceremony due to a head of state. His exile was splendid and fruitless. There was little chance of his return and as a pretender to the throne he proved a dismal failure with little if any domestic support. Bajazet sought to gain favour with the Order by proposing a lasting peace in negotiations that would take place in Constantinople. In December 1482 an agreement was made between Bajazet and the order that they should receive 10,000 gold ducats per annum indefinitely, while Djem was to receive an annual pension of 35,000 Venetian ducats. In order to gain its support the Order was presented with priceless relics, including the arm of St John. Djem was now becoming an embarrassment rather than an asset to the Order and was sent to the Order's house in d'Aubusson's Langue at Bourgneuf. He seems to have left on the best of terms with the Grand Master and the Order and in effect gave them *carte blanche* to negotiate whatever they could gain for him from his brother.

Djem's efforts to gain support from amongst the Christian leaders failed miserably but it did gain the attention of Pope Innocent VIII, a man who more than fulfilled the popular perception of Renaissance Popes as immoral, greedy and cruel. Innocent demanded that Djem be handed over to him and the Order faced breaking its promise to Djem or its oath of obedience to the Pope. The papacy won and Djem was handed over in 1488 and in return the Order was saved from further ingresses on its western property by papal interference.

Pope Alexander VI (1492–1503), a late fifteenth century Italian bronze medallion. Diameter: 1 11/16in (43mm). This scion of the Borgia family was to become the epitome of all that was wrong with the Renaissance papacy. He was appointed to numerous posts in the Church in his early teens by his uncle, who would become Pope Calixtus III. Through political acumen and nepotism, he became the maker of Popes before becoming Pope himself. Having risen through his family ties he now rewarded his relatives and supporters. He had seven acknowledged children and perhaps four others, who were to find themselves senior appointments within the Church. As he said, "Who are we to trust if not our family" and "Oh what would Rome be without a plot?" (Metropolitan Museum of Art, public domain)

Djem remained in comfortable confinement until the accession of Rodrigo Borgia, as Pope Alexander VI. Charles VIII of France began his rampage through Italy in 1494 and by January of the next year had seized Rome. The Pope and Djem were both forced to seek safety in the Castel St Angelo. Charles sought to gain control of Djem for no obvious reason and he was handed over by the increasingly desperate Pope for what should have been a period of six months. It was reported in February 1494 that Djem had died at Castle Capuana near Naples of reasons unknown but possibly associated with his eating and drinking. Who killed him or whether he was indeed murdered is unknown. Bajazet was pleased to welcome home his brother's body and his remaining household. He could certainly have done the deed, as could Pope Alexander VI on his behalf. It was an unhappy end that left a stain on the reputation of d'Aubusson and the Order.

The sad history of Djem and Bajazet had at least provided the Order with a degree of safety from attack for the immediate post-siege period. In 1495, conflict between the Ottomans and the Mamelukes broke out once more, further saving Rhodes from Ottoman ambitions. In 1499 the Ottoman forces were sent against Venice with an army landing at Friuli. This led in 1500 to the Pope declaring another Crusade in defence of Christendom with d'Aubusson as Captain General of the Holy League. The Crusade came to nothing as the European powers were too concerned with their own affairs but there was a limited and ineffectual naval campaign, with the Order fighting alongside the Venetians.

The current Hospital was built soon after the siege of 1480 and is a most impressive building. There is one large open ward as well as smaller private rooms, each provided with its own fireplace, for more important patients. The wide balconies would have provided shade and a breath of fresh air, especially important in the hottest part of the year. I would like to think that a fountain in the courtyard would have cooled the air and provided a melodious tinkling. It has been suggested that the hospital was designed upon Islamic principles and practice and although there is no evidence to support this assumption, there are some similarities. (Author's photograph)

The work of the Order was not solely military and throughout this period the Hospital played an important part in its duty towards fellow Christians. The Czech pilgrim John, Lord of Lobkowicz, described the treatment to be found in the Hospital during his stay in Rhodes in 1493.

> Now the Master of Rhodes has endowed that house, that any man being Christian, of whatever lowly or great rank, who shall come there, if he be sick and ask for it for God's sake, should at once be taken in; and there he is at once provided with medicine and other necessities, to wit food and drink and bedclothes. If an important person, he is given a room of his own; and if any lesser man, then there is a fine hall, very long, and in it made beds in double row, and on some of them sick people are lying. And these beds are well made with clean white bedclothes, and on each bed there is a red cloth

> blanket, for there it is not so cold as [in Bohemia]. And near each of these beds a door opens upon that balcony and there too he has a privy .... Also at that time I saw how the sick were served their meals in silver dishes, and they drink too from silver spoons. And none need pay anything for his stay there, except he freely of his goodwill gives anything to the servant that has waited upon him.[36]

The sick, of whatever rank, were provided with servants and the medical staff included two doctors who conducted rounds twice a day. There was an apothecary and a pharmacy providing whatever medicine was prescribed, irrespective of cost. The Hospital naturally had an extensive herb garden attached to it. The Hospital absorbed between five and ten percent of the Order's annual revenues, not an insubstantial amount. When the Order settled in Malta they built their Hospital in Birgu in a single year, an indication of its central importance to their purpose.

In 1503 d'Aubusson died after 27 years as Grand Master; his successor was Emeric d'Amboise who was also the Prior of the Langue of France. It was also the year when a raiding fleet of 16 Ottoman vessels attacked Rhodes. Fortunately, the Order's galleys under Diego Almeida caught up with them, sank eight ships and captured two more, at the loss of only one of their galleys, sunk by a careless gunner who blew off the bows of the ship when a powder barrel exploded. The Order had another ship constructed in its place, as it recognised the importance of its fleet in both defending the island and maintaining the struggle with their numerous enemies. In 1510 a great victory was achieved over a Mameluke convoy with 15 great ships and galleys captured, although a bitter dispute erupted between the two principal commanders – de l'Isle Adam and Andrea d'Amaral. It is doubtful whether d'Amaral ever forgave his superior officer, whose caution led to the victory and who had overruled the more aggressive and impetuous d'Amaral.

D'Amboise died in 1512 and his successor Guy de Blanchefort did not survive him long, dying on the return journey to Rhodes in October 1513. Guy had intended that the Order should choose their own Grand Master, before the papacy with which they had had an increasingly difficult relationship imposed a candidate. The Order elected Fabrizio del Carretto who had proved his bravery again and again during the siege of 1480, principally as the Commander at the Tower of St Nicholas. He was to be responsible for building one of the most ambitious and modern defences, the Tower of Italy, which still stands in a remarkable state of preservation.

Bajazet's rule had come to an unhappy end when he was deposed by Selim Yavuz who also murdered his enemy's sons. Selim was faced with a rival to the leadership of the Islamic world in Shah Isma'il, a Persian

36 Anthony Luttrell., The Hospitallers' medical tradition 1291–1530, p.70, in Malcolm Barber (ed.), *The Military Orders: Fighting for the Faith and Caring for the Sick* (Farnham: Ashgate Ltd, 1994)

Safavid. Selim 'the Grim' first defeated his Persian rival in 1514 and then his Mameluke enemy in 1516, annexing Egypt and executing its leader Tuman Bey in 1517. It was clearly essential that the sea route from Constantinople to Syria and Egypt was free from interference from the Order if the expanded Ottoman Empire was to be governed effectively. Rhodes had to be captured and the threat from the odious Order removed.

Selim's successes led to regular warnings of imminent attack from the Grand Masters. In January 1515 Carretto warned Henry VIII of England of an invasion force of 50,000 waiting to descend on Rhodes. He maintained a regular correspondence with Henry and insisted on the return of Docwra the Prior of England, which Henry refused. In 1520 Henry had promised to send a force of 1,000 men to reinforce the island, a promise that was never kept despite the support for it by Cardinal Wolsey. Pope Leo X added to the pressure on Henry, urging him to send to Rhodes the thousand well-equipped infantry promised and all the money raised by the Order in England but denied them by the cash conscious King. Fortunately for the Knights, Selim died suddenly in 1520 while preparations were being made for the assault, he was succeeded by his young and ambitious son Suleiman. Del Carretto died in 1521 to be succeeded by Villiers de l'Isle Adam. The Order had been preparing for another siege since 1480; the successes of Selim and the arrival of a new young Sultan intent on employing his father's war machine against Islam's enemies made that siege inevitable.

A sixteenth century portrait of Philippe Villiers de l'Isle Adam. He was, as his name suggests, a French knight. Born in Beauvais he was of the same family as Grand Master Jean de Villiers who had led the order when it lost Acre in 1291. He was also connected to formidable figures in contemporary French politics including the *Connétable* de France, Anne de Montmorency, and the man who would later be the champion of the Huguenots, *Amiral* Coligny. De l'Isle Adam joined the order soon after the siege of 1480 and progressed gradually through to the higher ranks. He was Captain General of the Galleys by 1510 and became Grand Prior of France by 1515. (Public domain via Wikimedia Commons)

It would be comforting to assume that the system of recruitment and promotion that the Order had developed over the centuries was bound to produce the right man at the right time. It had in 1480 and was to be the case again in 1522. It is certain that when left to its own devices the Order would always provide experienced and competent leaders but in the three sieges that the order had to face, on every occasion they were exceptionally fortunate in having not only capable and brave leaders but inspirational ones as well.

It was as Commander of the Order's sailing fleet that de l'Isle Adam achieved their greatest success at the Battle of Lajazzo in 1510, where he had fallen out with d'Amaral. The Order was attempting to catch a combined Ottoman and Mameluke fleet at Ayas near Alexandretta. A convoy was in preparation which was carrying a vital cargo of shipbuilding timber that the Mamelukes needed. Andrea d'Amaral, the Portuguese commander of the oar-powered galleys, sought to attack the enemy fleet in its anchorage. De l'Isle Adam demurred as his own clumsy sailing ships, unlike the galleys, were unsuited to operate so close inshore and with weak and contrary winds. De l'Isle Adam won the argument and on the next day when the enemy left their anchorage they were soundly defeated. The quarrel between the two men was to have profound consequences both before and during the siege.

When Fabrizio del Carretto died in 1521 there were three leading candidates for the Grand Mastership. The three were de l'Isle Adam, then on diplomatic duty in Paris, Thomas Docwra the Grand Prior of England, and d'Amaral, the Chancellor and Grand Prior of Castile. De l'Isle Adam remained aloof from the competition. D'Amaral who had been Carretto's deputy in the Convent expected to get considerable support, especially from the Langues of Castile and Leon who should have counterbalanced the French predominance. Docwra was attractive as a compromise candidate, as England might be considered a neutral in the internal politics of the Order. De l'Isle Adam won by a very slim majority, it is said by one vote, but over Docwra. D'Amaral failed disastrously to gain the full support of even his own Langue. It was reported later that d'Amaral had declared that de l'Isle Adam would be the 'last of the Grand Masters in Rhodes', words that if spoken, would come back to haunt him. His detractors pointed to this supposed statement as evidence of his treachery, rather than simply frustrated ambition. They reported that even before the second siege he was already in traitorous communication with the Turk. There was admittedly some dissent within the Order, in the Italian Langue in particular where the knights were concerned that in their absence the new Pope was distributing their Commanderies inequitably but this dissent was quickly suppressed and was not a threat to the Order, and it was certainly not traitorous.

If de l'Isle Adam had gained legitimacy and authority from this election it left d'Amaral bitter and discontented. De l'Isle Adam had still to return from his duties in France and this was no easy project. The small convoy that escorted him was subject to accident and attack. One vessel caught fire and was only just saved. His own ship was struck by lightning, nine men were killed and it was reported that his sword was burnt to a cinder, hardly a good omen.[37] He was then forced to escape from the clutches of the notorious corsair Kurtoğlu, who awaited him outside the port of Syracuse where his ships took refuge. De l'Isle Adam considered this little more than an attempt at kidnapping on the high seas by the Sultan himself. He slipped away safely from the clutches of the notable corsair and finally reached Rhodes on 19 September 1521.

37 And highly improbable as swords do not burn!

4

New defences

New Principles of Fortification

It was long assumed that the appearance of gunpowder artillery resulted in the immediate obsolescence of 'medieval' fortifications. It was also assumed that the expense of such weapons led to them becoming a royal monopoly. Thus, the rebellious feudal lords were left to tremble in their crumbling castles, as they faced the royal roaring of crown cannons. Feudalism thus came to an end and the nation state came into existence. Although an appealing and apparently logical explanation it is of course, *mostly* nonsense. The earliest firearm can be dated to about the mid-fourteenth century but they only began to appear as a significant factor in sieges in the last quarter of that century. Medieval fortifications continued to stand up against early gunpowder artillery very successfully for at least a century before it became apparent that new technology required there to be a significant change in defences. This was to take advantage of the new weapons, as well as to defend against them. Even then 'medieval' fortifications often proved remarkably resilient in the face of the most modern weaponry. Many factors other than the system of the fortification could determine the outcome of a siege.

The siege of 1480 was fought with medieval gunpowder weapons against medieval fortifications, while the second siege was fought with more 'modern' weapons against fortifications that were in the process of transition from medieval to modern. The ultimate expression of the new fortification system was the *trace Italienne* a system of flanking bastions set deep into the ground, surrounded by well-planned ditches and glacis. This was a system that was only to develop in the 1530s, a decade before the final and fatal siege of Rhodes, and a system which survived and flourished well into the nineteenth century. The Order attempted to construct fortifications that responded to the danger posed by the new artillery and the opportunity that the new artillery gave to the defenders especially the provision of flanking fire. It involved the repair and refurbishment of the old fortifications, as well as the construction of new ones on what were the latest principles.

Christopher Duffy in his excellent study of siege warfare considered the years from 1494 to 1660 as being of great importance. The early date assumed that the invasion of Italy by Charles VIII saw the triumph of 'new' artillery over medieval fortifications: this was not really the case. It was certainly true that the eruption of the French army accompanied by its artillery, that the rather dim and destructive king Charles VIII brought with him, had a profound effect on all those who observed it and it led to an arms race in Italy and beyond. The process of modifying and modernising fortifications to adjust to artillery was happening long before.

One response to incorporate the use of artillery into fortifications was the artillery tower. At its most basic level it can be seen in the simple circular Cow Tower defending the Bishop's Gate Bridge over the river Wensum in Norwich. It had relatively thin walls built with a brick facing and a mortared flint rubble interior. The tower, built in 1398–1399, is 15 metres high and fitted with splayed gun ports as well as arrow loops. The Château de Castelnaud has a most impressive late medieval gun tower integrated into its fortifications, as well as several horseshoe-shaped blockhouses. The castle at Fougères has a magnificent horseshoe-shaped tower built in 1480 provided with six tiers of guns, and the last gun tower in Italy was constructed in Assisi in 1535. Albrecht Dürer produced a design for a massive gun tower with two lower gun decks and a massive ditch, an illustration of which was published in 1527. These towers had battered, that is sloping, walls with thick masonry protecting the casemates for artillery pieces. Dürer's influential book *Etliche Underricht zu Befestigung der Stett Schloss und Flecken* (Treatise on the Fortification of City, Castle, and Palaces) was reprinted in 1530 and again in 1538 and was at least in part a response to the perceived threat of further Ottoman incursions into Christendom. It has been argued that it was Dürer's book that inspired Henry VIII's design for his magnificent Device Forts, but there is no evidence to support that contention.

The shape of fortifications underwent a transformation designed to meet the threat posed by artillery to the tall walls and towers of the medieval period. It was also seen as important to protect the walls by providing flanking fire against an enemy assault on them. In the 1440s the architect Leon Battista Alberti had already suggested that, 'The wall should be flanked by towers acting as buttresses every 50 cubits. They should be round, standing out from the wall, and somewhat taller, so that anyone venturing too close would expose his flank to missiles and be hit; thus the wall is protected by the towers and the towers by each other.'[1] In addition the 'medieval' hollow tower provided with comparatively thin walls could be lowered in height and the wall spaces could be: 'filled with a mixture of clay and straw, and packed down. Thus, the softness of the clay will deaden

1 Leon Battista Alberti (Joseph Rykwert, trans. with Neil Leach and Robert Tavernor), *On the Art of Building in Ten Books* (Cambridge, Mass.: MIT Press, 1988) pp.104–105.

the force and impact of the engines.'[2] This was an acknowledgement of an entirely new way to deal with projectiles. The new defences were not to mimic breastplates but cushions!

Alberti clearly recognised the important deadening effect of the material on the projectile. Hard armour can either deflect or defeat a projectile while soft armour could absorb the impact. This was the principle that lay behind different armours in the late Middle Ages, such as the steel breastplate and a padded jack. With higher velocity iron projectiles, the old 'hard' defence would eventually be replaced by the soft, with thick stone walls giving way to much thicker earthen ones. This was a solution that could be resorted to easily in the moist Northern European climes where earth of all sorts abounded. In the South where soil was thin and rock abounded it was more difficult to apply.

Using these ideas, medieval castles could be 'modernised' by adopting some relatively simple measures. Walls could be lowered and the thin crenellation replaced by thicker curved or bevelled parapets. The crenel is an excellent aiming point for an archer or crossbowman if the besiegers wished to keep the defenders' heads down. The crenel would be replaced by a splayed embrasure designed to protect an artillery piece and provide it with a wide field of fire. The stone machicolations or wooden hoardings would also be removed: they had lost their function now that creating a breach in the wall with artillery had replaced storming with ladders. The newly lowered walls could then be reinforced with a wide bank of earth, a process known as rampiring. This would provide space for a wide rampart, replacing the narrow wall walk, and upon which artillery could be moved and mounted, exploiting the opportunities provided by an embrasure. The disadvantage of this was that the earth placed a great strain on the stone walls. The consequence was that when the outer stone wall was struck the earth behind it could collapse. As Duke Philip of Cleves complained in the late fifteenth century, 'Whenever the guns batter the walls, the earth tumbles down with the masonry, which makes it all the easier for the enemy to climb the breach.'[3]

The transformation of a medieval to a more modern system of defence could be achieved quite quickly and at much less expense than building anew. The medieval castle at Tantallon in Scotland was transformed by the building of a gun tower fitted with wide-mouthed horizontal gun ports, while the towers and chambers in the curtain wall were filled with rubble to help absorb the impact of shot, the remaining towers were strengthened and forward earthworks were constructed to keep enemy artillery at a

2 Leon Battista Alberti (Joseph Rykwert, trans. with Neil Leach and Robert Tavernor), *On the Art of Building in Ten Books* (Cambridge, Mass.: MIT Press, 1988) p.104.

3 Christopher Duffy, *Siege Warfare: the Fortress in the Early Modern World, 1494–1660* (London: Routledge Kegan Paul, 1979) p.2.

distance.[4] The idea of concentric or layered defences could be adhered to by the addition of a wall placed between the wall and the usual ditch. Known as the *fausse braye,* they were quite common additions and one was included in the defences of Rhodes before the first siege. In the images in the Caoursin manuscript the *fausse braye* is far more prominent than it would appear in 1522 after the major re-modelling.

The successes of the 'invincible' French artillery that had amazed everyone ended at the siege of Pisa in1500. Although the high stone wall was breached, the Pisans had prepared another ditch and free-standing rampart which came to be known as the *retirata* or 'double Pisan rampart.' The collapse of the wall produced an, 'outer barrier to the interior ditch and the intact earthen rampart behind.'[5] This technique of double-defence was used with success at Brescia in 1515, Parma in 1521 and Marseilles in 1524. It was also used by d'Aubusson in 1480 and had been referred to as a useful ruse by both Juvencel and Christine de Pisan much earlier in the fifteenth century.

It was in the late fifteenth and the early sixteenth century in Italy that the full effect of the new artillery would be felt and a process of refortification began. The initial response to the new dangers posed by artillery was to bury the high walls of the castle in an even deeper and wider moat and to simplify and modify the corner towers to provide better fields of fire. The towers were now broad and 'tub shaped', fully integrated into the walls rather than standing proud from them. The best example is that of Fort Sarzanello that was completed between 1493 and 1502 by Francesco Giamberti. It was made up of two massive triangles one of which had towers set into each corner and set inside a deep ditch. It retained some outmoded features such as machicolations and a thin wall surmounted by crenels and merlons. It also had a purpose-built countermine gallery running around the turreted triangular half of the fortress at ditch level.

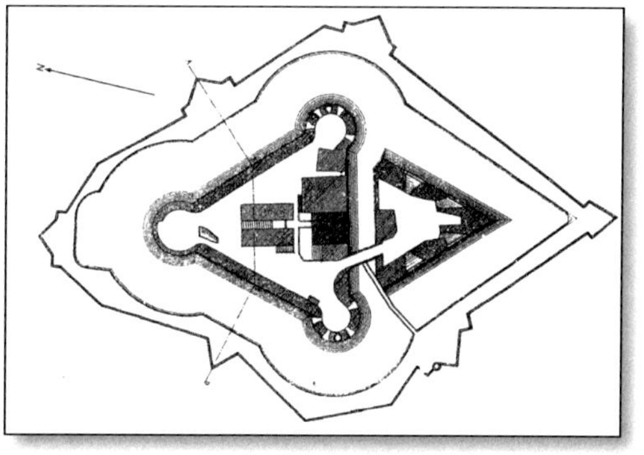

The fortress of Sarzanello was one more step in the development of the principle of the angled bastion, which would come to be the predominant feature of military architecture for well over 300 years. The triangular fortification on the left-hand side was provided with three tub-like bastions and set in a deep, dry moat. The angled bastion to the right was the next step in eradication of 'dead ground' which defensive fire could not reach. It is worth comparing this with the fortress of Salse. (Public domain via Wikimedia Commons)

The problem of providing fully integrated flanking fire was being addressed in several Italian fortifications, the Pogio Imperiale (1495–1513) and the fortress of Nettuno (1501–1503), where the gun chambers were carefully arranged to provide both crossfire and flanking fire. The castle walls were still high, although the lower level had a pronounced scarp which meant that the guns had to fire down on their attackers. This had two disadvantages; firstly, plunging fire meant that you

4 *Statement of Significance. Tantallon Castle.* Historic Environment Scotland. pp.15–16.

5 Christopher Duffy, *Siege Warfare: the Fortress in the Early Modern World, 1494–1660* (London: Routledge Kegan Paul, 1979), p.15.

would normally have a lower point of aim and secondly, the balls were less likely to ricochet, and instead would bury themselves in the ground.

The reconstruction of the defences of Rhodes occurred during this period of experimentation involving the modification and modernisation of old structures as well as the creation of entirely new ones. Quite clearly Rhodes was at the cutting edge of developments in military fortification.

The Refortification of Rhodes 1480–1520

The urgent business after the first siege was simply the equivalent of making a building watertight, repairing the worst of the damage to the walls and the Tower of St Nicholas. What was now needed was the development of new principles of defence that would acknowledge the destructive power of artillery, as well as exploiting its ability to defend, whether through counter-battery fire or by flanking fire. Funds and labour were not unlimited and it was clear that some sections of the defences, those least likely to be attacked, were left more or less in their original state. The section of the walls from St Paul's Tower to St Catherine's Gate was left virtually untouched. This was also true of a small section from St Catherine's Gate,[6] which would have originally been protected from attack by the sea. It had been constructed using funds from France while d'Aubusson was Grand Master.

The Marine gate was left in its medieval form consisting of two imposing round towers, which were surmounted by what were now obsolete but attractive machicolations. In neither siege did it come under attack as the harbour entrance was carefully protected. Although many of the Grand Masters left their coats of arms on new construction it is difficult to date with precision when the work was completed or whether it was begun by a previous Grand Master. (Albert Gabriel, *La Cité de Rhodes, 1310–1522 : Topographie, Architecture Militaire*, (Paris: E. de Boccard, 1921 & 1923))

The Langues were responsible for their own fortifications and their wealth and the interests of their priors determined what and when building work took place. The Grand Masters tended to prefer their own portions of the defences, so that the Gate D'Amboise was rebuilt under the eponymous French Grand Master and under Grand Master Carretto the Post of Italy was completely extended and modified on the most modern lines. What is surprising is that despite the somewhat piecemeal process the result was remarkably complete and coherent by the time of the great siege of 1522. D'Aubusson's 'master plan', which was followed by all of his successors wherever possible, would appear to have been based on the following precepts.

6 Or 'the Gate of the Mole'.

Widen the moat wherever possible and where necessary deepen it.

Construct *tenailles* to provide outworks to defend the inner wall from bombardment

Where no *tenaille* could be constructed to thicken the walls and make a *terreplein* (platform) for artillery.

Replace the crenellated parapet with thicker walls pierced with embrasures for large pieces of artillery, widening at mouth and protected with a mantlet.

Rebuild the four principal gates and towers to provide them with stronger and thicker walls and provide extensive opportunities for flanking as well as counter-battery fire. By the time of the siege only the Gates of St John, d'Amboise and possibly St Athanasius on the landward side were in use.

To provide enfilading fire along the moat at ground level where blockhouses and *caponiers* were built.

Smaller towers would be integrated fully into the defences.

The *fausse braye* would be incorporated in the tower defences and equipped with gun loops.

Where the walls and towers were lowered the ditch was dug deeper to maintain the overall height of the wall.[7]

The *fausse braye* adjoining the Tower of Italy. It is evident from this photograph how narrow the fausse braye was. It conformed fairly closely to the precepts of the Roman author Procopius, in that in width it was one-quarter of the height of the interior wall. It was also, of course, employed by Byzantine architects where it was known as the *προτείχισμα* or simply an outwork. (Author's photograph)

D'Aubusson did not forget his promise to the Franciscans to build them a monastery in the Jews' quarter dedicated to Our Lady of Victories. He also had rebuilt the synagogue that had been demolished in order to prepare the city for the Turkish assault.

It was clear that the ditch, *fausse braye* and walls were, as they stood, inadequate defences against modern artillery. One relatively straightforward decision was to widen the ditch providing a greater field of fire for the defenders and a bigger distance for attackers to cross. There is also some evidence such as the use of battered reinforcement to the base of a tower, that the ditch was also deepened, at least in some places. The most significant additions to the ditch were a number of *tenailles*. These were defensive works placed in front of the main defences. The name

7 NB in some areas the walls could not be lowered because the land beyond the defences was at the same height and if lowered would overlook the defences and the interior of the city.

derived from either a French or Latin word describing the two arms of pincers when opened. The *tenaille* was a massive obstruction to the direct fire on the wall by an enemy. It could also be provided with a parapet so that it could be garrisoned and act as an outward defence against assault. In some cases, the *tenaille* was provided with embrasures for the mounting of cannon, providing additional arcs of fire. The *tenaille* would have to be

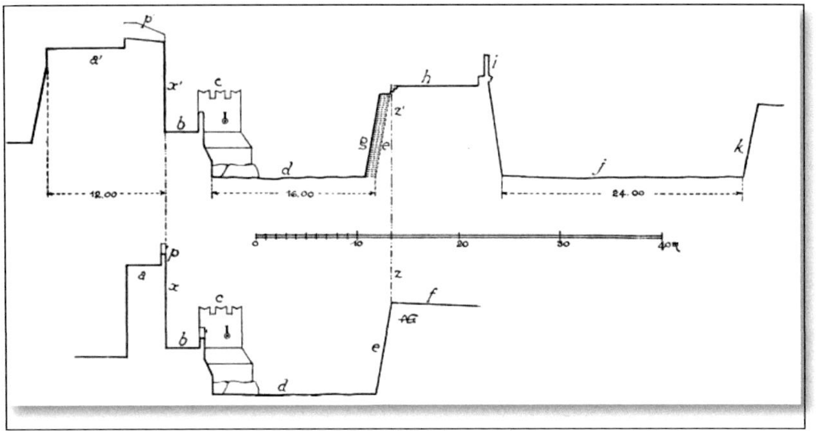

This illustration shows the principal changes to the defences between 1480 and 1522. The curtain wall was heightened and thickened to provide a wide rampart more suitable for the use of artillery. The thin crenellated parapet was replaced with thicker walls pierced by embrasures suited to modern artillery. A much wider ditch was dug and the *terreplein* was fitted with a relatively narrow parapet and firing step. There was no protection from the rear. If it was captured this would enable the defenders on the inner curtain wall and tower to shoot at the defenceless attackers. (Albert Gabriel, *La Cité de Rhodes, 1310–1522: Topographie, Architecture Militaire*, (Paris: E. de Boccard, 1921 & 1923))

A view from the Tower of the Virgin, the English Bastion, which gives an excellent view of the *grande tenaille* and its overall significance in the scheme of fortifications. (Albert Gabriel, *La Cité de Rhodes, 1310–1522: Topographie, Architecture Militaire*, (Paris: E. de Boccard, 1921 & 1923))

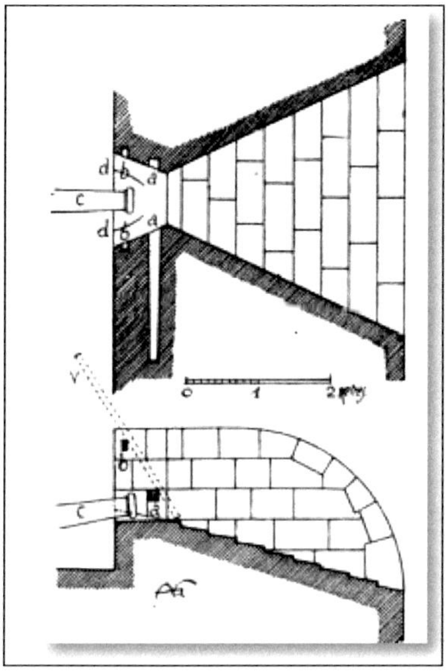

A cross section of the new embrasures. These permitted a wide field of fire as well as enabling the barrel of the gun to be depressed up to 15 degrees. It was protected from enemy firearms with a mantlet, or shutter, which could be locked in place. (Albert Gabriel, *La Cité de Rhodes, 1310–1522: Topographie, Architecture Militaire*, (Paris: E. de Boccard, 1921 & 1923))

One of the most novel innovations was the construction of *caponiers*, added by Grand Master Carretto and in this example dateable to 1514. These were small enclosed fortification in the form of barrel-vaulted chambers equipped with gun ports. They were set obliquely across the moat to provide flanking fire along it. Those at Rhodes might be the earliest examples of their type, although such fortifications were described by Franceso di Giorgio in his late fifteenth century treatises, where they are called *capannati*. In Dürer's illustration of 'modernised' fortifications he places a small circular pillbox in the moat, rather than a fully-developed *caponier*. Note the impressive embrasures in the Tower of Italy at the right rear of the photograph. (Author's photograph)

taken if the wall itself was to be assaulted. It was a clever addition to the concept of concentric defences.

The *tenaille* in front of the Tower of the Virgin is crescent-shaped but the principle on which such fortification was based remained the same. The first *tenaille* protected the south east corner of the defences, the second running from the Koskino Gate (St John) to the Gate of Spain and the last was in the North-West covering the Grand Master's Palace. The construction of the *tenaille* was achieved by simply leaving a large section of ground in place when widening the moat, so that the inner face of the *tenaille* was in fact the outer face of the original moat.

Those parts of the wall that were likely to face an assault were reinforced to make them considerably thicker, and pierced for artillery. The addition of a *terreplein*, the name given to the level space created from St John's Gate to the Tower of Italy, made up for the absence of a *tenaille* and enabled heavy guns to be manoeuvred and mounted along the wall. This was also the plan adopted for the wall from the Tower of Spain to St George's Bastion, where no *tenaille* was constructed. This was also where a section of the ditch was

St John's Gate, showing a three storied blockhouse enfilading the moat. Bronze artillery was expensive and lighter pieces and arquebuses could be used to bolster the anti-personnel defences. The amount of powder used by an arquebus was trifling compared to that necessary to provide a full charge for even small artillery pieces. The use of bronze perriers using smaller powder charges than their larger brethren also helped economise on precious gunpowder. Simon Pepper has argued convincingly, that before the availability of cheaper cast iron artillery, small-calibre pieces were a much more important feature of fortifications than previously thought.[7] (Author's photograph)

deepened significantly. The crenels and merlons on the parapet could be replaced by curved or bevelled parapets with embrasures for artillery and round firing loops inserted into walls for arquebuses and crossbows.

The Contributions of the Grand Masters

Pierre d'Aubusson was, according to the French chronicler of the civil and military architecture of City of Rhodes, the '*plus Glorieux des grandsmaitres de Rhodes*.'[9] He established the plan that would make the defences of Rhodes fit for a new age. His arms appear 40 times on the defences of Rhodes, more than any other Grand Master and an indication of his importance in the refortification of Rhodes. He had been made the Superintendent of Fortification in 1472 by Battista Orsini and after he became Grand Master in 1476, he continued to act in that role. He had devoted a considerable amount of time to the study of mathematics especially to its military application. The consequences of the siege in 1480 and of a disastrous earthquake the year after meant that there was much to rebuild and many opportunities to do so. His contribution to the defences was immense, beginning with the construction of the grand *terrepleins* which completely altered the face of

8 Simon Pepper, 'Firepower and the design of Renaissance fortifications.' *Fort*, vol.10 1982, pp.93–104.

9 Albert Gabriel, *La Cité de Rhodes 1310–1522: Topographie, Architecture Militaire*, volume 1 (Paris: E. de Boccard 1921), p.109.

The entrance to the Tower of St John, the responsibility of the Provencal Langue and commanded by Jean de Brinquier de Lioncel. D'Aubusson was responsible for its transformation into a strong artillery bastion soon after the end of the first siege. The Bastion is hewn from the solid rock and therefore has no firing ports below this level but is flanked by well-constructed blockhouses. The moat here is comparatively narrow but still deep and imposing. (Author's photograph)

Rhodes. He was also responsible for the strengthening transformation of the Tower of St Nicholas, the Barbican of England (1487), the Bastion of Spain (1489), and the Bastion d'Auvergne (1496). He was in control of the restoration of parts of the port curtain wall (1489), the strengthening of the curtain wall of the Mole of Naillac and of the rectangular bastion between the Tour of Italy and Port de Koskino (St John's Gate) as well as the New Bastion of St James.

The contribution of Pierre d'Aubusson's successor, Emery d'Amboise, was far less impressive. He reinforced the curtain walls near to the Tower of Italy added a *terreplein* and restored the walls of the counterscarps. He also rebuilt the Port d'Amboise which was completed in the year of his death. Fabrizio del Carretto continued the work of d'Amboise. It is worth recalling that Carretto had been the stalwart defender of the tower of St Nicholas in 1480, he therefore understood the vital importance of modern fortifications in the face of artillery bombardment! He strengthened the curtain walls, replacing the ancient parapets, worked to strengthen and mend the *terrepleins* but above all he was responsible for building the new circular Tower of Italy. Philippe Villiers de l'Isle Adam had too little time to achieve much before the second siege but he did oversee the transformation of the Bastion d'Auvergne following the plans of the Italian architect Basilio della Scuola. It was d'Aubusson who established the pattern of refortification that was to be followed by his successors. He had triumphed in 1480; in 1522 he came close to repeating his success – posthumously.

The ruins of antiquity that surrounded the Knights, including the remains of the Byzantine fortification, provided much of the material that was initially used. The massive ditches, quarried out of the living rock provided much more and the neighbouring quarries at Koskino and Malona also added to the store of material. The stone was oolithic limestone which was easy to quarry but hardened when exposed to the air. It was however subject to erosion when exposed to salt rich air especially on the curtain wall around the port. It is also very sharp and is very painful to fall on, producing nasty grazes that take weeks to heal. Marble was used for grander work and for the lintels in gun emplacements and this was exclusively reused ancient classical marble. At the beginning of the sixteenth century, it was reported that a hundred prisoners captured at sea could be seen working on the defences every day. In 1522 the Grand Master allocated three-quarters of them to work on the defences and the remainder to the needs of the Rhodians. The unit of measurement was *la canne* which was divided into 8 *palmes* and 16 *demi-palmes*, the unit of area was the *canne carée*.[10] These were the units traditionally used in France and were imported by the Knights from Provence.

The Italians have claimed an important role for themselves in the refortification of Rhodes. Firstly, it must be said that much of the work that was done was begun under d'Aubusson long before the first Italian engineer appeared on the island. There were certainly Italians working in Rhodes – but in the sixteenth century. The Venetian, Basilio della Scuola acted as a consulting engineer suggesting improvements to existing work. He left the plans for the Bastion d'Auvergne which were put into operation by Adam de l'Isle Adam, having returned to his patron Charles V on the death of Carretto. Matteo Giuenio, a Sicilian 'Engineer of the Religion', worked with Basilio and produced a relief map of Rhodes in 1521 that was sent to Pope Leo X. Grand Master Carretto asked for the services of Antonio di Pietro Abbondi, known as Scarpagnino, who was primarily a civilian architect, in 1516 but the Venetian Senate refused.

A Short Tour of The Key Defences

Tower of St Nicholas

Perhaps the most famous of all the defences of Rhodes was the Tower of St Nicholas. It had played a vital part in the siege of 1480 in diverting the Ottomans from their principal purpose. Their failure to capture it using boats and pontoon bridges was at a dreadful cost in lives and morale. It was inevitable that the rebuilding and refortification would be on a massive scale.

10 In modern units one palm equalled .262m (10.3 in) and the *Canne* would be 2.096m (82.5in).

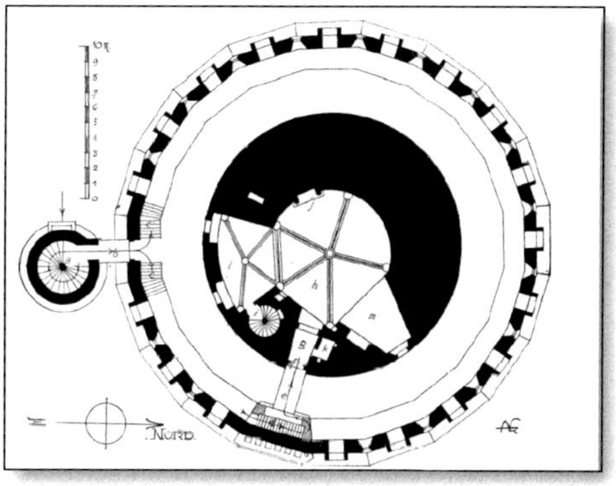

The original tower was an impressive structure consisting of a thick-walled tower surrounded by a circular wall. Access to the upper levels was by a separate tower. Construction started in 1464 and was completed, using a massive donation of cash by the Duke of Burgundy, in 1467. Its destruction in the siege of 1480 was almost total and it was clearly unsuited to sustaining a siege against modern gunpowder weapons. The response was to encase the old tower in what was almost an entirely new fortification. (Albert Gabriel, *La Cité de Rhodes, 1310–1522: Topographie, Architecture Militaire*, (Paris: E. de Boccard, 1921 & 1923))

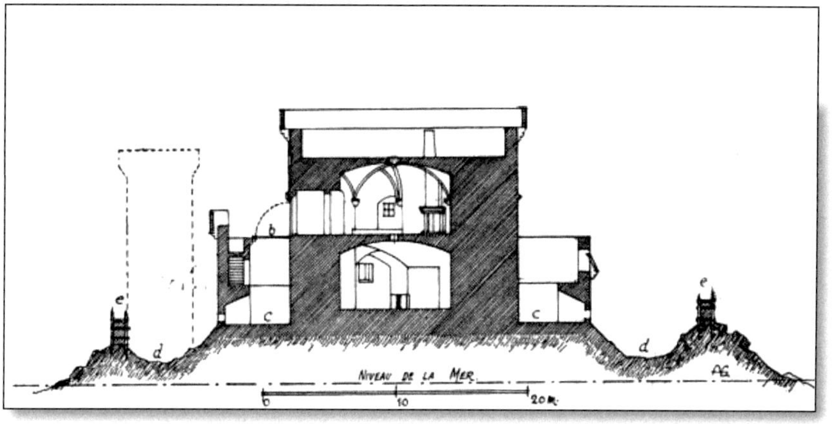

A cross section of the Tower of St Nicholas as it might have appeared in 1480. The access tower (removed for clarity) is indicated in dots. The additional defences, designed to keep an amphibious attack from reaching the walls, are well represented here. (Albert Gabriel, *La Cité de Rhodes, 1310–1522: Topographie, Architecture Militaire*, (Paris: E. de Boccard, 1921 & 1923))

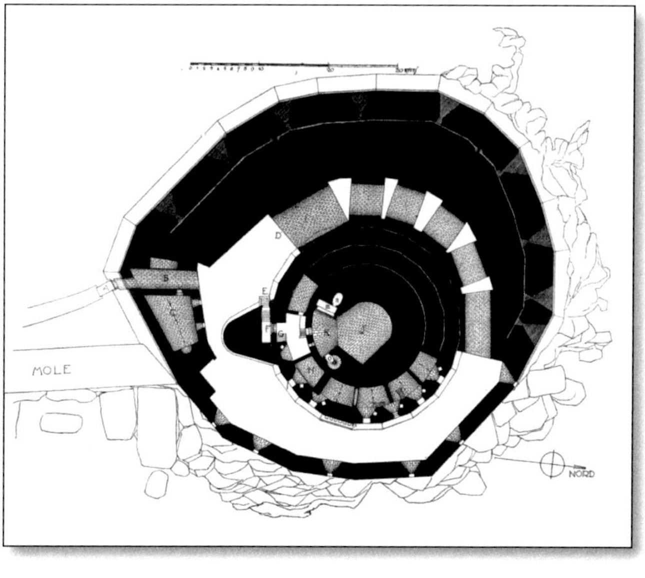

In 1480 the Ottoman forces had attacked the Tower of St Nicholas from the landward side and it was this which was dramatically reinforced with a massive gun platform with nine large embrasures for artillery which had a wide field of fire. Rather than merely being a tower, it was now a self-supporting independent fortification. The massive tall walls meant that an amphibious landing would have been nearly impossible. Ironically, by making it appear invincible it discouraged the Ottomans from repeating their mistake in the siege of 1480. (Albert Gabriel, *La Cité de Rhodes, 1310–1522: Topographie, Architecture Militaire*, (Paris: E. de Boccard, 1921 & 1923))

The Tower of Italy

The Tower and Bastion of Italy, sometimes referred to as the Bastion of Carretto, is perhaps the most impressive and intimidating of the defences because of its sheer mass and potent firepower. It was a complete rebuilding of the original round tower which was open at the rear. After the siege of 1480 it probably benefited, as did others, from forward works which were obliterated by the construction of the new artillery tower. The embrasures were protected by wide parapets in the lower circular gallery the embrasures were designed to sweep the ditch providing flanking fire. The casemate was provided with vents to allow the dense gun smoke in the gallery to disperse and escape. There was also access to a *caponier*, provided with loopholes. It was constructed between 1515 and 1517 under Carretto's Grand Mastership and is liberally decorated with his Coat of Arms.

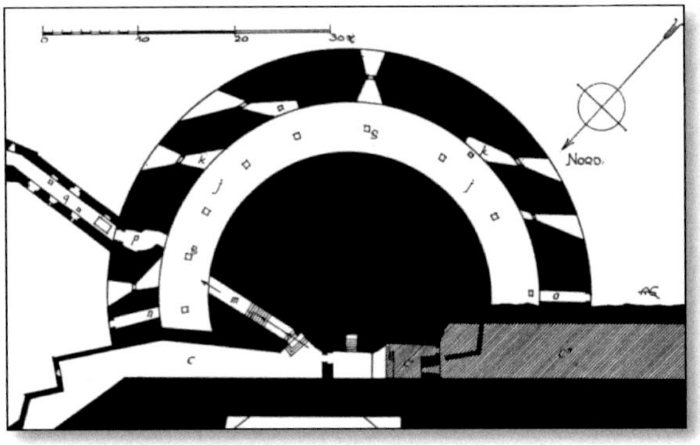

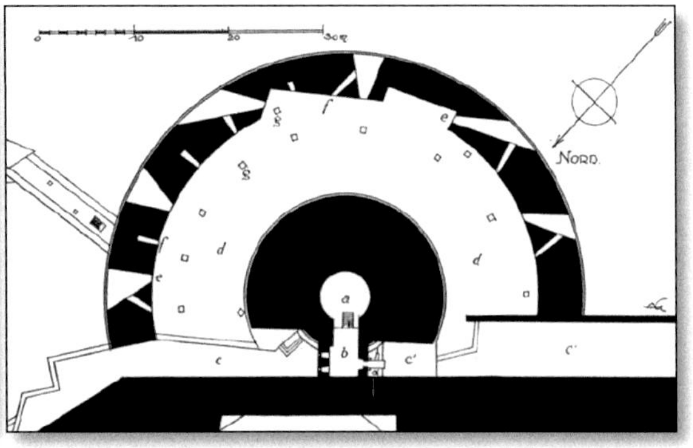

The Upper and lower plan of the Tower of Italy which show clearly how important flanking fire was considered in the new design. Only two of the embrasures/firing ports point directly ahead. (Albert Gabriel, *La Cité de Rhodes, 1310–1522: Topographie, Architecture Militaire*, (Paris: E. de Boccard, 1921 & 1923))

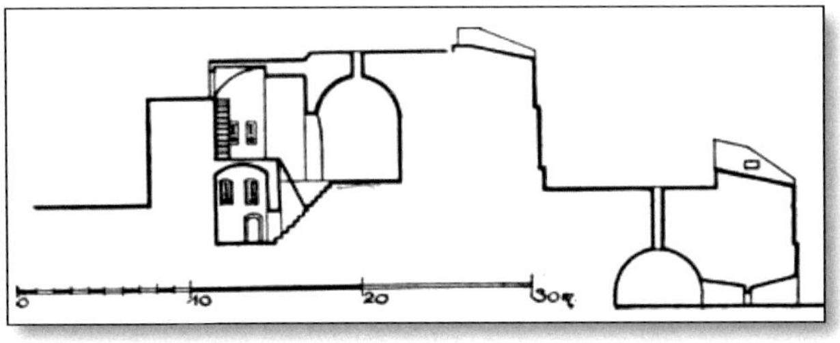

There are clear similarities between the Carretto tower and the Device Forts of Henry VIII of two decades later. There is no obvious direct connection between them and their purpose was different. This tower was defensive in nature while the Device Forts were meant to cover anchorages and harbours with their offensive firepower. They were however both attempts to exploit the opportunities and resist the challenge created by the artillery revolution. (Albert Gabriel, *La Cité de Rhodes, 1310–1522: Topographie, Architecture Militaire*, (Paris: E. de Boccard, 1921 & 1923))

D'Aubusson's Tower

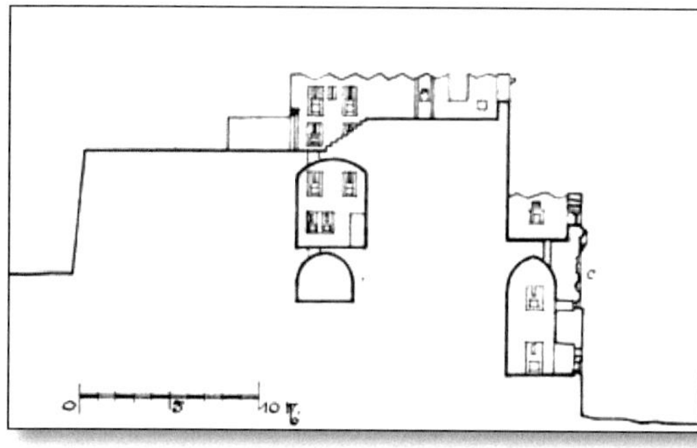

This impressive structure began as a tower detached from the curtain wall. Soon after the siege of 1480 it was transformed on the orders of d'Aubusson. The Tower was fully joined to the curtain wall and provided with a large rectangular outwork. This was built with two levels of gun ports, while two further 'gun decks› were provided by the original tower. Its purpose was to dominate the moat with small arms fire, while providing the greatest protection for its garrison. (Albert Gabriel, *La Cité de Rhodes, 1310–1522: Topographie, Architecture Militaire*, (Paris: E. de Boccard, 1921 & 1923))

Next to d'Aubusson's Tower is another bastion which developed from a circular tower. As can be seen it was joined to the curtain wall and had a polygonal ‹bastion' added to the face. Although unnamed and without any indication of which Grand Master was responsible for the re-modelling it is still impressive fortification.

Although this tower has no associations with a Grand Master and remains unnamed it is still an imposing structure. (Author's photograph)

Tower of St Athanasius

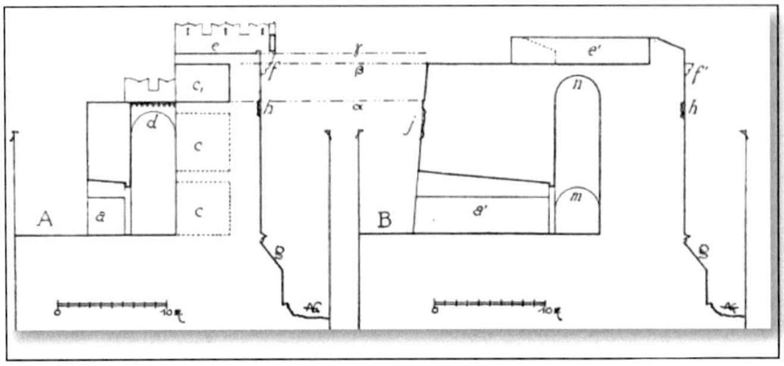

The Tower of St Athanasius was an example of the transformation that was accomplished when converting a weak medieval defence. The square tower on the left was part of the forward defences connecting the *fausse braye*. It was separate from the curtain wall, connected to it only by wooden bridge. To transform it, the interior of the tower was filled and the wall heightened, it was now completely connected to the curtain wall which had also been massively widened to provide a broader fighting platform upon which artillery could be deployed. A transverse passage integrated the tower with the existing *fausse braye*. The facing of the tower remained unchanged as did the *talus* (sloping wall) down to the ditch. (Author's photograph)

It is easy to see how the original tower of 1480 was transformed into a more powerful fortification. The corbelling to support the machicolations remain as evidence of the earlier period. (Author's photograph)

The city walls behind the *grande tenaille*. This photograph shows pretty much how the walls would have appeared in 1480. It is easy to see how important the *tenaille* was in protecting them from further assault in 1522, explaining why the Ottoman attack, on the latter occasion, concentrated on the massively reinforced bastions. Note how the towers were fully integrated into the defences and the thin crenellated wall replaced by deep embrasures. (Author's photograph)

View of the *grande tenaille* and the city wall behind. The tower on the far left is that of St Athanasius. (Author's photograph)

The Gate of St John

The Gate of St John began with the usual simple modest square tower, built in the mid-fifteenth century. A small angled bulwark was placed before it in the decades preceding the first siege. As a consequence of the siege the massive angled bulwark was built by d'Aubusson and completed before 1489. It is a solid structure and massively strong. The moat was narrow at this point but remains very impressive. It was flanked by a rectangular blockhouse on its right and a complex tiered system of defences, which swept the moat, on its left. (Albert Gabriel, *La Cité de Rhodes, 1310–1522: Topographie, Architecture Militaire*, (Paris: E. de Boccard, 1921 & 1923))

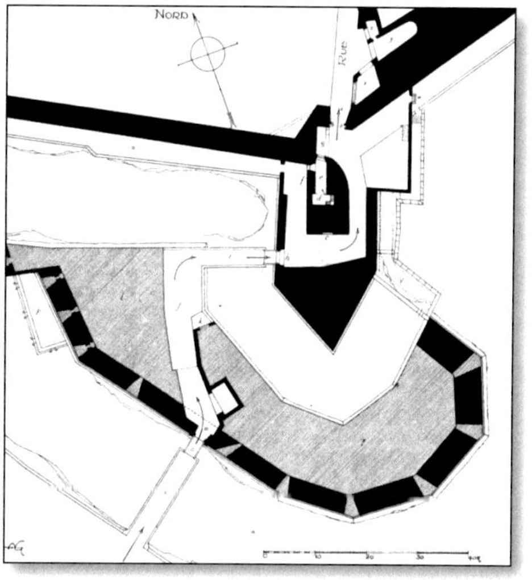

(Albert Gabriel, *La Cité de Rhodes, 1310–1522: Topographie, Architecture Militaire*, (Paris: E. de Boccard, 1921 & 1923))

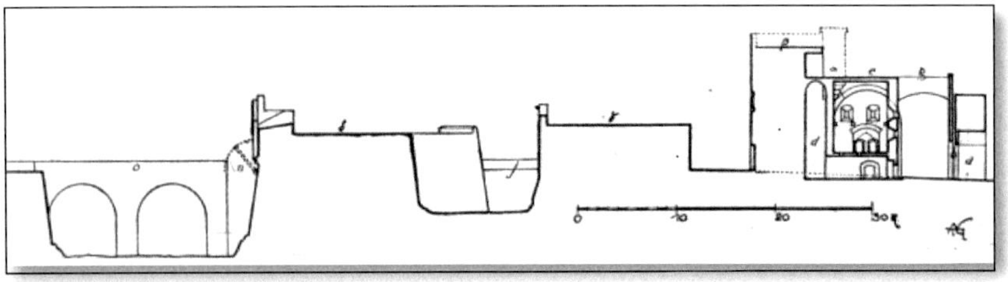

A plan of the gate, moat and bridge extending back to the tower. The depth and complexity of the fortifications that developed over the decade after the first siege made this gateway almost impregnable. (Albert Gabriel, *La Cité de Rhodes, 1310–1522: Topographie, Architecture Militaire*, (Paris: E. de Boccard, 1921 & 1923))

What is especially notable in this photograph are the ground level embrasures providing a wide field of fire across the moat. The gun chamber was provided with a ventilation chimney, essential with larger firearms as even if the muzzle is outside the venting of hot gas from the touch hole can be considerable. The later *caponier* on the flank of the tower interrupted the last of the ground-floor embrasures. As the inevitable great siege approached such additions had to be made to even recent constructions such as this tower. (Author's photograph)

Tower and Gate of The Virgin Mary, The Post of England

The original tower was similar to that of others of the defences – circular and detached from the curtain wall. It was constructed in 1441, a little after the Tower of Spain. It was modified by the additional of a polygonal bastion which was separated from the tower by a large ditch. There are two outworks flanking the bastion each with two floors. In front of this was constructed a crescent shaped *tenaille* which was faced with stone and provided with embrasures for artillery.

The Tower of the Virgin seen from the other side of the moat. (Author's photograph)

The Tower and Bastion of Spain

The Tower and Bastion of Spain dominated the moat, this time with low lying gun ports that would sweep the ground in front of them. At the upper level the embrasures would have added to the carnage. (Albert Gabriel, *La Cité de Rhodes, 1310-1522: Topographie, Architecture Militaire*, (Paris: E. de Boccard, 1921 & 1923))

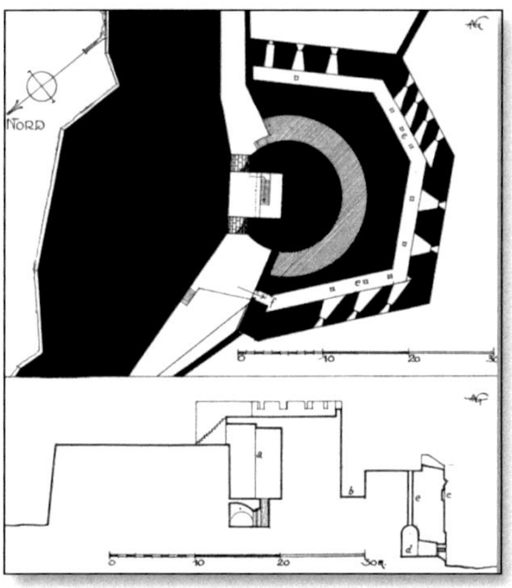

The original tower was, as in other examples, originally open to the rear. The bastion had four faces which were provided with numerous embrasures primarily aimed at providing flanking fire at two levels along the ditch, which lay on its left flank between the *fausse braye* and the *terreplein*. (Albert Gabriel, *La Cité de Rhodes, 1310-1522: Topographie, Architecture Militaire*, (Paris: E. de Boccard, 1921 & 1923))

This image was taken from the other side of the moat and shows how near it is to the Bastion of Spain. It also shows the carefully shaped bow (or stern) of the *petite tenaille*, faced with fine masonry and interposing itself shield-like between the besiegers and the curtain wall. Just visible is the *fausse braye*, about halfway down the curtain wall. (Author›s photograph)

The view from the Tower of Spain to the Tower of the Virgin. This excellent photograph demonstrated the importance of the *petite tenaille* in interposing itself between the Ottoman attackers and the curtain wall. The *fausse braye* is also much in evidence. The new curtain wall had been broadened and new embrasures for artillery installed. The small rectangular towers connecting the fausse braye look entirely inadequate defences compared to the later additions. The great depth of the moats is also apparent. (Albert Gabriel, *La Cité de Rhodes, 1310–1522: Topographie, Architecture Militaire*, (Paris: E. de Boccard, 1921 & 1923))

St George Bastion – Bastion d›Auvergne[11]

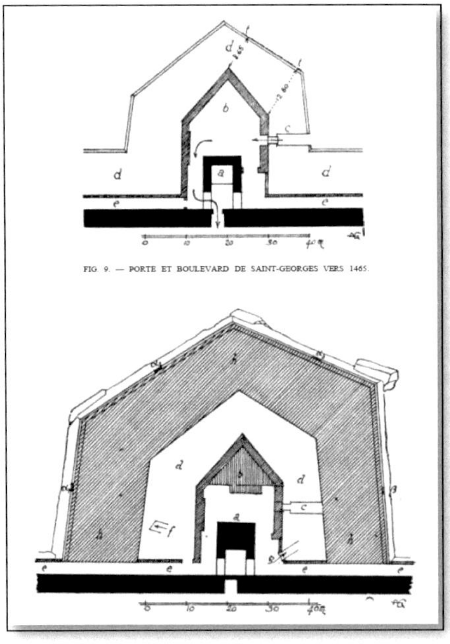

The original small square central tower was constructed in the early decades of the fifteenth century, it was open to the rear and only connected to the curtain wall by wooden ladders. As with the Gate of St John, a modest angled bulwark was first added. It was greatly enlarged by d'Aubusson but it was the work of the engineer Basilio Della Scuolla under de l'Isle Adam that produced the final form. The fortification was thrown forward producing a massive promontory upon which were placed numerous artillery pieces. It was to play an important part during the siege of 1522. (Albert Gabriel, *La Cité de Rhodes, 1310–1522: Topographie, Architecture Militaire*, (Paris: E. de Boccard, 1921 & 1923))

11 Albert Gabriel considered the term 'bastion' to be *impropre* as he preferred the term *boulevard* to describe the complex outwork that protected gateways. It is not a term that would find much favour with a modern audience, who would probably think it referred to a rather grand street. The bastion has been defined as a projecting part of a fortification built at an angle to the line of a wall, so as to allow defensive fire in several directions.

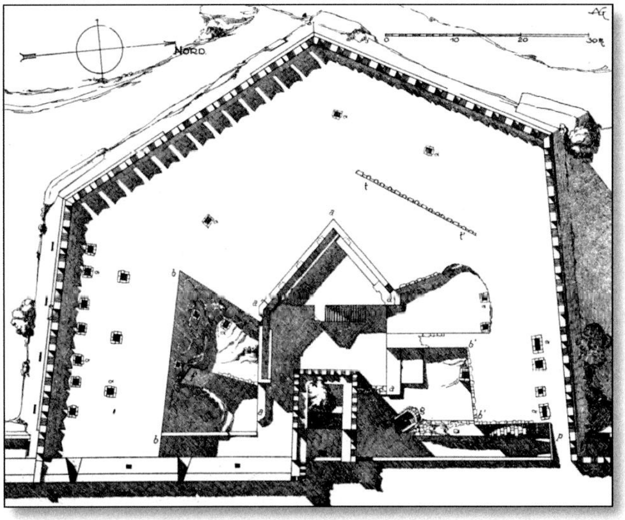

Plan view of the bastion. The original small rectangular tower can still be seen as can the first bulwark placed before it. (Albert Gabriel, *La Cité de Rhodes, 1310–1522: Topographie, Architecture Militaire*, (Paris: E. de Boccard, 1921 & 1923))

The ground level embrasures would sweep the moat with devastating fire to which would be added the fire from the main battery above and then small arms fire from the battlements. (Author's photograph)

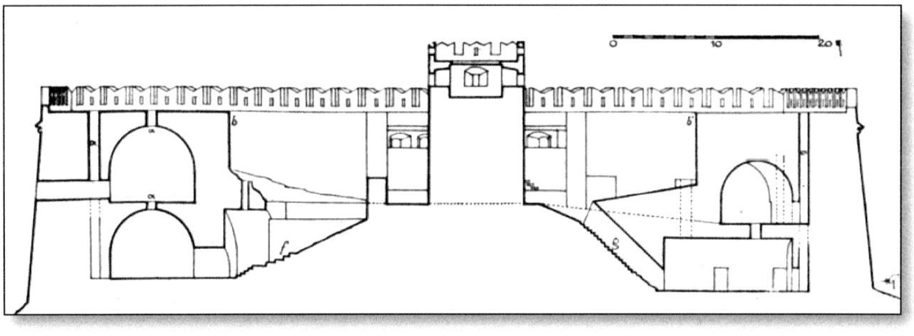

A plan view from the rear of the bastion. The extensive underground works become clear providing extensive storage space as well as firing points from which to cover the moat. There were internal chimneys included in the plan to aid ventilations especially of those spaces where forearms were being used. There is a remarkable amount of gas produced from the touch hole when a gun is fired even if the barrel protrudes beyond the emplacement. (Albert Gabriel, *La Cité de Rhodes, 1310–1522: Topographie, Architecture Militaire*, (Paris: E. de Boccard, 1921 & 1923))

Amboise gate and Grand Master's Palace

The view along the moat to the two massive towers of the Amboise Gate. (Author's photograph)

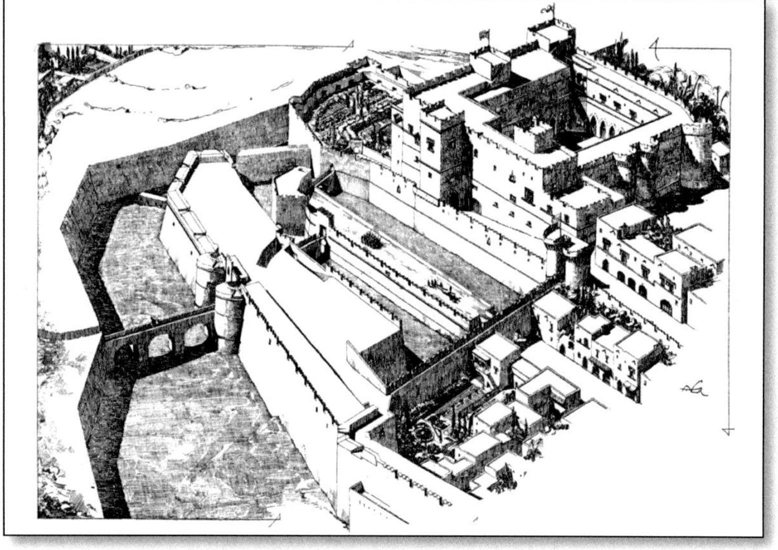

The current Grand Master's Palace is a piece of fascist theatrics meant to provide a summer residence for King Victor Emmanuel and Mussolini, although neither gentleman visited. Although it contains archaeological remains including superb mosaics and many classical pillars it owes more to Disney than d'Aubusson. The gate and bastion form a complex multi-layered defence. At this point the *fausse braye* which had been a companion to the main curtain wall ended. (Albert Gabriel, *La Cité de Rhodes, 1310–1522: Topographie, Architecture Militaire*, (Paris: E. de Boccard, 1921 & 1923))

The bridge and Amboise gate. (Author's photograph)

The moat to the left of the Amboise gate from the middle of the bridge. This gives an indication of the massive dimensions of this space. The end of the *fausse braye* can be seen at the bottom of the curtain wall in the middle of the picture. (Author's photograph)

The view in the other direction gives an excellent impression of how the massive fortifications dominate the space. Towards the end of the moat can just be seen the *caponier* and its gun ports, a late addition by Grand Master Carretto. (Author's photograph)

The *caponier* of the Post of France is a very early example of the type, it enfiladed the ground facing the Amboise gate. It does not extend the full width of the moat. It is an interesting design with a sloped roof and four firing ports. When walking the defences, it became apparent that the defenders were determined to pour down small arms fire from as many directions as possible on any attacking force in the moat. This *caponier* was perhaps an afterthought but a very unpleasant one. To the right of the *caponier* is the Battery of Olives, a small two-storey artillery tower built by Grand Master Amboise in 1511. (Author's photograph)

St Peter's Tower and Bastion

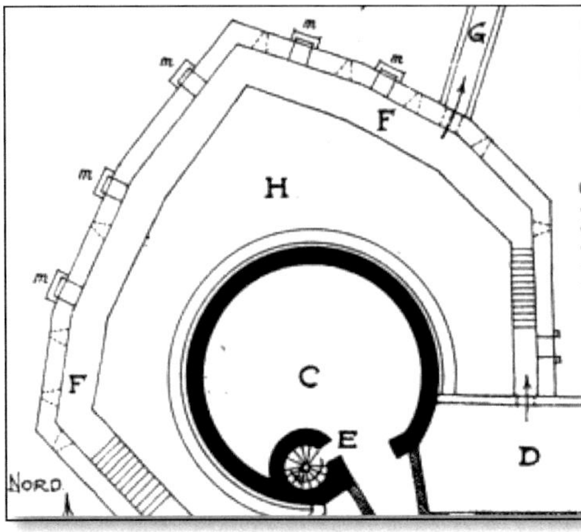

The tower itself is 13 metres in diameter and is connected directly to the curtain wall and is embellished with the devices of Pope Pius II as well as those of Grand Master Zacosta. It was modified with the addition of a polygonal bastion or outwork provided with a parapet with crenels and merlons as well as embrasures and arrow loops. Steps from the wall walk allowed access to the *fausse braye*, an oft-forgotten but important part of the defences. (Albert Gabriel, *La Cité de Rhodes, 1310–1522: Topographie, Architecture Militaire*, (Paris: E. de Boccard, 1921 & 1923))

The Tower and Defences of St Paul

The Tower was built by d'Aubusson in 1476, probably with funds given by Pope Sixtus V, whose Coat of Arms, together with those of the Grand Master, were placed on it. The bastion with gun ports was added after the first siege. (Author's photograph)

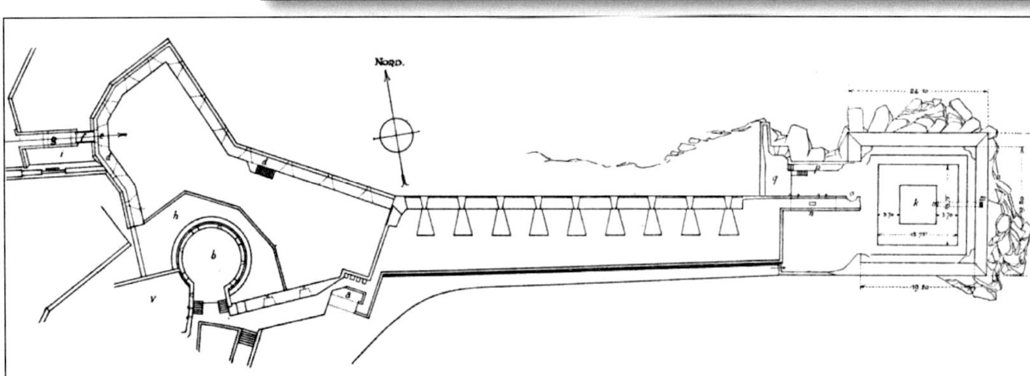

The Tower of St Paul on the left, with its new bastion and gate. The battery defending the mole is in the centre and the Tower of Naillac at the end. These defences covered the entrance to the Mandraki and the mole leading to the Tower of St Nicholas. The 'thickening' of the original 1480 fortifications produced not only more substantial defences but ones that exploited the firepower of the new artillery. (Albert Gabriel, *La Cité de Rhodes, 1310–1522: Topographie, Architecture Militaire*, (Paris: E. de Boccard, 1921 & 1923))

Naillac Tower

The Tower of Naillac was destroyed in 1863 during an earthquake. It was originally built upon the remains of an Hellenic structure at the extreme rocky end of the mole. It was built by Grand Master Naillac hence the name and controlled the entrance to the harbour, closing it with a chain which stretched to the Tower of Windmills. Albert Gabriel shows a rectangular tower surmounted by an octagonal turret in his reconstruction. The mole itself, constructed by Grand Master Flavian, was strongly reinforced, producing a continuous defensive structure with embrasures for artillery and small arms. (Albert Gabriel, *La Cité de Rhodes, 1310–1522: Topographie, Architecture Militaire*, (Paris: E. de Boccard, 1921 & 1923))

Between 1480 and 1522 the fortifications underwent continuous modification and modernisation presenting their attackers with a much tougher nut to crack. Rhodes at the time of the second siege probably possessed the most advanced fortifications of any city in Christendom. In addition Rhodes' defences mounted some of the most advanced weapons, including the surviving piece brought back with the Grand Master Adam specifically for service in the Tower of St Nicholas. The modification of the curtain walls, the widening of the ditches, the use of *terrepleins* and the massive rebuilding of all the key towers and gates into powerful bulwarks or bastions left no weak points to exploit. It is hardly surprising that ultimately the Ottoman force would have to rely upon mining and a war of attrition, to bring the siege to an end.

Some Notes on Walking the 'Medieval Trench'

Having now spent much of a day in the 'medieval trench', as it is described by the guidebook, surrounding the city of Rhodes, I can assure the reader that it is not a trench, nor is it a moat. A moat is, to my mind, narrow, damp and overgrown, as those used to British castles would understand it. This 'moat' feels much more like a quarry with almost vertical sides, impossible to scale, on each side. In places it is easy to see how what was already a deep moat was made even deeper as the Order's slaves dug deeper into the solid rock upon which the fortifications were built. With the 'moat' varying from 20 to 70 metres wide, the Order would have little problem in supplying the stone necessary to conduct the complete modernisation of their defences.

If the moat is impressive enough, what is even more so is the phenomenal size of the *tenailles*, the fortifications constructed by the creation of the extra-large moats. These were so brilliantly constructed as to make them appear like stone battleships protecting the main walls from attack. Although they might appear to be rather crude in construction, they were well-finished with fine ashlar masonry and strongly built embrasures for heavy artillery. The ends of the *tenailles* were also profiled to ensure that they did not provide 'dead ground' for any enemy unfortunate enough to find themselves there.

Being at ground level made me especially aware of the attention paid to providing a clear field of fire from bastions, *caponier*s and rectangular blockhouses, which were designed to provide covering fire across the moat. The assumption that it was the introduction of the *trace Italienne* that introduced the concept of flanking fire is clearly incorrect. The lower gun ports of the Tower of Italy, for example, as well as many of the other bastions, were clearly designed to protect the gun crew from direct fire from across the moat, while providing flanking fire along it. I was reminded of a gun position on Juno beach in Normandy, which was blind facing seawards but open to the flank, which gave it a clear field of fire along the beach and seafront. It was invulnerable to allied seaborne firepower and took a heavy toll on the Canadian tanks as they drove up the beach.

Portrait of Sultan Mehmet II

Portrait of Selim 'the Grim'

Plate A

See Colour Plate Commentaries for further information.

Detail of a cavalry action

Detail from the "The Battle of Pashan Begins"

Plate B

See Colour Plate Commentaries for further information.

Tower on the curtain wall of the city

Hospitaller 'Bombarde-mortier'

Plate C

See Colour Plate Commentaries for further information.

The attack on the Tower of St Nicholas 1480

Plate D

See Colour Plate Commentaries for further information.

The final Ottoman assault of 1480

Plate E

See Colour Plate Commentaries for further information.

The defences on the flank of St John's Tower of the Post of Provence

Plate F
See Colour Plate Commentaries for further information.

Grande Tenaille

Plate G
See Colour Plate Commentaries for further information.

The Carretto tower

Plate H
See Colour Plate Commentaries for further information.

The Tower of St Nicholas

Plate I

See Colour Plate Commentaries for further information.

Suleiman the Magnificent

Portrait of Tadini da Martinengo

Plate J

See Colour Plate Commentaries for further information.

Ottoman depiction of the siege of Rhodes 1522

Plate K
See Colour Plate Commentaries for further information.

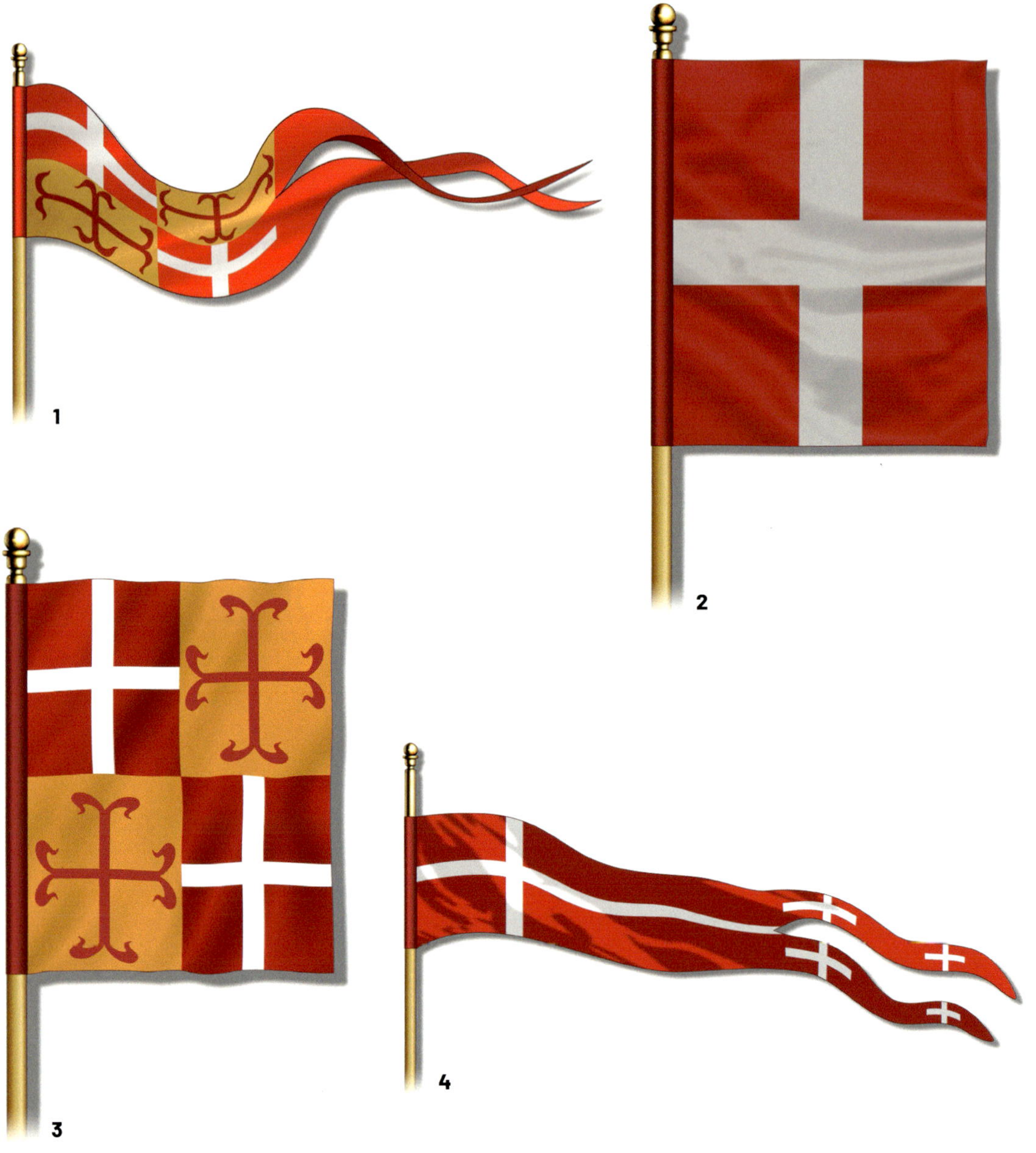

Plate L
Hospitaller Heraldry
See Colour Plate Commentaries for further information.

Plate M
Flags of the Langues
See Colour Plate Commentaries for further information.
Colour artwork by Anderson Subtil © Helion & Company

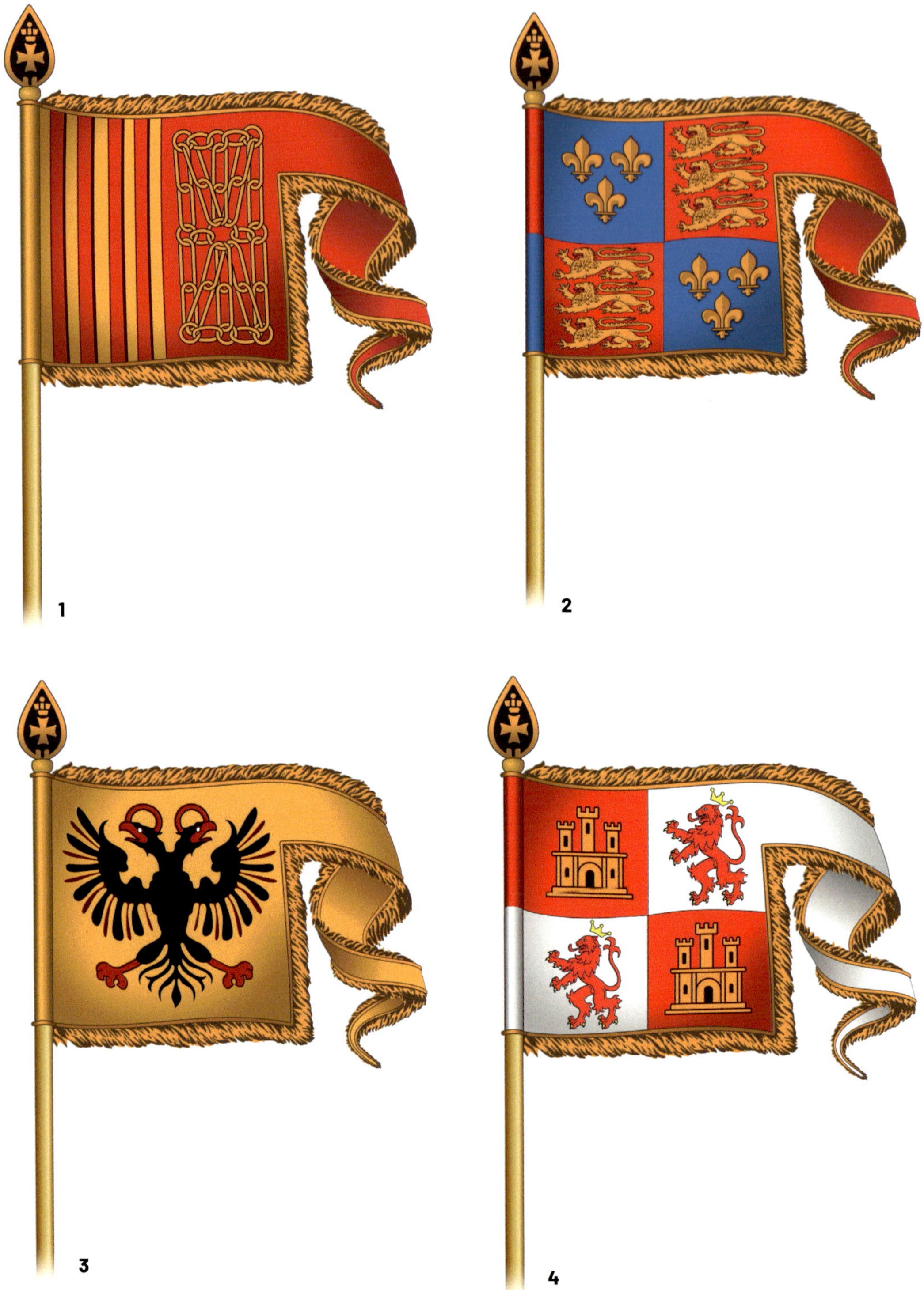

Plate N
Flags of the Langues
See Colour Plate Commentaries for further information.
Colour artwork by Anderson Subtil © Helion & Company

Pierre d'Aubusson 1

1476 1503

Emery d'Amboise 2

1503 1512

Guy de Blanchefort 3

1512 1513

Fabrizio del Carretto 4

1513 1521

Philippe Villiers de L'Isle-Adam 5

1521 1534

Plate 0
Grand Masters' Arms
See Colour Plate Commentaries for further information.
Colour artwork by Anderson Subtil

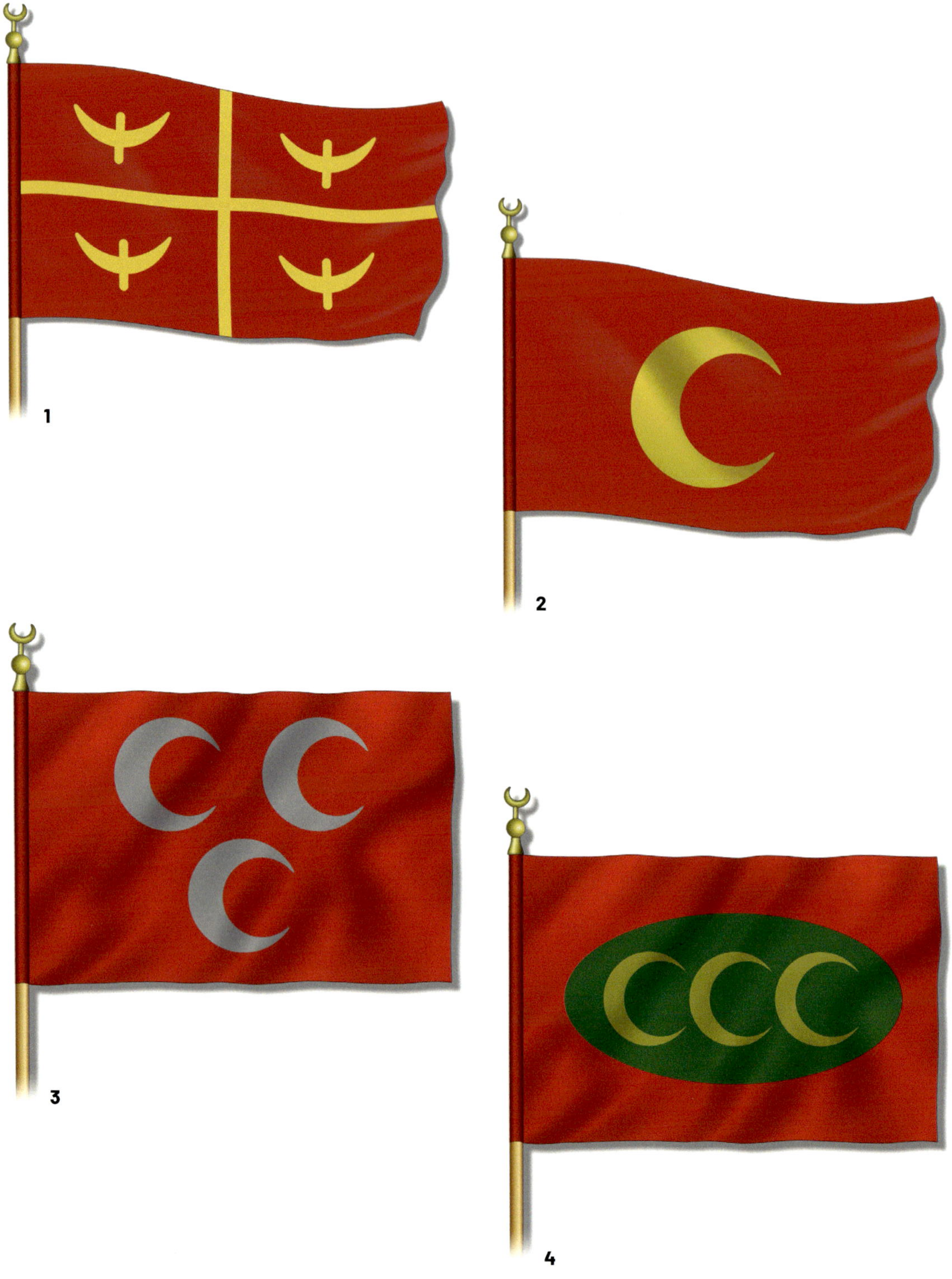

Plate P
Ottoman Heraldry
See Colour Plate Commentaries for further information.
Colour artwork by Anderson Subtil © Helion & Company

5

'New Artillery'

What was the 'artillery revolution' that ostensibly made the walls and towers that had defended cities and their rulers for centuries, useless? It has been associated with the events that accompanied the invasion of Italy by the French king Charles VIII. The eminent historian Geoffrey Parker, one of the principal authors of the revived 'Military Revolution debate', is in no doubt as to its importance:

> The catalyst of major change was the French invasion of the [Italian] peninsula in 1494–5. Charles VIII brought to Italy an army of 18,000 men and a horse-drawn siege train of at least forty guns. Even contemporaries realised that this marked a new departure in warfare: in 1498 the Venetian Senate declared that "the wars of the present time are more influenced by the force of bombards and artillery than by men-at-arms" and frantically set about acquiring arms.[1]

The oft-repeated description of the new artillery by Francesco Giucciardini, provided a brilliant summary of the very tangible impact that French artillery had in 1494 and how these pieces differed from their predecessors:

> The largest pieces of the artillery we are speaking of, were called bombards, and from that time were spread through Italy, and made use of in sieges. Some of them were made of iron, and some of bronze, but they were of so large a size, that, on account of the little experience of the gunners, and clumsiness of their carriages, they were moved from place to place very slowly, and with great difficulty, and for the same reason were very unhandy when placed against

1 Geoffrey Parker, *The Military Revolution: Military Innovation & the Rise of the West, 1500–1800* (Cambridge University Press, 1996), pp.9–10.

> the walls of a town. The intervals between the firings were so long, that a great deal of time was lost, and little progress was made in comparison to what we see these days. This gave time to the besieged to cast up ramparts and fortifications behind the breaches at their leisure. But, notwithstanding all these impediments, the violence of the saltpetre, of which gunpowder is made, was such that, when these weapons were fired, the balls flew with so horrible a noise, and stupendous force, even before they were brought to their present perfection, that they rendered ridiculous all the instruments, so much renowned, invented by Archimedes and others, and used by the Ancients in sieges of towns.
>
> But now the French brought a much handier engine, made of bronze, called a cannon, which they charged with heavy iron balls, smaller without comparison than those of stone made use of heretofore, and drove them on carriages with horses, not with oxen, as was the custom in Italy. And they were attended with such clever men, and on such instruments appointed for that purpose, that they almost always kept pace with the army. They were planted against the walls of a town with such speed, the space between the shots was so little, and the balls flew so quick, and were impelled with such force, that as much execution was done in a few hours, as formerly, in Italy, in the like number of days. These, rather more diabolical than human instruments, were used not only in sieges, but also in the field, and were mixed with others of smaller size. Such artillery rendered Charles's army very formidable to all Italy.[2]

Paolo Giovio described the movement of the artillery train through Rome. Here it was deployed successfully to intimidate the Pope who had ensconced himself in the Castel St Angelo:

> More than thirty-six guns, mounted on carts [carriages], induced astonishment and fright among everyone. They were drawn by horses, at incredible velocity, over flat ground and on slopes. The biggest of these, two and a half meters in length and two thousand kilograms of bronze in weight, were named cannons, and fired an iron ball as large as a man's head. After them followed the culverins, half as long again, but with a narrower barrel and a smaller shot. Falcons of different dimensions ended the parade. The smallest of them threw a ball similar in size to an orange .... The pace of cavalry could even be equalled by artillery carthorses, across plains, due to the tremendous skill of carters and masters.[3]

---

2 Francesco Guicciardini, *The History of Italy*, (Princeton: Princeton University Press, 1984), pp.147–149.

3 Paolo Giovio, *Le Historie del Suo Tempo* (Venice: Appresso Domenico de'

The key features of this new artillery could be summarised as follows:

> That they used lighter, more manoeuvrable bronze guns (rather than built up wrought iron pieces or cast bronze bombards)
> Iron balls were substituted for stone (iron has three times the density of stone) and were shot at higher velocities
> They were hauled and fired from their own gun carriages (rather than carried, dismounted and placed on wooden beds)
> The use of trunnions had become common: these simple devices allowed a gun to be laid quickly and accurately using a quoin or wedge between the barrel and a transom in the trail of the gun
> Horses were used as draught animals in contrast to the oxen preferred in southern Europe
> One further addition, often overlooked, was the development of the limber a simple two-wheeled axle fitted to a trail for the draught animals. This could be attached to the trail of the gun using a simple hole and pintle system. The unwieldy poorly balanced gun carriage was now converted into a stable four-wheeled cart

The consequences were that such weapons gave artillery much greater firepower and increased mobility:

> The rapidity and the efficiency with which French gunners could move, aim, and fire their guns represented an absolute, frightening novelty. The practice of positioning numerous guns near the walls, the simultaneity of the explosions, the saturation bombardments, the use of iron cannonballs, and the immediate infantry assaults were unprecedented in Italian Renaissance warfare. According to de Commines, Venetian senators were incredulous about the French way of seizing towns, which was simply "new, in Italy".[4]

Although the impact, literal and metaphorical, was great it was not as novel as it appeared to contemporaries. Robert Smith and Kelly DeVries in their magisterial study of Burgundian artillery are duly sceptical of Guiccardini:

> The mistake that Guiccardini made, which has been followed by all those who have relied on his statement .... was to attribute French success to revolutionary types of gunpowder weapons,

Farri, 1555), 59rv. In Fabrizio Ansani., "This French artillery is very good and very effective," 'Hypotheses on the Diffusion of a New Military Technology in Renaissance Italy', *The Journal of Military History*, 83 (April 2019), p.361.

4 "This French artillery is very good and very effective," Fabrizio Ansani, 'Hypotheses on the Diffusion of a New Military Technology in Renaissance Italy', *The Journal of Military History*, 83 (April 2019), p.364.

> iron cannonballs, and light, moveable carriages drawn by horse. In fact, none of these were new or revolutionary in 1494. The French gunpowder weapons were the same as those which had been in existence for half a century.[5]

The major innovation in artillery took place in the last quarter of the fifteenth century. It has often been assumed that this was a change from wrought iron guns built on a hoop and stave system to bronze guns. This is not the case; bronze had been used from the earliest time to cast guns and such guns are well represented in medieval manuscripts. The comparative absence of medieval bronze guns can be explained simply by the fact that bronze guns could be, and were, melted down and recast. For example, in 1433 it was recorded that 49 guns were melted down to cast a single gun weighing 3,904lb for the Compte de Saint-Pol.

The real change was in the internal architecture of the gun and its use of new cast iron ammunition. The large calibre barrel with a sub-calibre chamber would now be replaced by a constant diameter bore with the metal being at the thickest at the breech end and gradually diminishing towards the muzzle. The stone ball would be replaced by an iron one and the much higher pressures induced could be managed using cast bronze, exploiting the full potential of this wonderful material. This new weapon did not supersede all others, in practice wrought iron guns continued in use on a very large scale. Additionally, some bronze guns continued to be cast with sub-calibre chambers and thin-walled barrels, for shooting stone balls. Even the new bronze guns could be divided into two complementary types: a long-barrelled, narrow bore gun for longer-range and field work, and a shorter-barrelled larger bore gun for close and siege work.

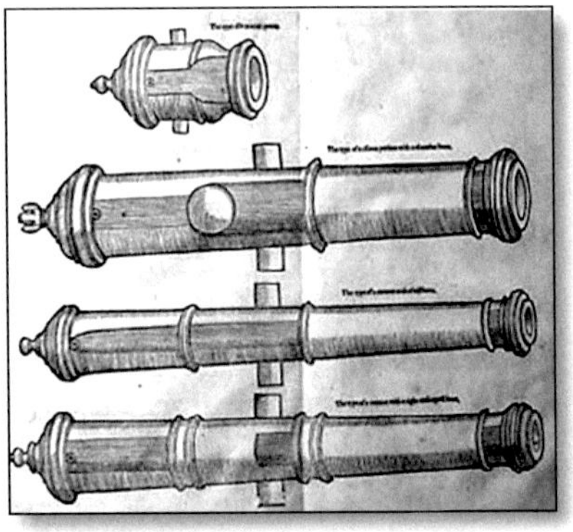

The principal types of cast guns, as illustrated in *Three Bookes of Colloquies*. They are, from top to bottom, mortar and perier (which both fired stone shot) and then a culverin and a cannon. Note the sub-calibre chamber in the mortar and perier as well as the unusual conical chamber in the culverin. There was much debate and dispute, as well as rubbish, talked about the design of the internal shape of the breech – Biringuccio has some choice words to say about the claims or boasts of his colleagues. (Nicolò Tartaglia: *Three Bookes of Colloquies* (London: John Harrison, 1588), pp.34–35)

The length of the barrel was calculated in calibres, that is the ratio of the diameter of the bore to the length of the tube of the barrel, measured from the muzzle to the touch hole. Cannons were on the whole large-bore weapons and had barrels of about 15–25 calibres, shooting iron shot and with the thickness of metal at the breech rather less than the diameter of its shot. Culverins providing the medium and field guns had barrels considerably longer than a cannon at over, and sometimes well over, 25 calibres. To add to the confusion some guns were called culverins or demi-culverins, while a falconet firing much smaller shot could be of a culverin type. The use of calibre to describe bore diameter was the result of an attempt to standardise bore diameter for a firearm known as a caliver.[6]

5 Robert Smith and Kelly DeVries, *The Artillery of the Dukes of Burgundy* (Woodbridge: Boydell, 2005), pp.43–44.

6 For the full explanation of its origin please see Jonathan Davies, *The Tudor Arte of*

López-Martín in his doctoral thesis identified the 1480s as the key period in development as bronze guns begin to develop their own design philosophy. He highlights the bronze pieces on display in Neuchâtel which can be precisely dated to 1488. These were also identified as important by Robert Smith from the Royal Armouries in his article on late medieval artillery.[7] With multi-faceted barrels, as were many of the late medieval bronze pieces, the Neuchâtel guns are in many respects very simple in design, with the metal thickest at the breech and thinnest at the muzzle. They were cast with trunnions, and concluded with a convex cone cascabel and a fitting for a vent cover. Perhaps the most important feature is the bore, which was of a constant diameter. They are of the form that would, in its fundamentals, be seen in use for almost four hundred years.

Although the fundamental shape of the barrel was now decided, the external appearance was not. A faceted shape was quite commonly cast in the late medieval period. The Norwich Great Hospital gun has a faceted octagonal barrel which turns by half of one flat about half way along the barrel. Faceting was one form of decoration the other was twisted faceting and barley stick forms, as well as exuberant and often beautifully detailed decorations. These were a gesture towards the aesthetic sensibilities of the age and would not have added to the strength of the barrel.

One of the most important innovations was the trunnions – the 'axle' around which the gun pivots. This was probably invented in the Duchy of Burgundy, although Venice has also claimed this honour, and it has also been attributed to the

Two late medieval field guns illustrated in the Swiss Schilling chronicle in the decade when many of the features of the new artillery were beginning to appear more widely. Both guns have cast bronze, part barley twist and part round, barrels. One is mounted in a wooden bed with a tiller attached, the other is fitted with trunnions and has a cast tiller. It is easy to see how the tiller fitted to the wooden bed on the right-hand gun could have led to the development of the barrel with a cast tiller on the left-hand piece. Both guns seem to be using cartridges rather than loose powder, indicative of the early adoption of this practice. This was especially sensible for field pieces that may have had to go into action quickly. The gunner on the right is using a pricker to clear the vent and prick the cartridge. Both guns have a towing ring which would suggest that they were not provided with limbers. The metal ladle seems to be of iron; they were usually of copper or brass to avoid sparking but this would not matter greatly with a bronze barrel. The ladle could be used mainly for loading loose powder, as a cartridge could simply be rammed down the barrel. (Diebold Schilling, Berner Chronik, vol. 3 p. 347. (1474-1484). www.e-codices.ch. courtesy of Burgerbibliothek Bern)

Tudor Warre, 1558–1603, volume 3, Retinue to Regiment series no.22, (Warwick: Helion & Co, 2023), p.273

7 Robert D. Smith, 'All Manner of Peeces: Artillery in the Late Medieval Period', *Royal Armouries Yearbook*, vol. 5 (2002), pp.130–138.

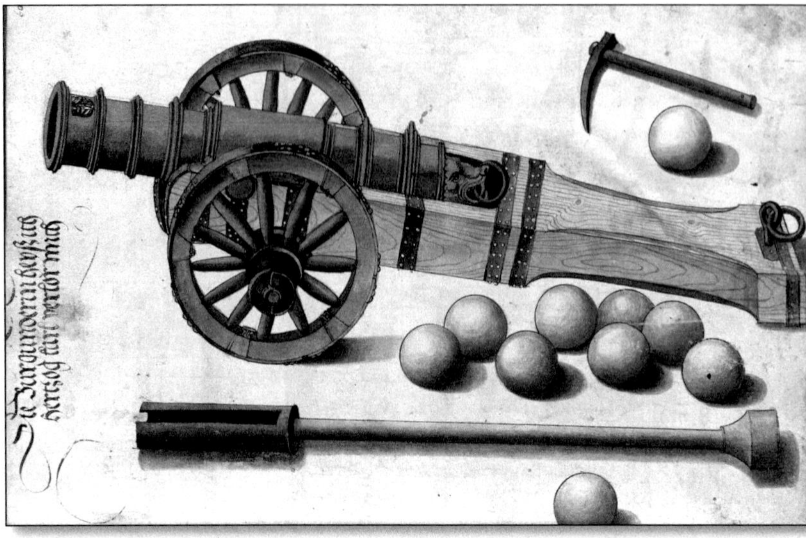

This cannon perrier illustrated in the Zeugbuch of Kaiser Maximilian demonstrated the advantages of trunnions and the 'modern' carriage. The trunnions enabled the gun to be elevated or depressed easily but they also transmitted the recoil force from the gun into the wheeled carriage. The whole piece would recoil and need to be re-laid but the carriage made it easy to move. Guns could be relocated along the rampart and reloaded under cover, before being wheeled to a shuttered embrasure, fired and then withdrawn, a form of the preferred 'shoot and scoot' tactic! (Zeugbuch Kaiser Maximilian I. Bayerische Staatsbibliothek München, Cod. icon. 222 p. 0115. Courtesy of the Bavarian State Library)

famous French artillerists the Bureau brothers. Carman refers to an entry in the archives of Lille referring to the making of trunnions for a serpentine in 1465.[8] The evidence for Burgundy comes from a small number of guns lost to the Swiss in 1476 and guns with trunnions are illustrated in the Swiss Chronicle of Diebold Schilling.[9] The earliest dateable piece belonging to the Order that was cast with trunnions can be dated to 1478 making it one of the earliest.

The development of the blast furnace in Europe in the late fourteenth century, meant that relatively cheap cast iron shot could be made on a very large scale. The casting of iron shot was certainly an easier task than casting iron barrels and was in use on a large scale far earlier, with medieval wrought iron guns such as the sling using iron shot in the late fifteenth century. Biringuccio claimed that iron shot was unknown in Italy until the arrival of the French in 1494.

The cannon-perier, although it appeared very similar to a cannon, was very different in its design. It was very economical in metal and powder use. The sub-calibre chamber held a small charge suited to a comparatively less

8 W. Y. Carman, *A History of Firearms* (London. Routledge & Kegan Paul, 1955), pp.34–35.

9 Diebold Schilling, Amtliche Berner Chronik, vol. 3 p.347.

Rhodes is littered with piles of stone cannon balls, usually neatly arranged and evidence of the long Ottoman occupation and not necessarily the siege. What is most apparent is their uniformity of size and the quality of their finish, which is remarkably high. In the West the labour cost of making such projectiles was another reason for abandoning their use, although the Portuguese with their new empire continued to use them. (Author's photograph)

dense stone rather than an iron projectile. This system produced relatively low barrel pressures allowing for a thinner, lighter barrel and therefore a cheaper gun. This characteristic of high breech and low barrel pressure was particularly apparent during the Middeladlercentret trials of their bronze gun. The disadvantage of this design was the expensive manufacture of stone balls which had to be hand carved from a single block. A stone that was not entirely round could cause a catastrophic failure of the gun. The price of labour in most of Europe made stone shot more expensive than iron. Stone shot was a perfectly satisfactory projectile for shooting at ships, or for counter-battery fire against field fortifications of wood and earth.

One weapon that shared some of the features of the cannon-perrier was the mortar. The use of high angle fire and indirect fire to discomfort the enemy was well understood in the Middle Ages. Mortars may have been used at the Siege of Constantinople in 1453 on the advice of the Sultan, and seven accompanied the army to the siege of Belgrade. The trebuchet provided direct fire against walls and indirect fire against the castle or city within. Biringuccio declared unequivocally that mortars, 'are not esteemed by us moderns.'[10] This is a strange conclusion to draw as high angle fire using large diameter projectiles appears to have been an aspect of siege warfare throughout this period. One of the largest pieces recovered from Rhodes was the bombard/mortar that could have been used in the siege of 1480.

Casting Bronze Cannon

Until about 1500, guns and bells were cast with the open end facing down. In a cannon where the metal is thickest and volume greatest the cooling will be slower. As the metal at the top freezes, it blocks any more liquid bronze feeding into the spaces caused by contraction lower down and it would also stop any more gas escaping. This is why tin was commonly added at the end of the pour to keep the metal liquid for longer. Ideally the cannon, like a bell would be cast muzzle down to reduce these problems, as in the early days it was.

Casting breech down and muzzle up seems to have first taken place at the end of the fifteenth century probably because of the contemporary

10 Vannoccio Biringuccio, *The Pirotechnia*, (New York: Dover Publications Inc., 1990), p.227.

observation that so much dross, spots of tin, air and gas floated or bubbled to the top of the casting, which would potentially seriously weaken the breech. The advantage of casting a large bronze gun is that a thick mould and heavily packed earth or sand would act as an insulation permitting a freezing process slow enough to allow the escape of gas and permit more feeding of metal to offset shrinkage. Bell founders did not change their methods. This was partly out of tradition but also because the very large core of the bell is hollow and there is much less gas pressure in the mould, usually producing a better result.

The great advantage that muzzle-up casting gave was to increase the density of the metal at the breech; meanwhile all the dirt, dross and scum would (hopefully) float to the top. The considerable weight of bronze meant that in a long barrel the metal would be under significant pressure, stopping gas bubbles from nucleating and thereby reducing porosity. A three-metre long cannon with a 300mm head of bronze above it, would create a pressure at the breech of 280 kN/m^2 or 40 psi (rather less than three atmospheres). The consequence of this would be a stronger and more importantly a safer piece. Much higher pressures could therefore be sustained enabling dense iron shot to be fired at high velocity.

The new gun that was the product of these changes was far more formidable than the older stone-throwing weapons. The high velocity iron projectile was far more destructive and the gun itself far more manageable and capable of a much higher rate of fire. In a list of artillery required to support an English Army in 1513 the number of rounds recommended to be fired per day for the larger pieces varied from thirty to forty; this compared with the five rounds a day suggested for the bombards which were also part of the artillery train. The rate of fire for bronze guns was comparatively low only because of the danger of overheating the barrel.

Table 1: List of artillery required to support an English Army of 15,000 foot and 3,000 horse 1513.[11]

Name	Weight of iron shot (lb)	Weight of powder (lb)	Rounds per day
Bombard	260	80	5
Curtow	60	40	40
Culverin	20	22	36
Nuremburg piece	20	20	30
Apostle	20	20	30
Lizard	12	14	37
Minion	8	8	NA
Pot gun	56 (stone)	40	NA

11 Letters and Papers, Foreign and Domestic, Henry VIII, Volume 1, March. 1513 (State Papers Henry VIII.,7, f. 51. R.O. 1726. [4633.] ORDNANCE.)

These new pieces did not make the iron or bronze bombard irrelevant, even if it was by most measures obsolete. They would continue to be used in the West well into the sixteenth century and by the Ottomans for far longer. If their stone ammunition and enough manpower to handle them was available, then they could still be a valuable addition to any siege battery. The 'obsolete' wrought-iron gun also continued to be used on a large scale. As Robert Smith has proved by analysing contemporary documentation, studying remaining pieces and through practical experimentation, such guns were viable and effective weapons of their time and remained so until there were enough 'modern' weapons to replace them. Although all the pieces associated with Rhodes in museums are bronze, Hedenborg in his account refers to iron guns as well as bronze and the illustration in Caoursin from 1482 show similar numbers of bronze and iron pieces.[12] On the barrels of both types of cannons can apparently be seen 'hoops,' which had a practical use in the construction of the wrought iron guns but were purely decorative in the case of bronze weapons.

It is clear that the defences of Rhodes in 1480 were quite inadequate. What saved the day was the leadership of d'Aubusson and the determination of the leaders and the weakness of their enemies. The revolution in artillery that took place in precisely the period between the two sieges required that the defences had to undergo a massive refurbishment as well as considerable amount of new building, based on new ideas.

Ottoman Guns in 1522

The Ottomans are perhaps the power most associated with cast bronze bombards. They are referred to in the siege of Corinth in 1446 and above all at the successful siege of Constantinople in 1453. On that occasion the Ottomans had over a dozen monster cannon, used to breach the five-metre thick and twelve metre high defences of the city. The siege guns of Sultan Mahomet II were cast in Adrianople from scrapped cannon, under the supervision of the renegade Hungarian, Urban. This use of foreign experts was quite common. Leonard of Chios recorded that, at the siege of Constantinople, Ottoman engineers were assisted by Greeks, Italians, Germans, Hungarians and Bohemians. The assumption could be made that the Ottoman use of Christian expertise and continued use of the bombard, was evidence of backwardness, but this is not the case by any means.

The Ottoman siege train certainly contained bombards but it also contained a wide range of other, what might be described as, 'modern pieces'. Bourbon very helpfully records the following weapons in the

12 J. Hedenborg, 1854 Geschichte der Insel Rhodos von der Urzeit bis auf die heutigen Tage, ΚΒ΄ Εφορεία Προϊστορικών και Κλασικών Αρχαιοτήτων, Mss. KK 5090–5094.

Ottoman siege train of 1522. We can assume that he could correctly identify the weapons and the projectiles that were fired at him!

> First there were 6 great guns cannons perriers of brass [bronze] that shot a stone of three foot and a half. Also there were 15 pieces of iron that shot stones of 5 or 6 spans [12 inch diameter approx.]. Also there were 14 great bombards that shot stones of about 11 spans [32 in]. Also there was 12 Basilisks wherof they shot but with 8 that is to wit 4 shot against the post of England and Spain [each] and 2 against the gate of Italy the other 2 shot sometime against St Nicholas Tower. Also there was 15 double guns casting balls as basilisks [same diameter]. The mean [smaller] shot [guns] as sacres and passovalanti [falcon-falconet] were in great number. [13]

He also refers to twelve mortars deployed during the siege at various points, of which one was broken.

The cannon perriers that he refers to were not ideally suited to bombarding a well-built stone fortification. These pieces were economical but the stone shot was fired at lower velocities than the iron and the shot itself was likely to fragment on stone defences rather than smash them. It was a weapon more suited to defence than attack.

The basilisks were perhaps the most formidable siege weapons at the disposal of the Ottomans. They were named after a legendary reptile so deadly that it could kill with a single glance or breath. These were exceptionally long-barrelled guns cast of constant diameter bore, firing iron projectiles at high velocity. Both surviving examples are constructed of wrought iron and have a fairly smooth exterior. This is itself somewhat perplexing. The Ottomans were clearly capable of casting massive guns from bronze and the design of the basilisk would be highly suited to casting. Is it simply that the bronze examples were recast or was wrought iron preferred? One of these monster guns is 7m in length and the other even longer at nearly 7.5m, they both have a similar bore of 24–25cm and would have fired a projectile weighing about 42kg. Both were forged in 1517 and might well have accompanied the expedition of 1522. What is surprising is that neither was equipped with trunnions. As with the bombards they were

The Dardanelles Gun is a magnificent representative of the Ottoman bombards that captured the imagination of Christendom in the conquest of Constantinople. It is 5.18m (204in) in length with a bore of 63.5cm (25in) and would have fired a stone projectile weighing about 300kg (661lb). It is in two parts, the sub-calibre breech with a bore diameter of 23cm (9in) and the full calibre barrel, joined by a screw mechanism. It was made in 1464 and the evidence suggests that it was cast like a bell, muzzle down. Although truly impressive guns, their glacially slow rate of fire and their lack of flexibility made them far less a threat than their size would have suggested. (Gaius Cornelius. Public domain, via Wikimedia Commons)

13 Jacques de Bourbon, *Grande et Merveilleuse, & Trés Cruelle Oppugnation de la noble Cité de Rhodes*, (London: 1524), page unnumbered.

provided with lugs and rings to secure them to substantial wooden beds. Perhaps in a prolonged siege this mattered less but it would suggest a certain backwardness when compared to the pieces employed by the Order.

The 'double cannons' firing iron balls have no obvious surviving extant examples although they are likened to basilisks. Jacque de Bourbon was equating the Ottoman pieces to European types and it is therefore not unreasonable to identify these guns with what were the largest guns of this type in service in the West. William Bourne provided an impressively comprehensive list of ordnance from a much later date.[14] His 'Old Double Cannon' had a bore diameter of 8¼ inches a length of 12 ft and a shot weighing 70lb. Caruana in his list of Tudor artillery refers to a cannon Royal firing shot of 60–68lb with a calibre of 8–8¼ inches.[15] This corresponds to the Curtow referred to in a list of English ordnance from 1513 which fired shot weighing 60lb. It would seem probable that an Ottoman 'double cannon' could have fired iron shot weighing 60–70lb from an 8inch bore barrel about 12 feet long. In the absence of an extant example, it would be safe to assume that these guns, like the basilisks, were not fitted with trunnions. The mortars referred to by Bourbon would have shot projectiles varying in weight from 200–300kg. There is no surviving Ottoman example but there is one belonging to the Order which would have fired a similar weight stone ball.

Hospitaller Ordnance

We are extraordinarily fortunate in that several of the Order's guns were left on the island in 1522 and given as a present to Napoleon III in 1862 by the Turkish Sultan. This was no doubt in return for French participation as an ally in the recent Crimean war. Napoleon III had an academic interest in artillery and was the author of the first serious study of artillery, published in 1846. To these 'trophy' guns can be added some guns belonging to the Order found in Museums in Istanbul and Europe. Hedenborg also provided a detailed description of the fortification and the disposition of some of the artillery.

An illustration from *Recueil des croniques et anciennes istoires de la Grant Bretaigne* by Jean de Wavrin (Royal 14 E IV BL f.28v.) (*c.* 1470 to *c.* 1480). The mounting for the bombard-mortar illustrated here is clearly inadequate to meet the massive recoil forces that would be generated on firing. (By kind permission of the British Library)

14 'List of Ordnance' from William Bourne, *The Arte of Shooting in Great Ordnaunce* (London, 1587), pp.65–71.

15 Lists of artillery dated 1535–1563, quoted in Caruana *Tudor Artillery*, p.13–14.

The earliest piece in the collection of Hospitaller guns at the Musée de l'Armée in Paris was almost certainly present at the siege of 1480. It was, according to the description around the muzzle, cast at Chartres in 1478 on the command of Louis XI by his Master of Artillery, Jahan Chollet. It was a gift to Pierre d'Aubusson and was accompanied by substantial funds which were used to reinforce the Tower of France and the Tower on the Windmill mole. In 1481, after the siege, Louis had four more pieces cast at Orleans, weighing 2,700 livres (1322kg) for service against the Turks, the enemies of the Catholic faith. It was in many respects a traditional design and was almost certainly cast muzzle down. It has a sub-calibre chamber (diameter 15cm) with a barrel bore 23cm in diameter, weighs 1603kg, and would have fired stone shot. The fore-part of the barrel is divided into three sections indicated by simple mouldings which are decorative rather than practical. They are intended to mimic the appearance of wrought iron guns where the larger hoops stand proud of the others. The rear of the breech is flat, without a decorated cascabel, which would appear on later pieces. If the gun was mounted on a wooden bed, the rear of the breech would have butted against a substantial wooden frame designed to absorb the recoil and this is why it would have had to have been flat. This gun is fitted with very early examples of trunnions which would have enabled the gun to be elevated or depressed and would have transmitted the recoil to the substantial wooden cheeks in which they rested. It is a peculiar combination of old design elements together with the very latest innovation. (Author's photograph)

Die Katerie was a bronze bombard, and the gift of Pierre d'Aubusson. It was cast by Georg Endorfer at Innsbruck in 1487. It bears the Arms of Sigismund of Austria and the legend 'My name is Katerie, beware of my strength, I punish injustice, Jorg Endorfer cast me'. It displays an unusually early pair of dolphins (or lifting lugs), which were used to hoist the piece at roughly its point of balance. It also has cast 'rings' along the barrel and a swollen 'midriff' which are reminiscent of the shape of wrought iron bombards. It has a sub-calibre powder chamber and like the piece above would have fired stone shot weighing about 70kg. The rectangular projections are for seating it in a wooden bed. It is an impressive collection of old and new features and indicates how capable gun founders were in producing very large cast bronze pieces by the end of the fifteenth century. The flat breech end would have butted against a wooden recoil mounting. The gun is 3.65m long with a bore of 39cm, it weighed a magnificent 4,597kg. Hedenborg identified the piece as being in or near the tower of St Paul. (Author's photograph)

Decorated with fleur de lys in its mid-section this fine piece clearly has a tapering barrel, although it is a perrier with a sub-calibre chamber and fired stone balls. The rather clumsy and over-large trunnions, as with other earlier examples, were parallel sided and positioned mid centre of the barrel. Later they were placed lower and were more cone shaped to enable them to self-centre the barrel in the carriage. The exterior, especially the breech end, mimics the appearance of wrought iron guns. I assume that this was not for aesthetic reasons but reflected a common understanding that this shape gave greater strength, which of course it didn't. (Author's photograph)

This is one of the last pieces of artillery belonging to the Order at Rhodes and dateable to the second siege. It carries the Arms of Grand Master de l'Isle Adam and must have been cast in 1521–22. It is a complex casting with each section consisting of sixteen facets all of which are offset from the previous section. Faceting was quite a common feature of late medieval pieces, and continued into the first decades of the sixteenth century. The trunnion is set slightly lower than the other guns but is still parallel sided. There is significant muzzle flare which indicated an understanding that this was often the weakest portion of the barrel as it was subject to casting flaws, including migration of tin. It was almost certainly cast muzzle down in contrast to the earlier pieces. It has a bore of 14.5cm and its tapering barrel would have fired iron projectiles weighing about 10kg. (Author's photograph)

This piece has a projecting lug at the breech end that would probably have fitted into an elevating arc, a traditional system which would soon be replaced by a simple elevating wedge or quoin placed beneath the breech. (Author's photograph)

One of the most unusual survivals is a gun that was cast specifically for service on the Tower of St Nicholas. It was cast with the Arms of Grand Master Emery d'Amboise (1503–1512). There is a Latin inscription that translates as *For the defence of the Tower of St Nicholas*. It is very similar to the other perriers of the period and is a workmanlike piece, with trunnions, a flat cascabel, and with cast rings on the chase. It is 2.55m long with a bore of 23.2cm and weighs 1427kg. According to Hedenborg it was one of a number of guns with an inscription dedicating them to the defence of St Nicholas. How many guns remained after the gift of 1862 is unknown but they could be double the number presented to Napoleon, if Hedenborg's account is to be trusted. (Author's photographs)

There are two other very long cannons associated with Pierre d'Aubusson, one faceted and the other round, both dateable to before 1489 and both now found in the Istanbul Military Museum (Askerî Müze). They are fitted with round and faceted projections from the cascabel to fit an elevation arc and trunnions positioned halfway up the barrel and near the point of balance. These contrast with the later cannon perriers which reflected some aspects of older medieval designs, such as the external finish.

Two other very long-barrelled guns dated to between 1498 and 1515, are to be found in the collection of the Musée de l'Armée in Paris. Both have long tapered barrels which although they appear to have reinforces, that is a stepped appearance in barrel diameter, this is actually achieved by a change in decoration, as the reduction in diameter is constant from base ring to muzzle. The longer, which is faceted, has a tiller at the cascabel for use with an elevating arc. It is 5.4m overall with a bore of 16.5cm, and weighs 3343kg. It would have fired a projectile weighing about 13kg. Its exceptionally long barrel would place it in the category known as the basilisk. The shorter piece would have fired iron shot weighing 15kg and has a simple flat base ring suggesting that it was mounted between two cheek pieces and elevated using a quoin or wedge. According to Hedenborg this piece was to be found in the Post of Italy

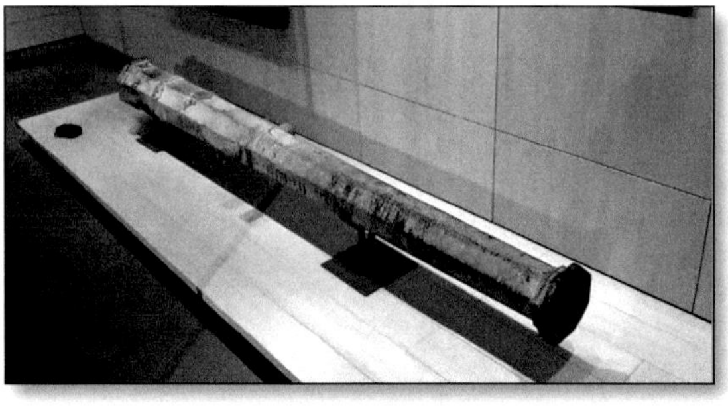

One extraordinary survival is a demi-culverin that was probably cast by Alessandro Gioardi in Italy for the Order of St John, on the orders of King Henry VIII. It is a fine long-barrelled faceted piece, useful for land or sea service. It bears the Arms of Phillipe Villiers de l'Isle Adam, Grand Master 1521–1534, and a poor cast of the Coat of Arms of England. The vent had been enlarged by use, then reamed and screwed to fit a replacement bronze or possibly iron pierced screw bolt. It is very similar in form to the faceted gun found in the Askeri Museum. Such guns were estimated to have a maximum range of three-quarters of a mile, with a point-blank range of 250 yards. This gun is currently in the Museum of St John in Clerkenwell, London.
Overall length: 109¼in (2.775m), length muzzle to touch hole: 100in (2.55m), diameter of bore 3.15in (80mm); diameter of projectile: 3in (76mm),[16] weight of projectile: 3¾lb (1.7kg). (Author's photograph)

16 The normal windage for Italian pieces was one twentieth of the bore diameter

Philippe de l'Isle Adam came to England to raise support for the order. In 1528 he met Henry VIII who promised him 20,000 ducats (ducats being the trade coin used in Europe at that time) towards an expedition for the recovery of Rhodes. In the end, this gift took the form of nineteen bronze cannons, of which this is probably one, as well as 1,023 cannon balls. Brother John Sutton, one of the Knights of St John, brought the cannons to the Order's new home of Malta, travelling via Syracuse in Italy. Later the Order took the cannons to Tripoli, but in 1551 after six days of fighting, Ottoman forces captured it from the Knights and seized the cannons. The Ottoman forces took some of the cannons, including this one, to Cyprus, where they used them in the Siege of Famagusta in 1571. Over three hundred years later, in around 1906, a sponge-diver happened to find this cannon, half buried in sand and mud in Famagusta harbour.

One other probably Hospitaller gun is today in England and this is a falcon barrel that may have been cast on behalf of Emery d'Amboise, who was Grand Master of the Order of St John from 1503–1512. The presence of what may have been his emblem on the barrel, *not* quartered with the Cross of the Order, would suggest that it was cast prior to 1503. The Genoese gunfounder Gregorio I Gioardi has been identified with the polygonal ordnance cast in 1499 and currently in the Fortress of Sarzanello, which included an octagonal falcon and a polygonal culverin and saker. The capital 'G', in Lombardic script, on the barrel surrounding the touch hole is associated with Gregorio I Gioardi. (Author's photographs)

We do not have detailed records of all of the pieces that were used by the Order in the siege of 1522 but the guns that have survived can be used to draw some tentative conclusions. The cannon-perrier was clearly a popular choice as it combined hitting power against ships and siege works with economy of material and propellant. At the same time the Order was employing the most modern long-barrelled weapons firing iron shot. The Order showed a willingness to use the latest technology, such as the trunnion and dolphin, while on occasion still employing the older style of exterior finish. What is also apparent is the piecemeal nature of the armament or re-armament of the defences of Rhodes. Pieces came from across Europe, France, Italy and the Empire, as gifts or commissions. This was entirely to be expected as the idea of a class of gun, mass produced to the purchaser's specifications could only be found in an individual gun founder's workshop for a single contract. Compared to the Ottoman weapons, those of the Order were certainly more 'modern' and provided a better balance of throw weight and velocity.

It is easy to stray down the technological determinist's path when explaining the outcome of a battle or a siege. In the siege of 1480 what were medieval defences resisted the most modern gunpowder weapons. In 1522 the Order could probably boast superiority in artillery technology with a higher proportion of modern pieces and yet it lost. The Ottoman guns may have severely damaged the 'modern' fortifications but it was the extensive undermining of the walls that was more conclusive in making the city indefensible. Guns mattered and fortifications mattered but they were part of a much larger equation.

Artillery performed key roles in a siege as Peter Purton pointed out:

> The purpose of such a bombardment varied. It might have been to keep the garrison's heads down to enable an assault on the walls to be launched, or to damage the physical structure of the defences, or to terrorise the population: all these objectives were part of medieval as well as modern warfare and nothing has changed there.[17]

It was one thing to knock walls down and metaphorically to kick the door in, quite another to capture the city – eventually it would come down to a hand-to-hand fight, unless the garrison chose to surrender.

17 Peter Purton, 'Ancient, Medieval and Modern: Continuity and Change in Siege Warfare', on *Academia.edu* page unnumbered.

6

Military Engineering

It is often, and wrongly, assumed that military engineering was a 'modern' innovation and that early-modern and medieval armies consisted only of fighting men. They, just as a modern army does, relied on engineers to mend and build bridges, clear obstacles, construct fortifications and prepare for an assault. Civilian craftsmen could be co-opted to provide the wide range of skills required, while unskilled labourers could be used as pioneers. Christine de Pisan, one of the most extraordinary women in the medieval world, provided an invaluable treatise on the art of war, drawn mostly from the Roman author Vegetius, as well as clearly benefiting from advice provided by contemporary military professionals. Written in 1410, her book gained a greater audience after print editions by Antoine Vérard in 1488, and William Caxton in 1489. She provided a detailed, though theoretical, account of the stores and personnel required to conduct a siege. The following section gives a good indication of the preparations needed for such an expensive and complex operation:

> XXVII
> Other equipment [required for a siege]
> First of all thirteen hundred shields, two hundred lanterns, and thirty other lanterns, sixteen feet tall, bound with great bands of iron to place in the ground.
> Item, twenty-seven thousand ropes [wicks] covered with pitch to burn in these lamps.
> Item, for mining, four hundred pointed spades for the foot soldiers, if they break theirs, one thousand wooden shovels, four hundred scoops to empty water, twelve large iron hooks, each with two loops.
> Item, fifteen hundred baskets, all with provisions, two lanterns.
> Item, a thousand large iron bars a foot and a half long and twelve smaller ones.
> Item, four barrels of nail; those in one of which will be half a foot long, another four fingers, another three and another two.
> Item, three equipped forges, two ropemakers, two leatherworkers, wheelwrights, two wood-turners to make plugs [tompions] for the

> cannons. Two carts filled with elm wood to make these plugs, three thousand bundles of iron, sixty bundles of steel, sixty measures of charcoal from dirt, of which three measures make two-sixths, two hundred sacks of wood charcoal for the workmen, two thousand pounds of spun rope to make cords for the machines [siege machines].
> Item, for the leatherworkers, forty tanned cowhides to make bases for the machines, twenty five rawhides to make slings for these machines, twenty-five rawhides to make girdles for those slings [trebuchets].
> Item, for the wheelwrights, wood will be taken when needed from what has been brought on the carts mentioned above.
> Item, to attach the ropes to the machines, leather strings bound with iron and other small things necessary for the machines will be prepared.
> Twenty-two barrels that can be locked.
> Item, eighty wheelbarrows shaped like stretchers to put stones in for the cannon barrels.[1]

The sieges of Rhodes required several major engineering feats. Firstly, a floating bridge that was used in the assault on St Nicholas in 1480, secondly, the construction of mantlets to protect the besieging artillery, and thirdly the preparation for an assault which involved filling the moats and providing ladders to scale the walls and debris. Christine de Pisan provided more insights into how these projects could be achieved. When it came to a river crossing, the commander would have good portable bridges made off site:

> He will have them brought on carts. Some of these can be made of empty barrels tied and attached to each other, with solid planks well hooked together placed upon them. Like a drawbridge, these can be placed in the water at once by the skill of clever artisans, with whom he will be well provided.
>
> Still others can be made by attaching boats to each other and then covering them with planks of wood well fastened together.[2]

There are numerous examples of 'floating bridges' contained in books such as *Bellifortis*,[3] designed to inform the technically minded. Invariably intended for peaceful river crossings rather than an assault, it was recommended that

1 Christine de Pisan., *The Book of Deeds of Arms and of Chivalry* (Pennsylvania State University Press, 1999), pp.121–122.

2 Christine de Pisan., *The Book of Deeds of Arms and of Chivalry* (Pennsylvania State University Press, 1999), p.52.

3 Konrad Kyeser (1366-1405), *Bellifortis* (strong in war): Munich. Bayerische Staatsbibliothek, Clm 30150, ff. 41v–43r, 67r/v.

the planking be covered with earth to encourage animals to cross. No such detail was necessary for the Turkish assault troops.

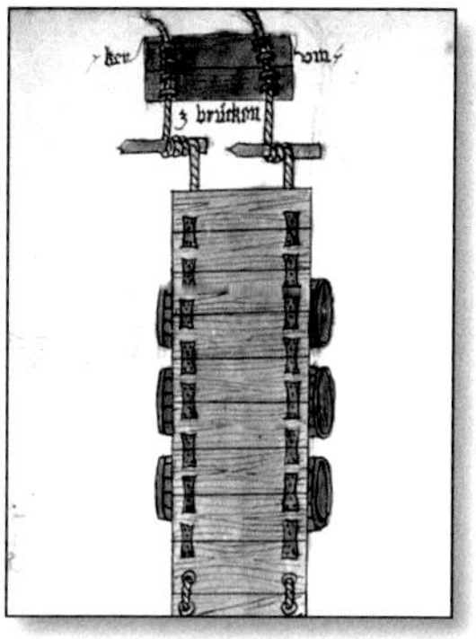

A floating bridge from the *Kriegsbuch* of Philipp Mönch. In this example he is using barrels as flotation devices. Part of the planking is held together with iron fixings and part with rope. There are two large stakes, used as land anchors, to secure the bridge to the shore as well as a plank section to bring men, horses and vehicles safely on to the bridge itself. Such constructions were everyday tasks for a competent military engineer. (Universitätsbibliothek Heidelberg, Cod. Pal. germ. 126 p.34)

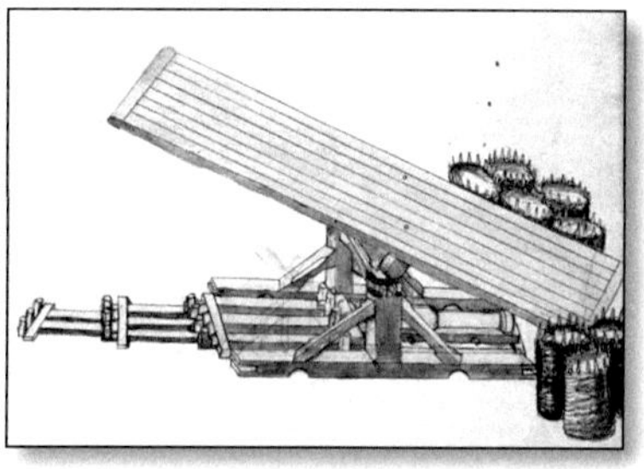

This illustration from Mönch's *Kriegsbuch* gives some indication of the efforts required to emplace even a small cannon. The gun itself is relatively small but still required an extensive and heavy timber construction to absorb the recoil of the piece. Gabions, earth-filled wicker baskets, can be seen providing a degree of protection on the flanks of the emplacement. A depth of a dozen feet of earth or more would be necessary to deal with high velocity iron shot. The massive wooden mantlet would protect the gun crews only from firearms and not artillery but would also provide an excellent aiming mark. Once in situ it would be nearly impossible to lay the gun onto another target without rebuilding the whole emplacement. (Universitätsbibliothek Heidelberg, Cod. Pal. germ. 126 p.87)

The assault when it took place would require ladders, and plenty of them. Establishing the height of the wall was essential or disaster would ensue, as it did at the assault on Leith in 1562. Christine de Pisan recommended using a piece of string attached to an arrow shot to the top of the wall. Alternatively, the length of shadow of the wall at a specific time could be compared with the length of shadow of a stick of a known length simultaneously. Both procedures posed problems and risks. The quadrant could be used to measure the angle from the observer's eye to the top of the wall and tower. If the distance from the bottom of the wall to the observer was known then the height could be calculated using a scale drawing or trigonometry, remembering of course to add the height of the observer.

Christine de Pisan went on to add a fairly comprehensive list of the 'small equipment for the attack':

> First one hundred picks, fifty goats-feet grappling hooks, sixteen bridge joinings, twenty four large and strong double ladders with four levels to support four men-at-arms together, from thirty to forty feet high, and on each ladder three pulleys at the upper end.

> Item seven to eight score of other ladders from twenty-four to twenty-six feet high and still other smaller ones[4]

Climbing up a high wall in armour was a nightmare at the best of times, but an essential activity if a town or castle was to be taken by storm. Medieval engineers came up with innumerable versions of scaling ladders. Two issues concerned them: firstly how to stop the legs of the ladder slipping at the bottom and secondly how to secure the ladder onto the top of the wall. There were also rope ladders and other lightweight examples designed for 'commando style' operations. During such a dangerous ascent it would have been vital for the attackers to keep up covering fire concentrating on any arrow slits or crenels, where an enemy sharpshooter might lurk picking off the ladder party. It was also sensible for the ladder party, responsible for bringing and lifting the ladder into position, to remain and protect those ascending with shields.

Mining

The mining, or rather undermining, of fortifications was an ancient practice and one employed throughout the Middle Ages. The use of such mines relied upon a nice calculation that had to be made between the strength of the fortifications above and the size of the excavated space below. This was not easy to assess, as the events at the siege of Rouen in 1592, where Fort St Catherine was the key to the defences, testified. Rather than bombarding the fort and scaling the ramparts, a mine was prepared. Unusually it was not gunpowder mine but relied on the fortification collapsing into the void excavated below. It failed impressively: 'The commanders believed that, without powder, it would all fall of itself (but) it sunk down so gently that without opening itself or falling in pieces, it only sunk down upon the ground, the bulwark remaining lower but not broken.'[5] Guiccardini provided a detailed description of a similar failure this time using gunpowder employed by Pedro Navarro's mine at the siege of Bologna in 1512:

> The mine at last being finished and the army drawn up in order for immediately giving the assault the same [mine] was sprung and with a horrible noise and violence lifted up the chapel and the wall in such a manner that, through the space between the ground and the wall thus heaved up by those that were without had an open view of the city within, and of the soldiers as they stood ready to defend it.

4 Christine de Pisan., *The Book of Deeds of Arms and of Chivalry* (Pennsylvania State University Press, 1999), p.123.

5 R. B. Wernham, *After the Armada – Elizabethan England and the Struggle for Western Europe, 1588–1595* (Oxford: Clarendon press, 1988), p.378.

> But the wall immediately sinking down returned sound and entire to the very same place whence the violence of the powder had forced it, and with all its parts as firmly connected as had never been moved.[6]

The availability of large quantities of cheaper gunpowder in the late fourteenth century should have revolutionised mine warfare but it seems that it was not employed for this purpose until much later. The first discussion of the use of gunpowder in mining has been attributed to the Italians Francisco di Giorgio Martini's in *Trattati di Architectura Ingegneria e Arte Militare* (Treatises on Architecture, Engineering and Military Art) and Mariona Taccola in *De Rebus Militaribus* (Concerning Military Matters). Mariano di Jacopo, more generally known as Taccola (died before 1458), illustrated barrels of gunpowder for demolition purposes and described the use of a fuse cord to detonate them. He also, and crucially, pointed to the importance of building a strongly mortared wall at the entrance to the tunnel to contain the explosion. This was a factor that the English soldiers mining the defences of Corunna in 1589 failed to consider and suffered the inevitable consequences. One very unusual role of a mine occurred at the Siege of Malaga in 1487. Francisco Ramirez de Madrid ordered a mine to be dug under a tower where he placed a short-barrelled gun firing upwards. The shot smashed the floor and the tower was entered by that route and captured. The first generally acknowledged use of a gunpowder mine took place on 27 November 1495, when the defences of Castelnuovo in Naples were breached by Francesco di Giorgio using such a mine, although it was some time before the garrison surrendered.

This first well-publicised success of a gunpowder mine led to its more general adoption. Pedro Navarro, a noted military engineer, used a mine in the siege of the Ottoman fortress of San Giorgio in Cephalonia, although the walls were also breached by artillery fire and the castle taken. In 1503 the Spanish fortress of Salses in Rousillon was besieged by the French who exploded a mine but although the wall: 'was thrown up into the air it came down as it was before, not leaning one way or the other.'[7] The defenders were more successful when they dug and exploded a countermine beneath a troublesome siege battery – blowing it to pieces.

Salses is a fascinating example of transitional architecture, constructed from stone and brick between 1497 and 1504 as a border fortification. It is rectangular with large round towers at each corner and semi-detached massive horseshoe-shaped bastions. It is all but buried in a deep ditch in a similar way to the Device Forts. It was a further step towards the *Trace Italienne*. (Par Ratheau *Château de Salses - Congrès Archéologique de France*, 1906 via Wikimedia)

6 Simon Pepper., 'The underground siege', *Fort* Vol.10 1982, p.36.
7 J. S. Bury, 'The Early History of the Explosive Mine, *Fort*, vol.10 1982, p.27.

There were many problems associated with mining. First was the availability of a skilled engineer and of men with experience in the difficult and dangerous work. Miners were inevitably recruited from communities that specialised in that activity. Extensive and specialised stores were also required for the miners, as recorded by Jean de Bueil in 1466.

> If by any chance you are in position to mine the walls, you will need the following: spades, wooden shovels, scoops for baling out water .... heavy iron pry-bars with two hooks, baskets with carrying straps, a thousand iron pegs a foot and a half long,[8] and depending on need, as many short ones.[9]

Collado recommended the use of augers rather than picks to remove material, in order to reduce vibration which would alert the enemy to the danger.

The geology of the area had to be understood to enable a judgement as to whether a mine could be dug and how long it might take. Chalk soil would prove quite easy to mine while sandstone or granite presented far greater problems. The objective had to be chosen carefully assessing the likelihood of success: this was particularly true of some of the massive bastions or bulwarks of Rhodes in 1522. Bringing down a single tower or a small section of wall was manageable but larger demolitions of an entire bulwark would be much more difficult. The starting point of the tunnel had to be chosen with care to avoid observation and retaliation by the enemy, which might therefore require a much longer tunnel than would otherwise be the case. Spoil had to be removed in large amounts and disposed of with care to avoid the enemy identifying and marking the progress of a mine. This was certainly also the case in the First World War where the appearance of chalk spoil would attract unwanted attention from enemy artillery. It was also difficult to navigate underground, especially if the tunnel was dog-legged. It was not until the middle of the sixteenth century that the magnetic compass became widely available.

The tunnel itself would have to be supported, lit and ventilated. Lighting would of course use up the available oxygen and providing ventilation by digging holes in the ceiling would give a visual indication of progress. In civilian mines a subsidiary shaft could be cut and a fire lit beneath it, which would lead to a substantial downdraft from the principal shaft, but this again was impossible in a siege. Pit props had to be made available in quantity and of a quality sufficient to resist the compressive forces of the weight of material above.

---

8 For connecting timbers?

9 Jean de Bueil (trans. Craig & Jane Taylor), *Le Jouvencel* (Woodbridge, The Boydell Press, 2020), p.138.

To avoid the catastrophic back blast from the charge when exploded the mine could zigzag and a section of the tunnel be backfilled. The dogleg in the tunnel was missing from early illustrations but is included in a book from 1492. The zigzag course would itself create problems as it was more difficult to establish the final position of the mine than if the mine followed a straight course. At the siege of Sarzanello in 1487 the explosion took place short of its intended target.

'The foundation of the mine disclosed & the place of greatest effect.' Although in principle a simple and effective tactic, there was so much that could and did go wrong when mining, even if the enemy was obliging enough to let one carry on undisturbed. The man-made tunnels that riddled Rhodes were an invaluable aid to the attackers but also to the defenders. (Vannoccio Biringuccio, *The Pirotechnia*, (New York: Dover Publications Inc., 1990), p.424)

Biringuccio provided a good description of the pains that had to be taken to make a mine effective:

> First, see that their beginning is distant from the place you wish to damage so that the defender may not sally out to interfere, so that he may hear or see the excavation as little as possible, and so that he may not know the place of certain attack and protect himself from it by making some cut or by limiting himself to a more restricted fortification or by countermining in such a way that the exhalation of your fire [explosion] must pass without effects and all your labour be in vain,
>
> These mines are made as small, narrow and twisting as possible, especially near the actual place that you wish to destroy. Exactly under the aforesaid spot dig out a space that is at least four *braccia* or more high and two in width, and its bottom surface should lie entirely above the entrance of the mine. In this space put open kegs full of good strong powder. At the foot of the kegs place a good thick fuse of twisted cotton .... having covered this fuse and powder with earthenware or wooden drainpipes, brick up the entrance very well, putting great pieces of oak stump across it or other beams so that, with the thick wall and those, it is as strong as possible in resisting the driving force of the fire.

He concluded in his usual forthright style:

> To show that they are masters, some men adorn their words when speaking of those things in order to colour their lies better with a thousand fables. But let them talk, for the perfection of this thing lies in having much good powder to make a great and strong fire. In

> having the space not too large and the entrance very well closed. All the rest is windy and useless verbiage.[10]

It was difficult if not impossible to hide the mine but arguably its very visibility could damage the morale of the defenders. It was almost inevitable that after the failure of bombardments and early assaults they would turn to mining, as took place on numerous occasions, for example at the siege of Boulogne in 1544 and of Leith in 1562. Once the enemy's intentions were clear there were two strategies that could be employed; one passive, the other active. The passive involved the identification of mines and their progress. This could be achieved through observation and the use of simple technology to register the vibrations caused by mining, such as a bowl of water. Vents could be constructed to allow the explosion to blow out, or a parallel expansion chamber could be constructed to allow some of the blast effect to be 'shared' and reduced.

Countermines could be dug to intercept the enemy mine and the enemy miners killed and the mine damaged with an explosive charge, a camouflet. A camouflet was used at the siege of Therouanne in 1513 and killed twelve of the defenders as well as thirty of the attackers. Attempts could be made to smoke the enemy miners out, or a stream of water diverted to drown them, as was successfully used at Exeter in 1549. Francesco di Marchi in the second half of the sixteenth century suggested mine-proof ramparts with a network of internal vents:

> A miner that knows how to use counter-mines constructed as they ought to be may stop the enemy miners, stifle them or destroy them or destroy their works in such a manner as to make it impossible for others to return to the same place, or if he please let them enter the galleries, block up the passages and take them prisoner, or kill them if thought proper.[11]

If the mine was successful then it could be devastating, Gabriello Busca described its victims as, 'either dead or deafened and astonished by such a horrifying event, trembling and with little heart to oppose any assault.'[12] In the case of the siege of Rhodes mining and counter-mining was extensive and intensive, for the simple reason that the Hellenistic city provided underground culverts, cisterns and drains that provided a man-made system of tunnels to be exploited.

---

10 Vannoccio Biringuccio, *The Pirotechnia*, (New York: Dover Publications Inc., 1990), pp.424–4.

11 Eric Brockman, *The Two Sieges* (London: John Murray, 1969), p.47, from M. Vallieres *A Dissertation on Countermines.*

12 Pepper, 'The underground siege' p.36. Busca, Gabriello., *Della Expugnatione et Difesa Delle Fortezze.* Libri due Turin 1585 Ch xxxvii p.149.

A drawing by Francisco di Giorgio Martini (1439–1501). Di Giorgio Martini was a true Renaissance man, an artist, sculptor, engineer as well as a civil and military architect. In this drawing he has placed a large gunpowder charge with a fuse, and charcoal brazier ready to light it, beneath this fortification. It is interesting to note his use of a dioptra or surveyor's transit, Egyptian levels and plumb lines to survey the castle mound. These were the skills that differentiated the 'professional' engineer from the careless amateur. A good grounding in mathematics and geometry were considered increasingly essential for the up-to-date master of the military arts. Di Giorgio Martini developed the use of mines and gunpowder in the Italian War of 1494–1498, in the service of Ferdinand II the King of Naples. (Courtesy of Lund Humphries)

Pyrotechnics

Gunpowder and the various associated chemicals were only not used in firearms but for pyrotechnic devices, for both military and civilian use. There are copious references and illustrations of these in contemporary manuscripts. Biringuccio provided an impressive compendium of such weapons including: 'mines, firetubes or trunks, fire pots, squibs, fireballs, rockets, shells, grapeshot, incendiary arrows' and, 'bronze balls that …. carry fire and break in many pieces when they hit.'[13]

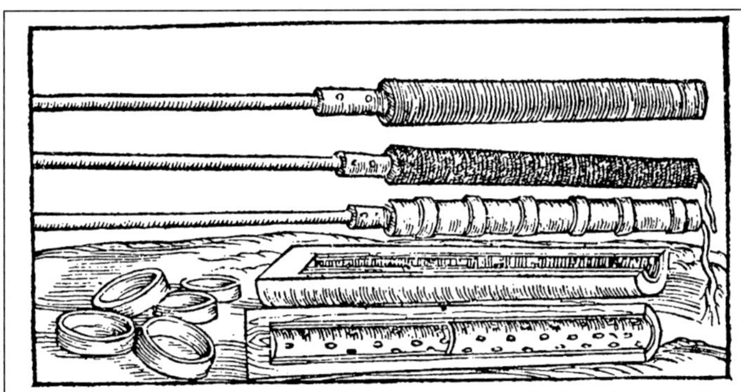

Fire tubes or trunks from Biringuccio's *Pirotechnia*. Ignited from the muzzle these examples seem to have reinforced barrels, the upper one clearly bound with wire. This was in order, I assume, to ensure that the casing did not break showering pyrotechnic madness everywhere. They were in effect extremely militant 'roman candles.' (Vannoccio Biringuccio, *The Pirotechnia*, (New York: Dover Publications Inc., 1990))

Fire tubes were short range flame throwers, useful for 'holding a gate' or 'forcing passage on a guarded bridge.'[14] In 1567 Richard Wright provided a detailed description of their manufacture:

> Item first for a trunk take serpentine powder 4 pounds,[15] and of saltpetre one pound, and of sulphur one pound and of linseed oil

13 Vannoccio Biringuccio, *The Pirotechnia*, (New York: Dover Publications Inc., 1990), p.403.

14 Vannoccio Biringuccio, *The Pirotechnia*, (New York: Dover Publications Inc., 1990), p.425.

15 Serpentine was very fine almost flour like gunpowder, made from dry mixing

> one pint and of Rosin 4 pounds and a little smith's dust [waste from the smithy floor?] and beat all these together small and then store them all rolled together and then take one pound of turpentine and melt it on the fire and then stir it with your hands again and so let it stand till it be dry and so lay them at length against that your trunk be surely bound for breaking. [For the casing] First you must see that your trunk be 20 inches long, 10 inches in compass, one inch and half high in the mouth. Then to lay first corn powder, then fill him 3 inches high and next take rosin 3 pounds and half and half a pound of corn powder and a little sulphur as small as a bean and then wrap canvas about it and so let it settle and thus you must order your trunks.[16]

Fire lances were small incendiaries that could be attached to lances or pikes and performed a similar role. Rockets could be made from rolled paper and one end folded to make a simple venturi tube. These could be fired at infantry or cavalry, 'since it is a fire that runs along the ground, and also endangers kegs of powder or barrels of munitions wherever they are found.'[17] Biringuccio illustrates incendiary weapons being shot from large calibre artillery pieces in order to scatter enemy formations.

Although clearly meant to engender panic amongst cavalry, the rather random scattering of the fire tubes would cause, at the very least, a modicum of confusion among anyone on the field. Gunpowder barrels and stores of powder were to be found everywhere, and to employ a weapon that scattered sparks indiscriminately would have been looked upon as a somewhat mixed blessing. (Vannoccio Biringuccio, *The Pirotechnia*, (New York: Dover Publications Inc., 1990))

Lad's English gunner's notebook[18] includes directions on how to make incendiary arrows, fire pots for hurling onto the decks of a ship, trunks (fire lances) and balls of wild fire. Fire pots were usually made from ceramic pots that were provided with handles for both suspension and the attachment of smouldering match cord to act as a fuse. Fire balls could be hurled and rolled at

the three main constituents, sulphur, charcoal and saltpetre. The corned powder referred to later was mixed wet and then sifted into different sized corns or granules. The difference between the two was similar to that between icing sugar and granulated in texture. Corned powder was considerably more powerful.

16 Ruth Rhynas Brown. 'Troncks, rockets and fiery balls: Military fireworks of the early modern period', *Journal of the Ordnance Society*, Vol.17 2005 p.26. *Soc of Antiquaries* Ms 94, 1 7r; 21.

17 Vannoccio Biringuccio, *The Pirotechnia*, (New York: Dover Publications Inc., 1990), p.432.

18 John Lad, 'A Rule of Gunners Art 1586 (his notebook)', pp18–36. Published in. Caruana, Adrian B, *Tudor Artillery 1485–1603* (Museum Restoration Service (Canada), 1992).

an enemy and could be made from metal or canvas. Richard Wright again provides a helpful description:

> First take an earthen pot and one pound of sulphur and one pound of rosin and scome [mix] them together in a mortar and then seeth [boil] them in the same pot, then take your ball and dip them in twice or thrice. So take them out of the pot and then make your touchhole and then hang them up on the sun. In the binding and trimming of them be sure to make them strong for it is very dangerous.[19]

The manufacture of fire pots was described by Biringuccio in some detail. The pots themselves had to be thoroughly dried to shatter on impact. Then they should:

> fill them a little more than half-full with coarse gunpowder which has mixed in it pounded Grecian pitch and at least a third of crushed sulphur. Then pour in a covering a *dito* thick of strained pig fat mixed with powder. This keeps it from falling out when it is thrown and keeps the fire slower until it reaches the enemy.[20]

After attaching a fuse, or setting fire to a corner of the pot, it could then be thrown, with the fearless warrior choosing his time carefully!

Incendiary weapons had long been part of an army's arsenal. The most well-known but elusive was Greek Fire, which should more correctly be called Roman or Byzantine fire since the Byzantines, who developed it, never referred to themselves as 'Greek'. It was unlikely to have been a mixture that included saltpetre but simply used rectified or distilled petroleum with a low ignition point. To this could have been added the distillate from resinous wood to thicken it and make it adhere to surfaces. Sulphur could be added to make the smoke even more noxious. Its liquid nature allowed it to be used in flame-throwers, either hand-held or ship-mounted.[21] The recipe for 'Greek' Fire had been long lost but Biringuccio provided a perfectly acceptable alternative – acceptable to all but its victims of course.

> A liquid composition is also made in a kettle in which are put pure pork fat, petroleum oil, oil of sulphur, live sulphur, double refined

---

19 Ruth Rhynas Brown, 'Troncks, Rockets and Fiery Balls: Military Fireworks of the Early Modern Period', *Journal of the Ordnance Society*, vol. 17 (2005), p.28.

20 Vannoccio Biringuccio, *The Pirotechnia*, (New York: Dover Publications Inc., 1990), p.434.

21 For a detailed account of the history of 'Greek Fire', please see J. R. A. Partington, *History of Greek fire and Gunpowder* (Cambridge: W. Heffer & sons, 1966), pp.10–21 & pp.28–32,

> saltpetre aqua vitae, Grecian pitch, turpentine, and some coarse gunpowder. Having liquefied everything well over a fire, stir it thoroughly with a stick so that it may be well incorporated, and to proceed to fill all the pots and vessels that you have with this composition in the desired amounts. Then put a layer of good gunpowder over them so that they ignite easily when desired, and let them stand. Use them when you wish, throwing them with slings, or tied with ropes or iron wire like a whip handle, or in other ways of throwing by hand.[22]

This was a multi-purpose composition that could be used to fill 'carcasses', incendiary balls or smeared on combustible surfaces such as bridges and gates.

22 Vannoccio Biringuccio, *The Pirotechnia*, (New York: Dover Publications Inc., 1990), pp.434–435.

7

The Ottoman Army

It has been said with reference to the Kingdom of Prussia that whereas all kingdoms have an army that only the Prussian Army had a Kingdom. What was perhaps true of Prussia was also true of Ottoman Turkey. The Ottomans were a nomadic band of raiding horseman who acquired a state. It was only after their conquests that they felt the necessity to establish the mechanisms by which their state could be governed. As with Henry VIII's England, the Ottoman Court and much of the civil administration would organise and accompany the Sultan to war and the army was bound in personal obligation to him. The senior commanders were also senior officials and advisers, sometimes connected by ties of marriage.

The army originally consisted of a large band of horseman equipped for raiding and conquest. They had, by the late fourteenth century, become a disciplined force that could be supplemented with peasant volunteers, both infantry and cavalry. Although the cavalry was in a sense the 'senior service', it was to be the infantry, and specifically the Janissaries, who were to impress their Western opponents.

This magnificent warrior is illustrated in a series about traditional clothing from across the world in 1580. His sidearm is a sabre but his principal weapon is his bow. On his back he has the partially 'wrap-around' shield that was also often used by Hungarian troops. There was considerable exchange of equipment and tactics between the countries bordering Ottoman territory and the Ottomans themselves. (Public domain, courtesy of Rijksmuseum, Amsterdam)

The Janissaries were at the heart of the army. Candali Kara Halil Hayreddin Pasha was ostensibly the founder of the Janissaries in the fourteenth century. Their name derives from the words *yeni cheri* or 'new troops.' They were a unique force recruited from subjects conquered by the Ottomans as a *devşhirmeh* (blood tax) following a practice sanctioned

This image comes from the same source as that above, a work entitled *Clothing of Ottomans*. The Ottomans were a source of fascination and fear for Christendom. There was no assumption of superiority, in fact quite the reverse. The triumphs of the Ottomans in their world contrasted with the chaos and disorder in the West engendered by dynastic rivalries and religious disputes. The posture of the soldier is almost identical to that of similar western models of captains, although he is wearing considerably less armour. Flowing robes are a considerable disadvantage in battle, especially in a siege where incendiary weapons are likely to be used. (Public domain, courtesy of Rijksmuseum, Amsterdam)

by Sharia Law. This asserted that, 'The conquered are the slaves of the conquerors, to whom their goods, their women and their children belong as lawful possession.' The Janissaries were not free men but slaves of the sultan, *kapı kulu* or *hünkâr kulu*, which was an honourable title.

The young Christian captives, usually aged between 10 and 17, after having been assessed as being sound in wind and limb, would be forced to convert to Islam and obey a harsh code of conduct demanding their complete loyalty to the Sultan. It was undoubtedly a severe system but one that provided considerable opportunities for personal advancement and was not, it seems, a future that all Christian parents viewed with horror for their sons. The boys could be enrolled in the infantry, the support troops or trained for service at Court; the opportunities were dependent upon talent and character. As Moslem converts, their social status and tax position would be better than their former Christian brethren.

In Istanbul the Janissaries performed a similar role to the Imperial Roman Praetorian Guard, as the defenders and sometimes creators of the Sultans, who both respected and feared them. On his accession the Sultan was expected to reward the Janissaries with substantial bonuses to keep their loyalty and demonstrate good lordship. They were only answerable to their own officers, and could cause collective chaos if they felt they had been slighted. Their discipline was not perfect and could lead to a confrontation with their commander. The hostility of the Janissaries to further operations far from home, forced even Selim the Grim to abandon further conquests in his Persian and Egyptian campaigns. After the capture of Rhodes, despite Suleiman's protestations they went on the rampage, raping and looting.

During Suleiman's reign the Janissaries numbered around 12,000 men who were available for overseas expeditions. Unmarried men were billeted in barracks where they were organised in messes of 10. 10 of these messes made an *orta* which equated to the standard company, although the strength of a company could vary from 100 to 300. There were 165 *ortas* which were commanded by officers who had risen through the ranks. The Colonel of a Regiment held the title of *Çorbaşi* (chief soup-maker) while his quartermaster was *Aşçi Başi* (chief cook). Although these titles may appear facetious, it highlighted the importance of food in pointing to the dependent relationship that existed between the men, their officers and the Sultan, whose title among the Janissaries was *bizi besleyen baba* or 'the father who feeds us'. It was not surprising that a mutiny was preceded and announced by the overturning of the very large cooking pot (*kazan*). The *Çorbaşi* had a lieutenant (*oda kethüdâsı*or *başodabaşı*) and a number of what might be equated to non-commissioned officers called *odabaşı* ('chiefs of barrack-rooms). There was also an imam and a scribe for the *orta*. In many respects it mirrored in size and organisation that of western infantry companies. The highest rank achieved by a Janissary was that of *Segban-Bashi* which was directly below that of the Agha.

Illustration by Lambert de Vos a Flemish artist in the diplomatic service of the Habsburg Empire, *c.* 1574. The personal guard of the Sultan was made up of 150 of the best bowmen known as the *solaks* and able to shoot left or right-handed. Their strung bows are more a symbol of office rather than a weapon as neither appear to carry arrows or a secondary weapon. Their distinctive Janissary head dress or *üsküfor börk* is well-represented, the diaphanous undergarment is something of a surprise and hardly campaign wear. Lambert de Vos, *Türkisches Kostümbuch* (Istanbul: 1574) (Public Domain via Wikimedia)

The *Agha* of the Janissaries (*yeniçeri agası)* was not a Janissary but was appointed from the court. He had his own palace in the vicinity of the Süleymaniye Mosque; he led his own council, the so-called *yeniçeri divânı*. This council included the five highest officers of the corps *başçavuş* (chief of the sergeants) who supervised the recruitment and training of new recruits. Finally, the *ocak* had its own bureaucracy headed by the *yeniçeri efendisi* (secretary of the Janissaries). He held the pay rolls (*kötük*) and was chief of the *Agha*'s chancery.

What made the Janissaries so feared was not only their finely honed martial skills, but their discipline in the face of terrible casualties. It was a common saying that, 'The body of a Janissary is but a stepping for his brother into the breach.'

The Janissaries had a distinctive march involving taking three paces forward, then a pause, followed by three more paces. This was a pattern that would maintain the dressing of the formation while at the same time stressing the inexorable nature of the advance. In the West, at a time when Roman discipline and order were so admired, the Janissaries appeared to be the true heirs to this tradition, just as their Sultan had adopted the titles of the Byzantine Emperors. What the Janissaries did not indulge in was the absurdly extravagant clothing associated with western troops, especially of the landsknechts, but commonly a style pursued by other 'professional' western warriors as well. The use of expensive fabrics and feathers, the slashing of doublets, hose and shoes and headgear that would be not out of place at Ascot in a later century, was the finery thought essential to attract others to the life and to make the *bravo bravissimo*.

Ogier Ghislain de Busbecq was a linguist, scholar, teacher, horticulturalist, herbalist and a diplomat in the service of three Habsburg emperors. His *Turkish Letters* were first published in part in 1581 and complete in 1589. They recounted the time he spent as Ambassador to the Court of Suleiman the Magnificent from 1554 to 1555 and from 1556 to 1562. His letters to Nichola Michault contain fascinating details about Turkish life and politics and made unflattering comparisons with Western practice. He never intended to publish his letters, which suggests that they contained his real opinions rather than polemic. He is credited with introducing the tulip and the lilac to western horticulture. This print by a European artist can be dated to 1557, at the time when Busbecq was in Turkey. (Public Domain via Wikimedia)

Ogier de Busbecq was a close observer and admirer of the Ottomans and contrasted the dress and conduct of the Janissaries that he saw in review order with that of western soldiers. He did allow for the extravagant use of plumes:

> When the cavalry had ridden past, they were followed by a long procession of Janissaries, but few of whom carried any arms except their regular weapon, the musket. They were dressed in uniforms of almost the same shape and colour, so that you might recognise them to be the slaves, and as it were the household, of the same master. Among them no extraordinary or startling dress was to be seen, and nothing slashed or pierced. They say their clothes wear out quite fast enough without their tearing them themselves. There

> is only one thing in which they are extravagant, viz., plumes, head-dresses, &c., and the veterans who formed the rear guard were specially distinguished by ornaments of this kind. The plumes which they insert in their frontlets might well be mistaken for a walking forest. Then followed on horseback their captains and colonels, distinguished by the badges of their rank. Last of all, rode their Aga by himself. Then succeeded the chief dignitaries of the Court, and among them the Pashas, and then the royal body-guard, consisting of infantry, who wore a special uniform and carried bows ready strung,[1] all of them being archers.[2]

Sir Nicholas Roberts in a letter to his uncle the Earl of Surrey in 1523 added to the description: 'They wear on their heddes a long white cap and on top of the cap a white Ostrich [feather] which giveth a great show.'[3] On occasion the Janissaries were seen to wear green and yellow cloaks as well as the usual headwear.

Three Mamelukes on horseback also from Jan Swart van Groningen's work *Suleiman with his Entourage*, dated to 1526. These fine horsemen are equipped with shields, lances and sabres but surprisingly not bows. The shield hung behind the back would be a useful defence against archers shooting from behind them. The shields and the pennons are decorated with crescents. (There is no truth to the myth that a billowing silk shirt would protect a galloping horseman's back from an arrow.) They are wearing *Zamt* headwear, described by Arnold van Harff, a late medieval German traveller, as, '... a high red hat, without a brim, about three spans high, with long wool hanging from it about a span long.'[4] Supposedly this style of hat was banned in 1517 after the Ottoman conquest of Egypt; if so, no-one was brave enough to tell these gentlemen.[5] (Public domain, courtesy of Rijksmuseum, Amsterdam)

---

1 Those on his right were left-handed archers and on his left the right-handed, so that they could bring their bow to bear on any enemy immediately. There was no disdain or fear of those who used the hand *sinister*!

2 Ogier Ghislain de Busbecq (Charles Thornton Forster, trans.), *The Life and Letters of Ogier Ghiselin de Busbecq* (London: Kegan Paul & co, 1881), pp.284–285. Project Gutenberg eBook.

3 Eric Brockman, *The Two Sieges* (London: John Murray, 1969), p.16.

Three mounted archers from a Dutch series of engravings by Jan Swart van Groningen entitled *Suleiman with his Entourage*, dated 1526. Horsed archers were an elite, capable of shooting at the gallop at a succession of targets, skills not easily learnt or lightly abandoned. The high stirrups allowed them to stand in the saddle and shoot in any direction, even directly downwards with the draw hand behind their back! As with all warriors of East or West they are shown with rather extravagant clothing and aggressive demeanour. (Public domain, courtesy of Rijksmuseum, Amsterdam)

If the Janissaries provided the strength of the infantry, the *spahis* provided the professional cavalry. They were known as the *Kapikula Süvarileri Ocaği* (Hearth of the Household Cavalrymen of Gate Slaves). They were formed from four corps recognised by their order of seniority and pay: The *Spahi Oghlans*; the *Silihdars* (weapon carriers); the *Ulufajis* (paid troops) and the *Ghurebas* (a mercenary force usually of non-Ottomans). The individual *spahis* had to provide five or six horsemen each, the *ulufajis* only two or three. The total force was about ten thousand strong, but fully mobilised it would number at least four times as many. They would also provide substantial contingents of 500 to 1000 men attached to the senior Viziers. The *spahis* and Janissaries were the Sultan's men; they received his pay and bounty and together provided an enormously powerful and mobile force that could not be matched by his enemies. Ogier Busbecq described in great detail the order, equipment, horses and tactics of the cavalry when he observed a parade of the Sultan's troops.

> I was accommodated with a window at the back of the house, commanding a view of the street by which the Sultan was to pass. From this I had the pleasure of seeing the magnificent column which was marching out. The Ghourebas and Ouloufedgis rode in double, and the Silihdars and Spahis in single file. The cavalry of the Imperial guard consists of these four regiments, each of which forms a distinct body, and has separate quarters. They are believed to amount to about 6,000 men, more or less. Besides these, I saw a large force,

4 Lugatism., *Headwear and Footwear in the Mamluk Sultanate*, posted June 20 2022, https://lugatism.wordpress.com/2022/06/22/headwear-and-footwear-in-the-mamluk-sultanate/

5 Albrecht Fuess, 'Sultans with Horns: The Political Significance of Headgear in the Mamluk Empire', *Mamlūk Studies Review*, vol. 12, no. 2, 2008 (Chicago: University of C hicago Press, 2008), p.71.

> consisting of the household slaves belonging to the Sultan himself, the Pashas, and the other court dignitaries. The spectacle presented by a Turkish horseman is indeed magnificent. His high-bred steed generally comes from Cappadocia or Syria, and its trappings and saddle sparkle with gold and jewels in silver settings. The rider himself is resplendent in a dress of cloth of gold or silver, or else of silk or velvet. The very lowest of them is clothed in scarlet, violet, or blue robes of the finest cloth. Right and left hang two handsome cases, one of which holds his bow, and the other is full of painted arrows. Both of these cases are curiously wrought, and come from Babylon, as does also the targe,[6] which is fitted to the left arm, and is proof only against arrows or the blows of a mace or sword. In the right hand, unless he prefers to keep it disengaged, is a light spear, which is generally painted green. Round his waist is girt a jewelled scimitar, while a mace of steel hangs from his saddle-bow. 'What are so many weapons for?' you will ask. I reply for your information, that he is trained by long practice to use them all. You will ask again, 'How can a man use both bow and spear? Will he seize the bow after he has cast or broken his spear?' Not so; he keeps the spear in his grasp as long as he can, but when circumstances require that it should be exchanged for the bow, he thrusts the spear, which is light and handy, between the saddle and his thigh, so that the point sticks out behind, and by the pressure of his knee keeps it in this position for any length of time he chooses. But when he has need of the spear, he puts the bow into its case, or slings it on his left arm across his shield. It is not, however, my object to explain at length their skill in arms, which is the result of long service and constant drilling. The covering they wear on the head is made of the whitest and lightest cotton-cloth, in the middle of which rises a fluted peak of fine purple silk. It is a favourite fashion to ornament this head-dress with black plumes.[7]

Using these tactics the Ottoman cavalry combined shock, with lance and hand weapons, and firepower, from their bows. Western cavalry in contrast tended to concentrate on only a limited range of tactical options.

In the countryside those who had received land from the Sultan had what might be called feudal responsibilities to provide horsemen for military service, dependent upon their assessed revenue. By Suleiman's reign the system was in disarray because of the rapid and confusing transfer of fiefs, often caused by deaths in action. Ottoman conquest led to the granting

6 A reference to a small lightweight shield made from cane but with a metal boss at the centre.

7 Ogier Ghislain de Busbecq (Charles Thornton Forster, trans.), *The Life and Letters of Ogier Ghiselin de Busbecq* (London: Kegan Paul & co, 1881), pp.213–214.

of land as fiefs, providing the Ottoman government with a ready-made garrisons if needed.

In addition to the professional and feudal troops were the large irregular forces that could be deployed. These were the *akinji* (cavalry), *azabs* (infantry), as well as the Kurds. The *akinji* numbered about 30,000 and were freebooters, found mostly on the borders with the Christian countries and they served without pay. The *azabs* could number up to 40,000 in wartime and served in garrisons and with the fleet as well as in the field army. The *bashibazookis* were unpaid volunteers in search of booty and mayhem. Their name derived from the Turkish word *başibozuk*, meaning 'damaged head', as they were deemed incapable of organised fighting. The *azabs*, *bashibazookis* together with any other 'riff-raff' would precede the Janissaries into the attack filling the moats and breaches with their dead. If they survived they would be rewarded with booty, but were otherwise treated as cannon-fodder.

In addition to these there were the gunners, sappers and logistical troops upon which the army depended for any sustained operations. These support arms were extensive and well provided for and would have made any western commander green with envy. The *cebeci ocağı* was responsible for the manufacture, repair, maintenance and supply of arms and armour to the army and was recruited from boys raised by the *devishirme*. Cannon were cast in facilities in Istanbul and in the conquered territories including Buda in Hungary, Timişoara in Romania, Shkodër in Albania, and Pravishte in Greece. This was supervised by the 'Artillery Furnace' which was responsible for all aspects of the ordnance apart from gunpowder manufacture. The artillery was transported by a separate corps of artillery drivers organised on military lines and provided with extensive stables, barracks and manufacturing facilities.

The types of artillery pieces were as extensive as in the West and its nomenclature as confusing. David Nicolle identifies, among others, the basilisk like *baçaluşha*, the *balymez* a medium-weight long-range weapon and *holonborna* which possibly derived in name from the culverin and finally the *humbaraçila*r or mortar.[8]There was even a separate organisation responsible for the manufacture of hand grenades. Sultan Murad recruited a corps of miners whose title rather unfortunately translated as Sewers. The *Sakalar* or *Saka* were a corps of several hundred whose role was to provide water for men and horses and to serve the Sultan with Sherbert and cooling drinks on campaign.

The abilities of the Ottoman logistical services were more than impressive, especially when compared to the inadequacy, or even complete lack, of such provision in contemporary Western armies. This was made especially clear during the Belgrade campaign. Busbecq describes in detail the very original system by which the Turks clothed and paid their men.

8 David Nicolle, *Armies of the Ottoman Empire 1775–1820*, Men-At-Arms series, no 314. (Oxford: Osprey Publishing 1998), p.19.

> I now return to the point from which I made this digression. I mentioned that baggage animals are used in a campaign for carrying armour and tents. These for the most part belong to the Janissaries.... The cloth for the clothes I referred to is supplied by the State, and is distributed after the following fashion. The soldiers at nightfall are summoned by companies to the office for the distribution of such stores, where parcels of cloth are ready in separate packets according to the number of men in each company. They march in, and take their chance in the dark, so that if any soldier's cloth is of inferior quality to that of his comrades, he has nought to grumble at save his own bad luck. For the same reason their pay is not given them by tale [counted by number], but by weight, to prevent anyone accusing the paymaster of giving him light or clipped coins. Moreover, their pay is always given them the day before it is actually due.[9]

Busbescq also described in glowing terms how not only clothes but tents were provided for the ordinary soldiers. The common soldier in the West in contrast was expected to make shift for himself.

> The Turks take great care to have their soldiers in good health and protected against the inclemency of the weather .... for their health the State will undertake to provide. Therefore you may see a Turk better clad than armed. They are especially afraid of cold, and even in summer time wear three garments, of which the innermost one, or shirt, is woven of coarse thread and gives a great deal of warmth. For protection against cold and rain they are furnished with tents, in which each man is given just room enough for his body, so that one tent holds twenty-five or thirty Janissaries.[10]

The total mobilised strength of the army numbered about 200,000 but as a field force accompanied by servants, sutlers, volunteers and hangers on of all sorts it would number 300,000. This was the estimated size of the Ottoman army outside Vienna in 1529. It was not impossible that the estimates of 500,000, given for later expeditions in his reign, were incorrect.

The Ottoman Army and Firearms

There has for long been an assumption of 'western' technical and organisational superiority especially in the nineteenth centuries, which

9 Ogier Ghislain de Busbecq (Charles Thornton Forster, trans.), *The Life and Letters of Ogier Ghiselin de Busbecq* (London: Kegan Paul & co, 1881), p.222.

10 Ogier Ghislain de Busbecq (Charles Thornton Forster, trans.), *The Life and Letters of Ogier Ghiselin de Busbecq* (London: Kegan Paul & co, 1881), p.222.

however has little basis in truth in earlier centuries. Underlying all the reasons put forward to explain the Ottomans' inability to keep pace with the 'West', was an assumption that their deficiencies ultimately sprang from their conservatism, fanaticism, and despotism, which in turn stemmed from their culture and religion.[11] There is very little evidence to support this contention, especially in Suleiman's reign, when the Ottomans were remarkably open to many different influences and opinions. Even so, there has been a long-held, and incorrect, opinion that the Ottoman Empire unlike the 'West', failed to adopt gunpowder weapons with the same enthusiasm. This opinion is again based on little evidence. It seems true that gunpowder weapons were introduced from contacts with Christians in the Balkans in the late fourteenth century, however the Ottomans were using artillery and hand-held firearms extensively by the date of the Ottoman Hungarian wars in 1443–1444 and at Kosovo in 1448. There are many reasons why a society adopts, adapts or retains weapons and systems of warfare that challenge the technological determinist approach to such matters. The recent direction in which the military revolution debate has developed suggests a much more subtle and nuanced approach needs to made when considering these issues.

The continued use of their magnificent horn and sinew bows was given as evidence of Ottoman backwardness. As with the case of the English longbow, however, this can be attributed to its usefulness as well as to the important part it played in their culture. Veinstein also points to the stress Suleiman placed on expertise in handling firearms:

> We have no details on the process of the adoption of firearms and we know nothing about the reception of this innovation by the troops, who had already demonstrated their corporatist mind as well as their propensity to mutiny. It remains striking in this respect that, as late as the year 1551, Suleyman considered it necessary to request the aga, the head of the janissaries, to train his men, so that – the sultan says – "they will become experts in the use of the muskct". Equally striking is the fact that the sultan is said to have been anxious, at each of his visits to the barracks of the janissaries, to see all the officers shooting, according to their hierarchical order, in the training area, luxuriously laid out by the same sultan.[12]

In Europe firearms were admitted as unfortunately necessary accoutrements but unsuited to the gentler and more honourable hands of the officer class. Suleiman on the other hand clearly saw that it was a weapon to be employed

11 Agoston Gabor., Firearms and Military Adaptation: The Ottomans and the European Military Revolution, 1450–1800, *Journal of World History*, vol. 25, no.1 (March 2014), p. 87.

12 Gilles Veinstein., 'On the Ottoman Janissaries (Fourteenth-Nineteenth Centuries)' in Erik-Jan Zürcher (ed.), *Fighting for a Living: A Comparative Study of Military Labour 1500–2000*, (Amsterdam: Amsterdam University Press, 2014), pp.117–118.

and not snubbed by his officers. Encouragement in the use of firearms did not necessarily preclude the continued use of the bow. Henry VIII founded the Fraternity or Guild of St George in 1537 to encourage the use of both the gun and the bow. Suleiman's personal bodyguard was made up of archers just as Henry's was. Encouragement of the new did not exclude the continued use of an old and honourable weapon.

The Ottomans were certainly considered experts in the use of their magnificently powerful horn and sinew bows as described in helpful detail by Busbecq.

Detail from the 'Ottoman Army Entering a City', folio from a Divan of Mahmud 'Abd al-Baqi from the last quarter of the sixteenth century. The adoption and employment of firearms by the Ottomans has become an important issue in the widening Military Revolution debate. The illustration shows a rank of Janissary arquebusiers with their magnificent headgear and with shouldered arms acting as a princely escort. They appear to have pouches and sidearms, although the bell-mouths of their weapons are probably artistic licence. The Ottomans retained their archers for longer than the promoters of the Military Revolution debate would have wished, for the same reason that the English longbow continued in use – utility and tradition. The Venetians and the Japanese also continued to use their bows as they recognised that their qualities complemented the 'fiery weapon.' (Metropolitan Museum of Art, public domain)

> After dinner I practise the Turkish bow, in the use of which weapon people here are marvellously expert. From the eighth, or even the seventh, year of their age they begin to shoot at a mark, and practise archery ten or twelve years. This constant exercise strengthens the muscles of their arms, and gives them such skill that they can hit the smallest marks with their arrows. The bows they use are much stronger than ours,[13] and being shorter, are also much more handy; they are made not of a single piece of wood, but of the sinews and horns of oxen fastened together with a quantity of glue and tow. A Turk in good practice can easily draw the string of the very stiffest of them to his ear. Without training, however, the strongest man could do nothing with a Turkish bow. Indeed, if a coin be set between the string and the bow close to the notch [upper nock of the bow], none but an adept could pull the string so far as would suffice to liberate the coin. So sure is their aim, that in battle they can hit a man in the eye or in any other exposed part they choose. At the range where they are taught, you may see them shooting with so sure an aim that they surround the white on the target, which is generally smaller than a thaler,[14] with five or six arrows, so that every arrow touches the margin of the white, but does not break it. They seldom use a range of more than thirty feet. On the thumb of the right

13 I assume he is referring here to civilian bows, used for sport and not for war.

14 The Thaler or Joachimsthaler was a silver coin in circulation from 1520. It had a diameter of 40mm.

> hand they wear bone rings, on which the bowstring lies when they draw it, and the arrow is kept in its place by holding the left thumb [thumb of the right hand] in an upright position and joining it to the forefinger; so that their way of shooting is quite different from ours. The butt they use as a target is raised four feet more or less from the ground, and consists of a wooden frame filled with sand. Pashas and men with large households exercise their servants in this sort of practice at home, the more skilful being told off to act as teachers.[15]

According to Taybughi al-Ashrafi a competent archer was expected to shoot all his arrows into a three foot diameter (91mm) circle at 75 yards (68.58 m).[16] The overall length of a full-sized archery range varied from 165 to 265 yards (250–400 gez) which is comparable to the minimum required practice range for English longbow archers of 240 yards.[17] The maximum draw weight of the bow has been calculated as about 90lbs with the average being 60–75lbs.[18] This contrasted with the monumental draw weights associated with Turkish flight bows, used to compete in shooting for distance. The Ottoman war bow was also longer nock to nock than a flight bow, varying from up to 58 inches for the war bow to only 40–42 inches for flight bows.[19]

An early fifteenth century Burgundian traveller, Bertrandon de la Brocquière, compared Turkish bows and arrows with western ones, which I assume were of the English war bow type.[20] He wrote:

> for the Turkish arrows, as we know, are not strong, however strong their bows. Their bows are short and their arrows, too, and light. The iron is set into the wood [tanged rather than socketed arrowheads] and would not sustain a heavy blow .... In case of necessity, our archers could use the Turkish arrows, but they could not use ours because the notches are too narrow and the strings of their bows are too thick since they are made of gut.[21]

15 Ogier Ghislain de Busbecq (Charles Thornton Forster, trans.), *The Life and Letters of Ogier Ghiselin de Busbecq* (London: Kegan Paul & co, 1881), pp.252–254.

16 Equivalent to a 13cm circle at 10m for those of you wishing to emulate them.

17 W. F. Paterson., 'The Archers of Islam', *Journal of the Economic and Social History of the Orient*, vol. 9, no. 1/2 (November 1966), p.84.

18 W. F. Paterson., 'The Archers of Islam', *Journal of the Economic and Social History of the Orient*, vol. 9, no. 1/2 (November 1966), p.86.

19 W. F. Paterson., 'The Archers of Islam', *Journal of the Economic and Social History of the Orient*, vol. 9, no. 1/2 (November 1966), p.86.

20 Bertrandon de la Brocquière (Galen R. Kline, trans.), *The Voyage d'Outremer by Bertrandon de la Brocquière* (New York: P. Lang, 1988).

21 David C Nicolle., Cresting on Arrows from the Citadel of Damascus', *Bulletin d'Études Orientales*, 2016, t. 65, Mélanges en Mémoire de Djamel Eddine Kouloughli (2016), p.265.

A selection of Mameluke and Ottoman arrows in the Sali d'Armi of the Museo dell'Arsenale in Venice vary from 640–710mm (25–28 in) in length, somewhat shorter than most English war bow arrows.

An English report to the Court of Queen Elizabeth described in detail the extraordinary skill of a hundred Turkish horse archers in what was admittedly an 'entertainment'.

A pair of horse archers demonstrating the skills that were reported to Elizabeth in the dispatch below. (*Icones habitus monumenta turcarum Libri picturati* (1586/1650?) A 15 p.63. Courtesy of the Biblioteka Jagiellońska)

> A very long mast with a golden ball at the top of it was planted in the middle of the Hippodrome,[22] and on one side and the other in a straight line were planted two rows of trenchers [wooden plates] with a little blank [white target] in the middle, on rods six *quarte* high from the ground, and over against them was extended on the ground a log of wood representing a man. These marks were laid in order a good hand-cast apart. The horseman rode straight for them, and at the beginning of the course drew his sword, aimed a blow at the log, at once replaced his sword, shot an arrow at the ball on the mast, and at once taking another from his quiver shot it at the other mark, almost as the course was ending. This was done by all, always in one course. Then they ran with their arrows only, shooting the first at the first mark, and taking another smartly shot at the mast, and then did the same at the last mark, always at full speed, and returned to do the same feats with the left hand. Then some ran with shields, shooting the arrow with the right hand and holding the shield in the left, and then put the shield in the right and shot with the left, doing all this at unbroken speed. Others, with sword and arrow, shifting the sword to the right hand and the left, did marvellous things. Others after shooting their arrows, drew their swords, and rising from their horses touched the ground with one foot, struck a blow and remounted instantly with much dexterity, aimed a second arrow at the mark at the end of their course, doing it to right and left alike; and certainly very few shots went astray, some having in one course hit all the marks except the ball .... Very good were those shots when riding one after another they turned, looking backwards, and shot the arrow behind them, hitting the mark to the great marvel of everyone. .... They threw darts standing upright on the saddle, and then with their head on the saddle and their feet in the air. Then they turned somersaults from the croup to the saddle and back. The courses were all at full speed; and those who bore themselves thus honourably had many presents from his Majesty[23]

22 This was used in a practice known as the *Qabaq*.

23 *Calendar of State Papers Foreign: Elizabeth*, volume 16, 21 July 1582 News from Constantinople to Elizabeth I, (London: HMSO, 1909).

The evidence from these Europeans sources was that the Turkish archer was very capable but only practised at short range. Flight archery, that is shooting for maximum distance, was practised but solely for sport. The distances achieved and recorded both in Europe and in Turkey were extraordinary. In 1792 a secretary at the Turkish embassy shot, with a 160lb draw weight bow, a light flight arrow 415 yards into the wind and another 482 yards with the wind, an achievement observed by members of the Toxophilite Society. This distance pales into insignificance compared to the 972 yards achieved by the Sultan in 1798 and observed by the English ambassador. If this seems excessive there is no doubt that the best archers could easily shoot well over 800 yards. This was far in excess, probably at least double the range, of the best war bow archer.

The Turkish bow was a formidable weapon and must have taken its toll of defenders in both sieges, especially of those who were not protected by armour. During the post-victory occupation, the Ottoman armoury on Rhodes was supplied with 1,100 bows and 300,000 arrows including 2,805 fire arrows. This was indicative of a serious commitment to these weapons.[24] In the same way that the bow was integral to the English Army and society of the period so was the Turkish bow. They remained a part of their military equipment for a very good reason, not simply because of innate conservatism or a romantic adherence to tradition.

One arm of the Ottoman army that did not embrace firearms was the cavalry. They disdained to use the wheellock pistol, preferring to retain their bows until the snaphaunce system was available in the seventeenth century. Busbecq, the remarkably observant diplomat, explained why firearms were sometimes abandoned in favour of the bow, partly admittedly as a result of simple conservatism and the observation of tradition but also because the more complex wheelock firearms issued to cavalry were prone to damage and could not be readily repaired, making them useless. He reported an abortive attempt to employ temperamental wheel lock firearms by the cavalry regiment of the Grand Vizier:

So, a large part of the fire-arms having been rendered unserviceable, the men took a dislike to the weapon; and this prejudice was increased by the dirt which its use entailed, the Turks being a very cleanly people; for the dragoons had their hands and clothes begrimed with gunpowder, and moreover presented such a sorry appearance, with their ugly boxes and pouches hanging about them, that their comrades laughed at them, and called them apothecaries. So, since with this equipment they pleased neither themselves nor others, they gathered round Roostem [the Sultan's Vizier, Rüstem Pasha], and showing him their broken and useless fire-arms, asked what advantage he hoped to gain from them when they met the enemy, and demanded that he should relieve them of them, and give them their old arms again. Roostem, after considering their request carefully, thought

24 The armoury also contained 172 crossbows with 100,000 bolts, with 581 bolts per crossbow and 273 arrows per bow.

there was no reason for refusing to comply with it, and so they got leave to resume their bows and arrows.[25]

Whereas in Western armies the handgunner was superior only to the pioneer troops in the military order of precedence, in the Ottoman army firearms were issued to the elite troops – the Janissaries. The figures available are not complete but probably half of the Janissaries at the second siege of Rhodes were equipped with hand guns. In 1522 there were 4,500 arquebuses issued as well as 1,000 'trench guns', which I speculate were what would be called rampart or wall pieces (heavy arquebuses, *arquebus a croc*) in the West. The Janissaries also used volley fire which has been considered an essential factor in making firearms the decisive weapon on the battlefield. An illustration shows two ranks one kneeling the other standing, one loading one firing. Caspali, the acute observer and influential rabbi, also referred to the Ottoman ability to maintain continuous fire on an enemy. In the West the use of volley fire was in response to the poor marksmanship of the average soldier. This was a result of the lack of training which was a consequence of the contempt felt for him by his social superior. In the Ottoman army, marksmanship was appreciated, as was the marksman.

The Ottomans had large sources of copper, lead and iron. For bronze guns they had to rely on supplies of English tin in later years. The advantage of bronze guns was that they could be re-cast into new models, making them in some respects highly economic since they could be 'recycled'. After 1453 an imperial cannon foundry (*Tophane-i Amire*) was founded and operated in Istanbul. This state arsenal contrasted with the dependence of western rulers on individual gun founders and their foundries. The Ottomans, like many European sovereigns including Henry VIII, called upon talent wherever it was to be found. The famous, or infamous, Master Urban cast a supergun in Edirne for the siege of Constantinople. Germany, which with Italy was at the centre of the new cannon technology, exported two masters of the art, Jörg of Nüremberg and later Master George of Meissen, who had played such a strange part in the first siege of Rhodes.

Ottoman small-arms barrels were considered of very high quality; made from flat sheets of steel coiled into a spiral and welded, which made for a stronger barrel. This type of barrel could be used more safely with a heavier powder charge, giving a longer effective range. One way of calculating the use and effectiveness of Ottoman firearms would be to establish the causes of fatalities amongst the Order. There is unsurprisingly no record of the casualties that the defenders suffered by number, let alone by type of weapon. There are however a few occasions when Bourbon recorded the deaths and injuries to people of 'worth' in 1522 that reveal some important information.

25 Ogier Ghislain de Busbecq (Charles Thornton Forster, trans.), *The Life and Letters of Ogier Ghiselin de Busbecq* (London: Kegan Paul & co, 1881), pp.242–243.

Lord Prior of Saint Giles Prior John was hurt through the neck with a handgun & was in great danger of death but he escaped and was made whole
Sir Francis de Fresnol .... chief captain of the great ship of Rhodes .... he was slain at the [post] of Italy wounded with 2 strokes of arquebuses
John de la Tous .... being as the said bulwark with a stroke of artillery had his arm smitten away in great danger to have lost his life howbeit by the help of god he died not
Sir William Weston above said captain of the post of England & had one of his fingers stricken away with an arquebus
And he [Tadini] being on the bulwark of Spain to order all thing that was needed there came a stroke of handgonne from the trenches that smote out his eye & put him in danger of his life
le Beglarby de la Notilia had a stroke with an arrow
Gabryell de Pomerolles lieutenant to the lord master ... fell from the wall as he went to see the trenches in the ditches & hurt his breast & for fault of good attendance [poor care] he fell in a fever wherof he died
[The Turks] came upon the bulwark with their banners & fought sore & mightily with our men not with hands but with shot of handgonnes

Elements of an armour, German or Austrian c. 1480–90. This is a late fifteenth century collection of armour, probably intended to be hung over the tomb of a knight. It is incomplete but contains most of the key pieces and is one of the very few assemblages that survive to today. These defences consist of sallet and bevor, breastplate and backplate of overlapping sections with cusped and channelled surfaces. The backplate is notable for its elegant silhouette and its fluting that imitates the gathered folds of fabric.[26] The breastplate has holes for fitting an *arret de lance*. The tassets are small and would permit a great freedom of movement. If completed with arm and leg armour the knight within would prove difficult to disable, let alone kill. The effectiveness of the sallet/bevor combination in protecting the head, face and neck is obvious. Dimensions: H, as mounted, 35in (88.9cm), Wt 23lb 3oz (10.55kg). (Metropolitan Museum of Art, Public domain)

Many of these deaths and serious injuries were caused by firearms of one sort or another, although there is one reference to an arrow 'stroke' and an accidental fall which was poorly treated. That there are no references to deaths by 'handstrokes' is interesting, considering so many of the injuries recorded above took place during wild melees. This suggests that the armour that the Knights wore made them, if not invulnerable to hand-held weapons, at least provided enough protection so that they were unlikely

26 Metropolitan Museum of Art Catalogue

to suffer fatal wounds. What is surprising is how several of those critically injured survived and in at least one case, that of Tadino, recovered to full health. The reference to a death 'for fault of good attendance' indicates that one of the reasons for survival may have been the quality of the treatment provided by the Order. Their devotion to the treatment of the sick almost equalled their devotion to war. The stress they put on cleanliness, diet and comfort may well also have contributed to the success of their care.

Ágoton when considering the use of firearms by the Ottoman made some important points, warning against simplistic assumptions.

> All this said, one has to be cautious not to overstate the importance of weapons technology. In an age when standardisation of calibers and quality was only attempted but never achieved, and when there no major technological breakthroughs in weapons design and manufacturing, the quality of weapons remained of secondary importance relative to that of their quantity. Firepower and military superiority were achieved through the sheer numbers of weapons and troops, not so much by their quality. In battles and sieges the party that outnumbered its opponent in terms of deployed weaponry and troops had a good chance of winning the engagement, provided that all other factors were equal.[27]

Burcu Özgüven highlighted the interest that Ottoman Sultan Mehmet II had in classical authors and their insights into military practice in a similar way to his western counterparts. The Sultan received a copy of Roberto Valturio's *De Re Militari* from Sigismondo Malatesta in 1463, and later he came to own one of the first printed copies. It is unsurprising that the developments taking place in military architecture in both the West and in the Ottoman world mirrored one another, in both the deployment of artillery and the means to defend against it. There was also a shared interest in the application of geometry to architecture, both civil and military.

Kilitbahir, or Kilid-ül Bahir, Castle was built in 1463 and was designed to control the Dardanelles; it was a massive structure consisting of three connected hollow towers in a trefoil shape. The wall walk was six metres wide and suitable for mounting artillery while a further circular gun tower was added by Suleiman the Magnificent in 1541. It is unique in its layout, as there was a reversion to rectangular structures in later reigns. The castle demonstrated that the Ottomans were aware of the offensive and defensive use of artillery in fortifications. There is little or no evidence for the technological superiority of European armies over Ottoman armies; there was however a very significant difference between them reflected from their differences in politics, culture, geography and history.

27 Gábor Ágoton., 'Firearms and Military Adaptation: The Ottomans and the European Military Revolution, 1450–1800', *Journal of World History*, March 2014, vol. 25, no.1, p.108.

8

Armour and Arms

One of the most extraordinary collections of medieval armour ever found was recovered from Rhodes. Recovered rather than discovered, as there was no bricked-up vault or Tutankhamun moment. There may have been 'wonderful' things but more like the 'discoveries' found in a 'lost' trunk in the attic. A cache of probably several hundred pieces of European armour was found in Rhodes in the late nineteenth century. Another large hoard of European armour has also been found, this time in 1840 in Chalcis, the capital of Euboea which had fallen to the Ottomans in 1470.[1]

It has been suggested that the Rhodian hoard came from an armoury near St Paul's Gate or the Auberge d'Auvergne, although there is no evidence for either claim. No doubt there were many stores of armour held in various parts of the city, by the Langues or by the Order. The earliest reference I have found to a store of armour found in Rhodes was by the painter Eugène-Napoléon Flandin who noted in a visit to the Order's Hospital in Rhodes in 1844: '*entassés sans ordre armures, que la rouille devore et des canons hors de service*' (haphazardly piled up armour, devoured by rust and out of service cannons).[2] Rhodes was well-known as a source of classical artefacts during the Renaissance and later. After the Knights had sold some through their Commanderies in the West, Isabella d'Este acquired numerous Rhodian classical pieces as part of her extensive collection of art.

There had been an expedition by the British Museum to Rhodes in 1853 that acquired a large number of classical artefacts, but there is no reference to Hospitaller armour or even the cannon which were lying around, apparently in profusion. It was General Sir John Henry Lefroy who recovered a major collection of pieces of armour by 1866, although it is

1 Charles Ffolkes, 'On Italian Armour from Chalcis in the Ethnological Museum at Athens', *Archaeologia* 62, part II, 2 February 1911.

2 Jean-Bernard de Vaivre, 'Les Canons de Rhodes Offerts à Napoléon III' in *Actes du 21e colloque de la Villa Kérylos à Beaulieu-sur-Mer* les 8 et 9 Octobre 2010. Publications de l'Académie des Inscriptions et Belles-Lettres Année 2011 no.22, p.207.

not known from whereabouts in Rhodes. The pieces were first sent to the Rotunda Museum at Woolwich and in the 1920s to the Royal Armouries. He also brought back rowel spurs which had apparently been used as a form of caltrops to impale the advancing Ottomans. Other items were collected from Rhodes in 1880–1890 on behalf of the Louis Bacherau Art House in Paris. They remained as a collection until the 1920s, when they were sold and distributed into private hands and museums. The Metropolitan Museum of Art acquired a collection of about a hundred items in 1920, some of which were sold by Christies in 1961, either as duplicate examples or because they were considered 'unworthy'. Some of these items were purchased on behalf of the Society of St John in London where they remain.

Guy Wilson, then Master of the Royal Armouries, wrote of the 'hoard':

> When they assembled to fight they would have looked an odd mixture of shapes and sizes, some with complete and decorated harnesses, most with plain armour, some covering the whole body, others not. And we can now see, too, how much of their armour had been patched, repaired and altered during its useful life. For these were real working knights…[3]

There is very little evidence of the engraving and gilding one might associate with such a brotherhood. D'Aubusson clearly had a visually impressive armour which he used to show himself to the defenders, and as an act of defiance to the enemy. He discouraged personal ostentation in others and this insistence on modesty would have suited his character.

The collection of pieces is a remarkable survival, attributable to the climatic conditions at Rhodes and the indifference of its new Turkish 'owners.' The stock of armour was apparently at different times ignored, kept for display and it seems occasionally used for target practice by bored Ottoman guards! It is undoubtedly a representative selection, but representative of what? The pieces vary in age, from the early fourteenth to the early sixteenth century and from pieces that would meet the exacting demands of a knight or the desperate needs of an archer for any form of protection. Karcheski and Richardson have carefully recorded and described 187 Rhodian pieces identified from collections around the world. Their work has been invaluable, although there is quite naturally some debate as to all their attributions.

3 Walter Karcheski and Thom Richardson., *The Medieval Armour from Rhodes* (Woodbridge: Boydell & Brewer; 2003), p.v.

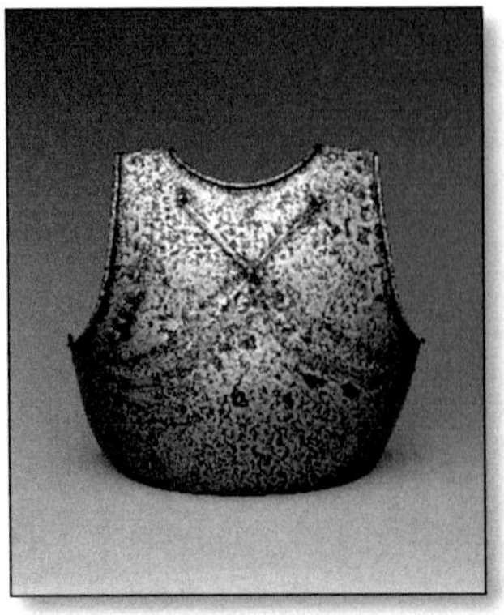

Breastplate *c.* 1420–1440 from the Rhodes hoard. This piece was purchased by the Metropolitan Museum of Art in 1928 probably from the Bacherau collection. There is a lot of evidence of rust damage although less than on some other pieces. It is probably of Italian manufacture. There appears to be a 'shadow' on the lower part of the plate indicative of it once being provided with a plackart plate reinforcement. There is a fitting for a lance rest and the V-shaped stop-rib was designed to stop all weapons, but arrows in particular, from sliding up the armour into the throat and face. The evidence from recent trials has shown this to be a most effective addition. The lack of decoration should not belie its effectiveness. (Metropolitan Museum of Art, Public domain)

Most of the early armour up to 1470 appeared to be of Italian manufacture; after that date Spanish and Italian predominate, with some German and Flemish pieces. It is a fairly representative selection of European armour of this period, although it is not a 'balanced' collection. There are, for example, a very large number of bevors compared to the number of helmets. It was also principally armour for those of lower rank, or no rank, that served alongside the Knights. Brockman makes the telling point that service in the sea-going 'caravans' meant that the Knights would have discovered that to be successful they had to fight as a crew and not as a crowd of individuals. This may have meant that they recognised the importance of armouring the least of their company as well as the great. The enthusiasm that their eastern enemies had for their bows also made armour invaluable for men of all ranks.

A sallet, made by Caspar Reider and dated to *c.* 1480. The sallet was the most common form of helmet discovered in Rhodes, usually provided with a bevor or with an intrinsic eye slit. Reider was a well-known armourer working in Mühlau, from 1452–99. It has a longish tail but not one as extravagant as on other known examples. Helmets were painted, for a variety of reasons but surviving examples showing this are rare as they were often polished by later owners to make them more 'authentic.' Dimensions: H 9½in (24.1cm), W. 9in (22.9cm); D 147/8in (37.8cm), Wt 6lb 8oz (2,948 g). (Metropolitan Museum of Art, Public domain)

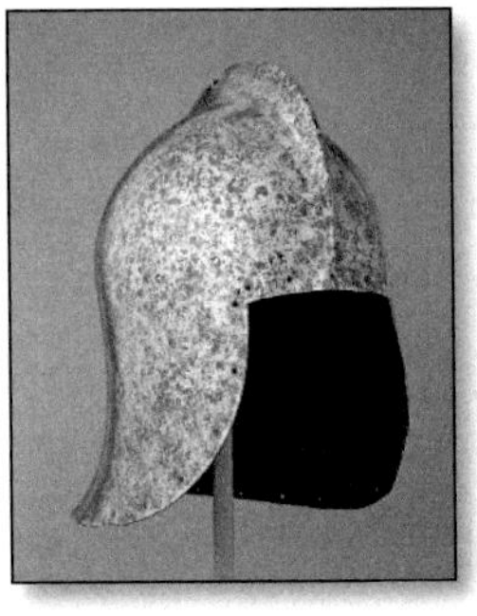

An Italian barbute sallet dated to *c.* 1510–1520. The armourer's mark shows it to be the work of Pietro Giacomo da Castello (documented as working 1485–1525), who was employed by the Dukes of Mantua. The design was inspired by a classical Greek helmet. The face could be fully exposed, as on this example, or have a 'T shaped' opening, which provided greater protection. Both styles were found in the Rhodian hoard. The reinforcing rib would have been of practical rather than solely decorative purpose.
H, without crest, 11½in (29.2cm), W 7 5/8in (19.4cm), D 10½in (26.7cm), Wt 4lb 3oz (1,899g). (Metropolitan Museum of Art, Public domain)

This peculiar looking sallet is German and dated to *c.* 1500–1510. It was purchased in 1920 by the Metropolitan Museum of Art from the Turkish national collection of arms and armour. This was held in the Byzantine Church of St Irene formerly the Imperial Ottoman arsenal which stored a vast quantity of captured equipment. It is certainly possible that this was captured at Rhodes. Mühlau and Innsbruck in Austria and Augsburg, Landshut, and Nuremberg in Germany became centres of armour manufacture. They were able to produce exquisite armour for an emperor or massive quantities of munition armour for an army. The diversity in date and origin of the Rhodian armour suggests that the Knights brought their own and that there was no attempt to provide a uniform style of equipment. This remarkable example has a sort of 'varifocal' visor with three pairs of eye slits
Dimensions: Ht 10½in (26.7cm), W 85/8in (21.9cm), D 121/8in (30.8cm), Wt 5lb 7oz (2,461g). (Metropolitan Museum of Art, Public domain)

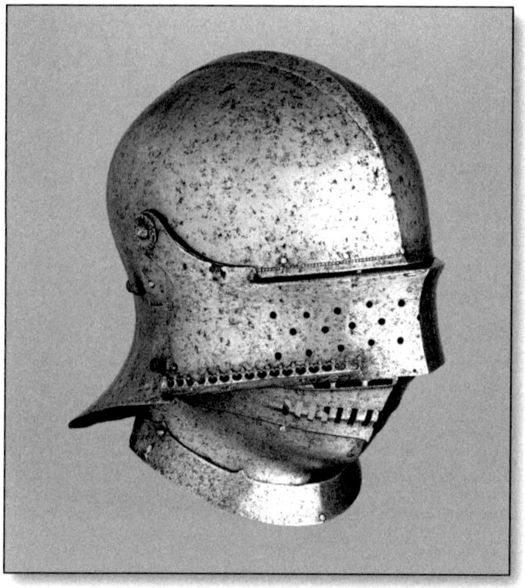

A sallet that once belonged to Emperor Maximilian I (1459–1519). This helmet was probably made by Lorenz Helmschmid the Imperial armourer to Emperor Maximilian I. It was captured by the Turks and kept in the Church of St Irene until sold to the Metropolitan Museum of Art in 1920. It was made around 1493 and is unusual because the bevor or buffe is intrinsic to the helmet and pivots at the same point as the visor. This helmet was probably captured when a castle armoury was looted on the march to Vienna in 1529. It has on it the armourers' marks of the Ottoman Imperial armoury identifying it as a trophy piece. The Victorian obsession with shiny armour was responsible for much destructive polishing. Anyone who owns armour knows how difficult it is to keep it lovely and shiny when any time is spent outdoors, or simply not in ideal conditions. Painting or simply blackening or browning armour would have been highly practical. It is noticeable that all the European armour in the Caoursin images is blackened.
Dimensions: H 12in (30.5cm), W 9in (22.9cm), D 12³/8in (31.4cm), Wt 4lb 15.7oz (2,261g). (Metropolitan Museum of Art, public domain)

In the Rhodian collection there are three armet helmets with full visors of Italian manufacture, three Barbute style helmets, one with a T-shaped face opening, the others with simpler horizontal ones. The most common form of a helmet in the collection is the sallet, with 12 sallets with visors as well as one sallet *alla francese*, that is with a skull drawn to a point and with a deep, wide, pointed tail. There was also one light metal skullcap or *mezza testa*, the simplest form of head defence. The collection also included five German sallets deep-brimmed and with either a short tail or a long tail drawn into a long point. These helmets were provided with an integral sight or a visor. There was one simple skull painted with a gold flame-like design on a dark brown background. There are 35 bevors or parts of bevors, indicative of their importance, acting in concert with the sallet to protect the face of the wearer. Dr Tobias Capwell considers this combination of sallet and bevor to have been the most practical, and probably that most commonly used by all classes of soldier.

There are several Italian breast and back plates as well as reinforcing plackarts. The early sixteenth century examples are fluted and have chisel-roped neck edgework. One exceptional piece (4.43 Catalogue) has the lower portion of the breastplate and the faulds decorated with small squarish pyramidal bosses, I assume to make the wearer look scarier. Other armours appear to be of a style and (low) quality associated with what would be commonly called Almain rivet. There are only a few examples of German cuirasses and these are rather later in date than most of the Italian types. Very rarely were breastplates found to have an *arret de lance,* (or the holes necessary to have one fitted): that is the lance rest essential for the use of one on horseback. Although there were cavalry in the Order, the vast majority of their fighting would have been aboard ship or in a garrison, making such an addition redundant. One breastplate (6.3) possibly of Spanish manufacture has a projectile hole almost dead centre slightly to the left of the ridge line. It may be damage from 1522 although a past librarian of the current English Order was told that bored Turkish sentries would take pot shots at armour with their modern weapons.[4] There are pauldrons, vambraces, couters, poleyns and cuisses aplenty but only a small selection of gauntlets, all of which are Italian and of mitten style. There are several shaffrons to protect the heads of barded or armoured horses including one (12.2) which is massively fluted.

This mitten gauntlet is of Austrian or German manufacture c. 1500. It has Ottoman marks indicating that it was a captured item, held as a trophy, as were other pieces of arms and armour associated with conquests both in the East and the West. In the collections of Rhodian armour only mitten gauntlets have been found. The determination of the Knights to protect their hands contrasts with the feeble, or completely absent, crossguards on Ottoman swords and sabres which would have left them open to serious hand injury. Length overall, 13¼in (33.7cm). (Metropolitan Museum of Art, Public domain)

The defensive quality of the armour varied considerably. Medieval steel was not as consistent as that of modern manufacture. There were attempts to improve its hardness by first quenching in cold water, which would create a very hard layer of martensite and then by tempering. This would be achieved by careful reheating, which made the metal less brittle or prone to fracturing. An analysis by Allan Williams of the 108 specimens of armour has shown that only nine were of iron, 61 were of low carbon steel (9 hardened) and 38 were of medium carbon steel of which 25 had been hardened.[5] This variation is hardly surprising, considering the age and varied origins of the armour.

What is very surprising is that although there is a great deal of evidence of repairing and reworking of armour, there is no observable battle damage on the pieces studied by Dr Capwell.[6] This may simply be, as he suggests, that the condition of the armour makes it difficult to establish whether it has been damaged. It could also be that the armour that was badly damaged was discarded and what remains is what was found to be serviceable after the battle. The Order was permitted to take personal arms and armour with them when Rhodes fell and this must have included their best and most serviceable pieces.

4 This is at present on display in the Museum of the Order in Clerkenwell, London.

5 Walter Karcheski and Thom Richardson, *The Medieval Armour from Rhodes* (Martlesham: Boydell & Brewer, 2003).

6 Author's conversation with Dr Tobias Capwell, 19 April 2023.

This is probably not the effigy of a Hospitaller Knight, as such effigies that exist show them in the habit of the Order or wearing a mantle with the Order's cross upon it. This effigy can be pretty precisely dated to the end of the Hospitaller occupation, because it is clearly unfinished as well as quite literally defaced. It is at present in the French consulate in the Street of the Knights. The knight's sword is a magnificent double-handed example, and his armour is complete except for his helmet – he would clearly have been a formidable opponent. (Author's photograph)

What is missing from this collection and for obvious reasons, is the great quantity of fabric armour that was an essential accompaniment to metal defences. There would have been inner liners to the helmets, and arming doublets to which the plate armour would have been attached. Padded jacks made from layers of linen and other materials as well as jacks into which metal plates had been sewn were commonly worn by infantry, especially by archers. Brigandines, in effect coats of plates sewn to a linen base, were very popular and effective and less exhausting to wear in hot weather than full plate armour. There was also no mail found in the hoard. Mail could have been worn in the form of shirts, sections of mail sewn to clothing to protect the armpits or as a skirt to protect the groin. It was also an important addition to the helmet, as an aventail or as a mail curtain to protect the throat and neck. This mail is likely to have been immediately recycled by their Ottoman conquerors, since mail was the basis of their system of armoured protection.

The armour of the Ottoman forces was very different from that worn by the Order which would have given the Knights a considerable advantage in close combat. The armour that had developed in the Islamic world reflected the conditions in which they fought and the equipment of their customary eastern adversaries. After the expulsion of the Christians from the Latin States in 1291 the principal opponents of Islamic armies would have been enemies armed and equipped in a similar manner to themselves. The Armies of Selim 'the Grim' had conquered Persian and Mameluke foes before encountering the Knights.

In the West plate armour had increased in weight and complexity, eventually covering the whole of the torso by the early fifteenth century. This had been, in part, a response to the threat of longbow arrows and crossbow bolts which had defeated mail and padded armour. Such armour gave almost complete immunity to sword blows, although mechanical

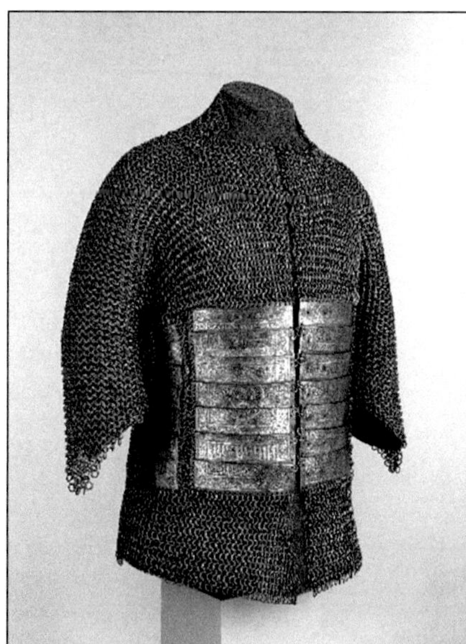

A shirt of mail and plate of Al-Ashraf Sayf ad-Din Qaitbay (c. 1416/18–1496), 18th Burji Mameluke Sultan of Egypt probably Egyptian, *c.* 1468–96. This armour is highly characteristic of that worn by both Ottoman and Mameluke soldiers in this period. Although this example is highly decorated it is in essence a simple mail shirt which has had 87 steel plates sewn in, forming two panels protecting the chest and the back. The mail consists of rows of solid flat section rings, connected by riveted rings. It was captured in 1517, long after the original owner's death and was sent as a war trophy to Istanbul. Dimensions: Height 31in. (78.7cm), W 54½in (138.4cm), Wt 25lb 2.4oz (11.41kg). (Metropolitan Museum of Art, public domain)

This turban helmet is from the late fifteenth century and is probably Persian in origin. The flutings and bulbous shape are reminiscent of a turban which explains its appellation. Just as the shape of the turban was indicative of religious devotion, a turban helmet could also be associated with a religious martial purpose, a *jihad*. This type of helmet was used by heavy cavalry from the fourteenth century onwards, this example is much later and is probably Persian or Anatolian. Dimensions: Ht 13¹/8in (33.34cm), Diam. 9½in (24.13cm), Wt 2lb 11oz (1,219g). (Metropolitan Museum of Art, public domain)

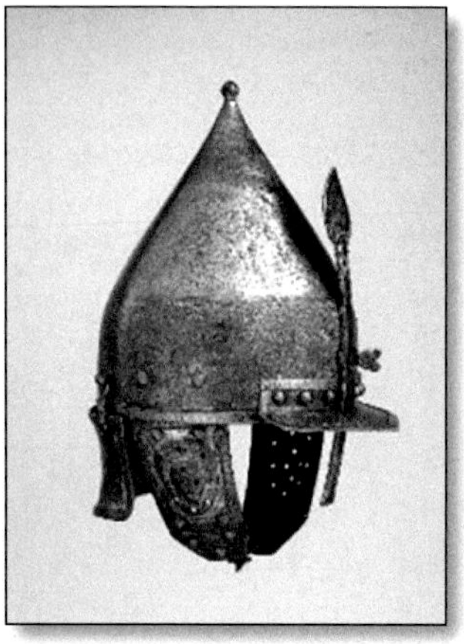

This conical helmet is of Turkish or of Turcoman style and dateable to *c.* 1500–1525. It has the original brim, neck defence, nasal bar and cheeks which would provide considerable protection. It is typical of Ottoman and Mameluke helmets of *c.* 1500. Dimensions: H, including cheek defence, 15½in (39.4cm), H, including nasal, 15½in (39.4cm), H, excluding cheek defence and nasal, 10in (25.4cm), W 8³/8in (21.3cm), D 10¼in (26cm), Wt 3lb 15.4oz (1797.4 g). (Metropolitan Museum of Art, public domain)

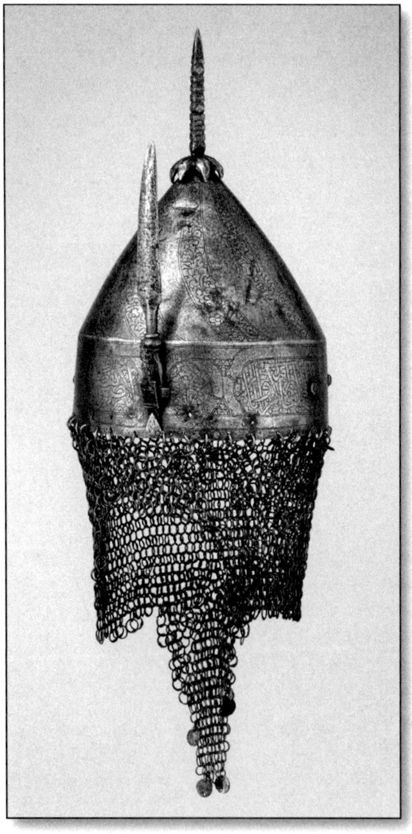

This Helmet is probably Egyptian in origin and is dateable to the early decades of the sixteenth century. It has the marks of the Ottoman arsenal, indicating that it was probably taken as war booty when the Mamelukes were defeated by Selim the Grim in 1517. The spear at the front, spiked top and mail are all later additions from North Africa. The Metropolitan Museum considers that this helmet was recycled for use during the Mahdi's revolt against Egyptian/British rule in the 1880s and 1890s, giving it a working life of almost four hundred years. Dimensions: H, including mail, 24½in (62.2cm), H 8in (20.3cm), W 8½in (21.6cm), D 8¾in (22.2cm), Wt, excluding mail, 3lb 3.8oz (1,468.5 g). (Metropolitan Museum of Art, public domain)

damage and even penetration could be achieved with maces and polearms swung with enough murderous force. Islamic armour had responded to the eruption of the Mongols into the region in the thirteenth century. The lamellar coats of plate were abandoned in favour of plates integrated as part of a mail garment. The *jawshan* consisted of overlapping breast and back plates joined together and articulated by mail. This was worn with a conical helm displaying varying degrees of decoration and complexity, including what is referred to as the 'turban' helmet or *migfer*. The *migfer* was eventually replaced by the *cicak* in the sixteenth century, this was similar to the burgonet in having an open face, a neck guard, an adjustable nasal guard and cheek-pieces.

This helmet is another product of the Royal Workshops in Istanbul, destined for the Court of Suleiman and dated to *c.* 1560. It is forged from a single piece of watered steel and decorated with Koranic script in gold. It is an excellent design and meant to deflect cuts from above. It also has a neck protector, nasal bar and cheek pieces. Although considered a 'parade' piece it was highly practical and could have been worn by the commanders of the Ottoman army in 1522. Dimensions: H 10¾in (27.8cm), Wt. 5lb 11oz (2,580 g). (Metropolitan Museum of Art, public domain)

The informative Fleming Ogier Ghiselin de Busbecq provided a fascinating insight into the rather haphazard approach to equipping the Ottoman soldiers with armour. He first noted:

> The convoy of armour, of which I spoke, is intended chiefly for the use of the royal horse-guards, as the Janissaries are lightly equipped, and generally do not fight at close quarters, but at a distance with muskets.[7]

Busbecq, it is important to note, was writing in the middle of the century when firearms were far more generally used.

> Well, when the enemy is near, and a battle is expected, the stock of armour is produced, consisting for the most part of antiquated pieces picked up on the fields which have been the scene of Turkish victories; they are distributed to the royal horse guards, who at other times have only their light shield to protect them. Where so little pains is taken to provide each man with a suit that fits him, I need hardly tell you that they are but clumsily equipped. One man's cuirass is too tight, another's helmet too big, a third gets a coat of mail too heavy for him to bear; one way or another no one is properly accoutred. Yet they never grumble, holding that a man who quarrels with his armour must needs be a cowardly fellow, and are confident that they will make a stout fight of it themselves whatever their equipment may be. This feeling is the result of their great successes and military experience.[8]

7 Ogier Ghislain de Busbecq (Charles Thornton Forster, trans.), *The Life and Letters of Ogier Ghiselin de Busbecq* (London: Kegan Paul & co, 1881), p.223.
8 Ogier Ghislain de Busbecq (Charles Thornton Forster, trans.), *The Life and Letters of Ogier Ghiselin de Busbecq* (London: Kegan Paul & co, 1881), p.223.

The Turkish soldiers were probably right in assuming that it was the man who was inside the armour that mattered and that armour did not make the man!

The Turkish bow is a wonder of both design and manufacture, and in many respects it was far superior to the yew bow. Made from horn and sinew with a wooden core, it is a far more technically sophisticated weapon than the longbow and has arrows that can achieve a very high velocity. Its arrows, on the other hand, are much slighter than those of a proper Western war bow and the arrowheads, although capable of penetrating mail and perhaps light plate would have great difficulty in penetrating well-designed western plate armour defences. The recent trials by Todeschini[9] have shown that even the best quality bows, shafts and archers would by 1415 face considerable difficulty when encountering good quality armour. In the context of eastern warfare however the bow could still win battles.

> Yet while the Ottoman conquest did look like a triumph of overwhelming firepower to Mameluke apologists, it was Ottoman mounted archers who outflanked the Mameluke defences on the approaches to Cairo to gain the victory (Ayalon 1956; Nicolle 1993).[10]

The Ottoman sword (*kilic*) possessed the same importance and significance in the Islamic world that the weapon did in Christendom. The curved blade was often of very high quality but it could only be used single-handed and the crossguard was narrow and provided little protection for the hand. It was best used for cutting rather than thrusting and could not compare in weight and size to the western arming and double-handed swords. The *yatagan* was, because of its light weight, of limited use in defence and was

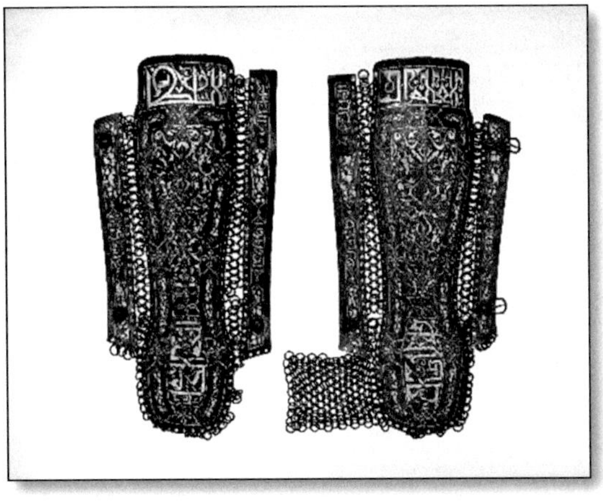

Legs are very vulnerable in combat and these leg defences, or greaves, were highly practical. Of Turkish manufacture and of the late fifteenth or early sixteenth century, they are the only known matching pair in existence. They use the usual combination of plate and mail which would make them lighter and more flexible than the equivalent western version. The back of the calf would still be exposed which would make it a target for an enemy taught to exploit it. Dimensions, of each: L 15⅝in (39.7cm), W 4¼in (10.8cm), Wt of 36.25.457 1lb 6 oz (737 g), Wt of 1990.229 1lb 10 oz (737 g). (Metropolitan Museum of Art, public domain)

9 https://www.youtube.com/@tods_workshop

10 Barton C. Hacker, 'Mounted Archery and Firearms, Late Medieval Muslim Military Technology Reconsidered', *Vulcan* 3, 2015 (Washington D.C., Journal of the Smithsonian Institution, 2015), p.52.

This *kilic* from the sixteenth century is highly characteristic of swords of this period and very different in both design and use from western weapons of the same period. These tend to be double-edged straight-bladed and fitted with a wider cross guard. This superb example has gold inlaid inscriptions 'to the glory of Allah and Suleiman'. It probably belonged to Suleiman and was manufactured in Istanbul between 1522 and 1566. As a hopeless romantic I would like to think that this weapon was worn by Suleiman at the time of the second siege, or perhaps made to commemorate his victory.
L overall 37⁷/8in (96.2cm), L of blade 30¾in (78.1cm), W 6¹/8in (15.5cm), Wt 2lb 5oz (1,049 g). (Metropolitan Museum of Art, public domain)

A short sword (*yatagan*) probably from the Court of Suleiman the Magnificent from the workshop of Ahmed Tekelü, possibly Iranian in origin and dated to *c.* 1525–30. It was made in the imperial workshop although the only thing that distinguishes it as a 'princely weapon' from others of the same design, is the quality of the workmanship and the use of precious materials. The designs are inspired by Chinese and Persian examples, exemplifying the range of the influences on Ottoman art in this period. It is an example of one of the earliest known *yatagans*, a weapon with a double-curved blade and lacking a cross guard. Why this absence was thought to be advantageous I cannot guess. An attractive weapon it has tended to be associated as a sidearm with the Janissaries.
Dimensions: L. 23 3/8 in. (59.3cm); L. of blade 18 3/8 in. (46.7cm); Wt. 1lb. 8 oz. (691 g). Materials: Steel, gold, ivory (walrus), silver, turquoise, pearls, rubies (Metropolitan Museum of Art, public domain)

A mid-sixteenth century mace, probably Turkish. The mace, as well as the war hammer was commonly carried by Turkish cavalry. The round or tear drop form was a common shape in the East, although flanged maces were not unknown. The spiral fluting on the shaft of this mace represents a style developed by the Mamelukes and then spread to other parts of the Middle East.[11]
Dimensions: Length 28in (71.12cm), L of head, 4½in (11.43cm), Diam. of head 3in (7.6cm), Wt 2lb 12oz (1256 g). (Metropolitan Museum of Art, public domain)

usually supplemented by a small shield. In the West the shield had been abandoned as full-armour was adopted. In addition to swords and possibly of greater use against an armed opponent were spiked war hammers, maces and polearms of a similar ferocity to those used by their Christian adversaries.

The Ottoman soldier was a fearsome figure in the imaginations of western Christians. Busbecq writing in the middle of the century stressed the logistical abilities of the Ottoman Army on its long campaigns to Persia and Egypt. He also pointed to the remarkable discipline and self-reliance that he saw demonstrated by the Ottoman soldier. He provided a glowing report on the Ottoman Army as well as giving a stern rebuke and warning to the Western forces that would face them. He felt his own rather dubious origins, as a legitimised bastard, and stressed the meritocratic aspect of the Ottomans that he felt produced a far more effective army.

> it is the patience, self-denial, and thrift of the Turkish soldier that enable him to face the most trying circumstances, and come safely out of the dangers that surround him. What a contrast to our men! Christian soldiers on a campaign refuse to put up with their ordinary food, and call for thrushes, beccaficoes [garden warbler or other fattened songbird considered a delicacy], and such like dainty dishes! If these are not supplied they grow mutinous and work their own ruin; and, if they are supplied, they are ruined all the same. For each man is his own worst enemy, and has no foe more deadly than his own intemperance, which is sure to kill him, if the enemy be not quick. It makes me shudder to think of what the result of a struggle

11 Metropolitan Museum of Art Catalogue

> between such different systems must be; one of us must prevail and the other be destroyed, at any rate we cannot both exist in safety. On their side is the vast wealth of their empire, unimpaired resources, experience and practice in arms, a veteran soldiery, an uninterrupted series of victories, readiness to endure hardships, union, order, discipline, thrift, and watchfulness. On ours are found an empty exchequer, luxurious habits, exhausted resources, broken spirits, a raw and insubordinate soldiery, and greedy generals; there is no regard for discipline, license runs riot, the men indulge in drunkenness and debauchery, and, worst of all, the enemy are accustomed to victory, we, to defeat. Can we doubt what the result must be?[12]

His criticisms of Christian soldiers, perhaps containing more than a smidgen of truth could not be levied at the Knights, Brothers and militia of Rhodes in 1522.

12 Ogier Ghislain de Busbecq (Charles Thornton Forster, trans.), *The Life and Letters of Ogier Ghiselin de Busbecq* (London: Kegan Paul & co, 1881), p.221.

9

The Siege of 1522

The Order Alone Again

In 1480 no European power was in a position to send aid to Rhodes and in 1520 the situation was little better. Spain united under Ferdinand and Isabella had become a major power in the Western Mediterranean but it was concerned with its empire in the New World. It was also in the business of completing the defeat and subjugation of the Moslem population in its own territories, as well as defending its borders. Portugal was engaged in acquiring a most extraordinary overseas empire across the Globe, which would have profound implications for the West. Eastern Christendom faced threats from the Turk as well as a new threat from a resurgent Russia, whose own Orthodox Church was no friend to either the Greek or Latin churches. Worst of all perhaps was increasing division in Christendom within the Church of Rome. In England the Lollards had proved troublesome to the establishment but in Bohemia the followers of Jan Hus, the Hussites, challenged not only the authority of the Church but the existing political order. The war that developed between 1419 and 1434 was a ghastly combination of Crusade and civil war and further weakened Christendom. Worse was to come as the result of a succession of Popes of dubious morals and limited authority beyond Rome, whose many vices and few virtues led to a demand for reform that culminated in Martin Luther's 'Ninety-Five Theses' of 1517.

Portrait of Emperor Charles V from *Libertas Germaniae*, by Hans Baldung and printed in Strasbourgh in 1519. The 19-year old Emperor looks young and vulnerable in this portrait, hardly up to the job of managing the greatest empire the West had seen since the fall of Rome. He faced discord, opposition and downright rebellion throughout his vast realm from his accession and could hardly be expected to come to the aid of Rhodes in 1522. He continued to struggle manfully with the role until finally separating the eastern territories from the western, creating in effect two empires, that of Spain and the Austrian Habsburgs. (Metropolitan Museum of Art, public Domain)

Emperor Charles V had succeeded to a massive empire which included Spain, the Netherlands, disparate German territories as well as the Indies and America. He was involved in securing Spain and her North African possessions against further attacks, including those of notorious corsair Barbarossa. In 1520 he became entangled in the bloody revolt of the *Comuneros* who objected to being governed by a Flemish monarch who could not speak their language. He was heavily embroiled in the religious conflicts with the developing Protestant movement as well as in a war with France over Italian territories. There was also unfinished business with the remaining Moslem population of Spain. His focus would not be on the defence of the eastern borders of the Empire, where he had never received any encouragement by those over whom he was ostensibly the suzerain.

Hungary was the principal Christian bulwark to Ottoman expansion, after the Balkans had been lost following the battle of Kosovo in 1389. Under Matthias Corvinus (1485–1490) Hungary had become a strong and respected power that could challenge the Ottomans in the field. The premature death of Matthias led to the disastrous reign of Ladislaus Jagello which led to a peasants' revolt in 1514 that ended in brutal massacre and perpetual servitude for those who survived. Ladislaus' death in 1516 left a child of ten, Louis II to succeed to a throne and a Kingdom weakened by internal dissent and the greed and ambition of its nobility. All was not lost and in 1521 Charles's younger brother Ferdinand married Anna the sister of Louis Jagello. In 1522 Charles handed over his Austrian Territories and dependencies to Ferdinand. This would not help Louis who at the age of 20 was killed on the field of Mohacs in 1526, an even greater loss for Christendom.

Henry VIII of England might have been expected to have provided support for the Order in 1522. He had been on the throne for thirteen years and was vigorous and bellicose. He had close, perhaps too close, connections with the Hospitaller Order and especially their Prior of England Thomas Docwra. Thomas had fought at the first siege of Rhodes when a young man and proceeded through the ranks in the English Langue becoming the Turcopolier in 1495. After numerous appointments he became Grand Prior of England in 1501 responsible for the 40 properties of the Order. In 1510 Henry refused him permission to leave the realm in response to a command from the Grand Master to reinforce the Priory. In 1513 Thomas accompanied Henry VIII in his expedition to France in command of three hundred men. As the Grand Prior he was a trusted servant of the Order and the English crown, acting regularly in England's interests as an ambassador and attending upon Henry at the Field of the Cloth of Gold in 1520. By May 1521 relations between the two kings had broken down and a year later Henry declared war on his former best friend. Henry VIII, although a loyal servant of the Church and a public enemy of Luther and his heresy, had no intention of employing his considerable resources in a war far beyond the boundaries of his own realm.

Illustration of a fifteenth century trade galley from a manuscript by Michael of Rhodes (1401–1445) dated to 1434. Michael of Rhodes was a fifteenth century sailor who it is thought was of Rhodian descent, although there is little evidence for that association. He began his career as a humble oarsman but rose to become Captain of a Venetian galley. He served in vessels around the Mediterranean and as far North as England and Flanders. His illustrations and descriptions of civilian vessels and warships in his manuscript are invaluable to historians. The illustration here is of a galley of Flanders or rather simply a *galia grossa* or large galley, used to carry a substantial cargo but also of use as military transport. Although a galley, what is most apparent is the large lateen sail commonly used in the Mediterranean. Even though the oarsmen would row in shifts the use of the sails was always preferred, both for speed and to rest the oarsmen for when they were essential. The large crews and small stowage space on a war galley meant that they could only remain at sea for a short period before requiring revictualling and especially the replenishment of their store of fresh water. (Public domain via Wikimedia Commons)
Length on the deck 121ft (36.9m), Breadth 21ft (6.12m), Height [above waterline?] 9ft (2.74m).

If there was to be found support for the Order anywhere it might be expected to come from within Italy. The region was extraordinarily wealthy and creative throughout the Middle Ages. It was at the heart of the Renaissance that would come to dominate European art and culture in all its forms for centuries ahead. Italy's wealth came from trade, manufacture and a sophisticated and effective banking system. It was also most likely to suffer from the depredations of Ottoman and Mameluke pirates. Much of the wealth flowed through the cities and territories that belonged to Genoa and to Venice.

Venice had prospered through dominating the eastern Mediterranean. It had used its power and influence to divert the Fourth Crusade against Constantinople in 1204, devastating its greatest trading rival, ostensibly in the cause of Christ. Venetian wealth came from trade with the Mamelukes and later the Ottomans, especially the trade in spices and other high value low volume cargoes, as well as the lucrative western Pilgrim trade. Its system of government, run by an elected Doge and the Council of Ten provided ruthless, competent and self-interested management of what was a well-armed trading corporation. The Venetians were only interested in engaging in conflict if it was to protect or expand its own interests. They often said of themselves, 'We are Venetians first and Christians second.'

The loss of Euboea (Negroponti) by Venice in 1470 had been balanced by the acquisition of Crete in 1489 but the greatest danger and the worst defeat was to come at the hands of the Christian League of Cambrai. The Venetian forces were defeated at the Battle of Agnadello in 1509 by a predominantly French Army under Louis XII. The Venetians lost two thirds of their army and even more importantly the value of the bonds fell by 40 percent. Selim's conquest of Egypt in 1517 put the vital port of Alexandria, that had been under the control of the Mamelukes, into the hands of the Ottomans. Worse still were the depredations of the Portuguese that threatened the very existence of the Indian Ocean and Persian Gulf routes to the spices of the East

Support for the Order would only be forthcoming if it was in the interests of Venice; they had been allied before but Rhodes could not rely upon Venetian assistance on every occasion. In 1521 the Venetians sought a rapprochement with Suleiman to avoid further threats to their diminished empire. Henry VIII joked with the Venetian Ambassador in 1518 that the Signory was 'linked' with the Turk and the ambassador retorted that this was: 'not of free will, but of necessity.' [1] In 1522 the Venetian Senate showed little concern for the besieged order but much for their own position, hoping that perhaps Christendom would come to her aid. Venetian self-obsession was made clear in this account of the deliberation of the Doge and the Council of Ten while the siege of Rhodes took place:

> Peace between Christians is greatly needed. Last year the Great Turk conquered Belgrade, Serimia [Servia?], and a great part of Hungary. During the last few months he has taken the fortresses of Scardona and Tuina (*sic*) in Croatia. He is now besieging Rhodes in person, with 300 sail and an army of 100,000 men, a terrible and fearful thing to every nation, however remote, but above all to the Signory, whose neighbour he is. The Republic is compelled to incur excessive expenditure for the defence of her possessions.[2]

The Serene Republic would not aid the Knights with a single soldier or pound of gunpowder if it endangered their precarious peace with the Sublime Porte.

The Portuguese had long pursued the wealth found at sea and were notable sailors. This tradition allied to the enthusiastic support for overseas trade with other European countries, from successive monarchs, created the conditions for further voyages of exploration. The epic voyage of Vasco da Gama to India in 1497–1499 led to a new strategy, the monopolising of the

1 CSP Venice March 15. 1518 Original Letter Book, St. Mark's Library, Letter no. 166. 1015. Sebastian Giustinian to the Signory.

2 CSP Venice August 8 1522. Deliberazioni Senato Secreta, v. xlix. p.112, tergo.516. The Doge and Senate to Antonio Surian, Venetian Ambassador in England

De Casu Regis Zyzymy (The case of Sultan Djem) printed in Ulm by Ioannem Reger in William Caoursin's *Obsidionis Rhodiae Urbis Descriptio* (1496) It was not only the Ottomans that the Order and Rhodians should fear. In 1481 a massive earthquake added to the damage caused by the siege. Within the old town the buttressing across streets to protect the domestic buildings from this threat is still present in places. The terror that such events caused is well-illustrated in the desperation of the figures in this image.

spice trade by controlling the sea routes across the Indian Ocean. By the second siege in 1522 Portugal had acquired control of the spice trade from India to the Persian Gulf a position which would have a profound impact on the future of Venice.

The Papacy was itself in a weak position politically, financially and morally. Leo X was a son of the de Medici family and saw the Papacy serving the interests of his famous family rather than the Church. He used his wealth to support a war that gained the Duchy of Urbino for his nephew. He was a great and extravagant patron of the arts but was neither a great theologian nor politician. As a means of restoring papal finances and completing the construction of St Peter's Basilica, he authorised the selling of indulgences which became the *casus belli* of Martin Luther. He seriously underestimated Luther and considered the dispute to be no more than a 'monkish quarrel.' His condemnation of Luther in 1520 as a heretic and his refusal to engage with papal critics made further conflict more likely. He sought an alliance with Charles V, ostensibly against the Turk but in practice to drive the French King, Francis I, out of Italy once and for all. Leo X died in December 1521 leaving the Papacy and Christendom weaker than ever.

Leo X's successor on the papal throne was Adrian VI, a Netherlander and protégé of the Emperor Charles V. He was accepted as a compromise candidate by the Church and during his short pontificate (January 1522 -September 1523) was able to achieve little. He did acknowledge the failures of the papacy and would have pursued a policy of reform but time, institutional inertia and the hostility of his opponents made it impossible for him to achieve anything. He was not even present in Rome until August 1522 when he arrived for his coronation, having travelled from Spain with little sense of urgency. His epitaph suited him well: 'Alas, even with the best of men, how much depends on the times in which he lives.' There was little hope that the papacy could provide either the means to reinforce the Order in Rhodes, or possessed the moral leadership to rally what was already a deeply divided Christendom. The Hospitallers could expect little aid from the powers in the West.

There was little hope for substantial reinforcements for the Order from overseas. The island had suffered badly in the years after the first siege. In 1481 a major earthquake damaged much of the city and led to many of the Jewish community leaving for more prosperous and stable climes. Plague followed in 1498–1500 which further decimated the population and led to the expulsion of all the resident Jews to Nice rather than allowing them to migrate to nearby Muslim Turkey. Jews remained but as slaves captured by the Order's ships and were employed in the rebuilding of the defences.

Suleiman the Lawgiver – a New Enemy

> Allah's Deputy on Earth, Lord of the Lords of this World, Possessor of Men's Necks, King of Believers and Unbelievers, King of Kings, Emperor of East and West, Emperor of the Chakrans of Great Authority, Prince and Lord of the Most Happy Constellation, Majestic Caesar,[3] Seal of Victory, Refuge of all the People in the Whole World, The Shadow of the Almighty Dispensing Quiet in the Earth.

Suleiman the 'Magnificent', or 'the Lawgiver' as he was known to his own subjects, succeeded to the blood-stained achievements of his father Selim the Grim. Selim had murdered his way to the throne and then used his power to conquer the Mamelukes and Persians and unite them under the Ottoman throne or yoke. Suleiman was fortunate in being the only son of Selim and successor to a much greater and more powerful empire than his father. He was not a bloodstained psychopathic tyrant, he was a cultured man, a poet and promoter of the arts and diverse learning, he was an able administrator and a diplomat who understood the opportunities and problems that faced him.

Suleiman had been kept at arm's length, literally and figuratively speaking, by his father for the safety of both. Appointed as Governor, some distance away from the centre of power in Constantinople, he avoided becoming a threat to his ageing but powerful father, thereby protecting

3 A reference to his conquest of Constantinople,

This bronze medallion of Suleiman was cast around 1520 in Venice. The relationship between Venice and Istanbul/Constantinople had always been difficult, even or especially when under Christian rule. Venice had to reach a compromise with the Ottomans if its lucrative trade and valuable territories were not to be lost. If this was cast in 1520 it might have been in the hope of gaining the favour of the new Sultan, his appearance is dignified and aloof. Mehmet II had also appeared on western medals and there was no sense of superiority in the West over Eastern rulers. Suleiman was considered to be a *vir illustris* (an illustrious man) a renaissance concept that could be applied to the great men of the past and the present, who were to be both feared and admired. This attitude to Suleiman was reflected in the Turkish letters of Busbecq (see Bibliography). Diameter: 5¹/8in (130mm). (Metropolitan Museum of Art, public domain)

his own life. Selim had of course challenged his own father twice; first in a failed military campaign and later by suborning the Janissaries and forcing his father's abdication. There is nothing to suggest that there was any affection between Selim and his son but Suleiman demonstrated personal loyalty and had no premature or deadly ambitions to replace his father, other than as a dutiful son after Selim's natural demise. This death was sudden and although unexpected was dealt with quickly and efficiently, avoiding the chaos it was assumed would follow. Inevitably some old scores were settled and the Janissaries flexed their military and political muscles, but order prevailed. Suleiman rewarded the Janissaries for their 'loyalty,' pardoned prisoners, executed a few evildoers and with the support of the administration, army and merchants came to the throne of a populous land of great wealth. His name, derived from that of the Biblical Solomon, was venerated and his accession was accompanied by encouraging auspices.

In the West the death of Selim was welcomed by all, as it had been felt that he would turn his attention to North Africa and possibly even the reconquest of Spain. Pope Leo X, when Selim's death was known for certain, commanded that the Litany and Common Prayers be sung throughout Rome by a barefoot congregation. The general feeling was that a 'fierce lion' had been succeeded by a 'gentle lamb.' Bartolomeo Contarini described the young Sultan on his accession thus:

> he is twenty-five years of age, tall, but wiry, of a delicate complexion. His neck is a little too long, his face thin, and his nose aquiline. He has a shadow of a moustache and a small beard; nevertheless he has a pleasant mien, though his skin tends to pallor. He is said to be a wise Lord, fond of study, and all men hope for good from his rule.'[4]

He was a cultivated man and noted linguist able to speak to his officers, many of whom came from the Balkans, in their own tongue. He appeared more interested in the history of the West and the opportunities to be found

4 R. B. Merriman, *Suleiman the magnificent* 1520–1566 (London: OUP, 1944), p.33

there than pursuing further conquests in the East. Although a true believer and a pious man, he wished to launch a *Jihad* against neither Christians nor Moslem heretics. He was still the 'Commander of the Faithful' and felt the responsibility that this brought strongly.

Much was expected of Suleiman, specifically to reverse the most obvious failures of his predecessors, the failure to capture Belgrade and Rhodes. The capture of Belgrade would give him complete access to the Danube and the capture of Rhodes would remove a significant irritant and be a final chapter in the bloody history of the Crusades. The Great Turk had good reasons to rid Rhodes of its turbulent monks. The Bâtard de Liège explained the thinking of Suleiman thus:

> The first and principal cause was that he considered and saw by experience that there was no other town nor place in the Levant that warred against him nor kept him in doubt but this poor rock of Rhodes. And hearing the continual complaints of his subjects as well of Syria as Turkey for the damages and prizes daily done of their bodies and goods by Christian men of war received because of Rhodes and the ships and galleys of the Religion. He drew the conclusion that if he might put the said town in his power and subjection that he should become the peaceable lord of all parts of the Levant & that his subjects should complain no more to him. The second [cause for attacking Rhodes was that] he would be following the example of his noble predecessors &would show himself very heir of the mighty victorious lord Sultan Selim his father.[5]

The author of this analysis was Frère Jacques de Bourbon, Bâtard de Liège. He was born in 1466, the natural son of the Prince-Bishop of Liège and joined the Order in 1503.[6] His arrival on Rhodes was propitious rather than planned and soon after the siege he committed his account to paper and then eventually to print. His account of the second siege was based on careful personal observation and is an invaluable source.

Belgrade was in a strategically vital position astride the Danube and the Save and was near impregnable. Besieged in 1440 and again in 1456 by Murad, the conqueror of Constantinople, it remained in Christian hands. Suleiman launched raids along the Hungarian frontier while calling for tribute from Hungary, a request which was of course rejected. The Hungarians pleaded to all those powers in Europe who might help, stressing the responsibility that they had taken for the defence of Christendom for so long and at such a high cost. They now asked for Christendom and especially the Emperor to come to their aid. Charles V faced rebellions in Spain, a new outbreak

5 Jacques de Bourbon, *Grande et Merveilleuse, & Tréscruelle Oppugnation de la noble Cité de Rhodes*, (London: 1524), page unnumbered.

6 His bastardy could no doubt be forgiven considering his sire.

of war with France, and a constitutional crisis over the Regency Council in Germany; added to this was the religious dissension caused by Martin Luther which threatened Catholic and Imperial authority. There would be no help from Charles V.

Suleiman's forces advanced inexorably towards Belgrade, supplied by massive camel trains as well as river transport. His progress to the siege of Belgrade was a triumphant one, on a route decorated with the heads of captured Hungarians. He used his impressive corps of engineers to construct pontoon bridges and then employed boats to enable him to cross the Save to reach the gates of the city. After a siege of two months the lower city was abandoned and although the Citadel held out, one of its towers was destroyed by mining. The few defenders left, half having already been killed or wounded, fell out among themselves as to the future course of action and on 28 August they surrendered. The Hungarian garrison was massacred, while the Serbians were allowed to go free. Suleiman returned to Constantinople in triumph but left his artillery with a garrison of 3,000 Janissaries. His intent on further conquest was obvious. The victory had not been a difficult one. His engineers, miners and gunners had transported an army across difficult terrain and then reduced the enemy defences with comparative ease and speed. He might have felt, with some confidence, that his next objective, the capture of the City of Rhodes, could be accomplished as easily, with a short sea interlude to break the journey. Although this is how the venture might have been presented by his land and sea commanders, it was not to be the case.

Suleiman was not to descend upon Rhodes without due warning and preparation. The diplomatic niceties had to be attended to first. The letter sent from the Sultan via the embassy of the Order in Constantinople began by listing Suleiman's many titles, including High Emperor of Byzantium. It continued by congratulating the new Grand Master on his appointment and trusting that he would rule well and profitably.

> I also mean to cultivate your favour; rejoice then with me, as a very dear friend, that following in the footsteps of my father, who conquered Persia, Jerusalem, Arabia and Egypt, I have captured the most powerful of fortresses, Belgrade, during the late Autumn; after which, having offered battle to the Kuffar [a pejorative term for his Christian enemies], which they had not the courage to accept, I took many other beautiful and well fortified cities, and destroyed most of their inhabitants either by sword or fire, the remainder being reduced to slavery. Now after sending my numerous and victorious army into winter quarters, I myself shall return to my Court at Constantinople.[7]

7 Eric Brockman, *The Two Sieges* (London: John Murray, 1969), p.114.

It was quite clear where Suleiman intended to lead his victorious army next. De l'Isle Adam replied, failing to employ the many titles that Suleiman claimed and pointed to his attempted abduction and assassination by a Turkish pirate and his embarrassing failure:

> I have right well comprehended the meaning of your letter which has been presented to me by your ambassador. Your propositions for a peace between us are pleasing to me as they will be obnoxious to Kurtoğlu. This pirate during my voyage from France tried to capture me unprepared; in which, when he failed, owing to my having passed into the Rhodian sea by night, he endeavoured to plunder certain merchantmen, that were being navigated by the Venetians; but scarcely had my fleet left their port, than he had to fly, and to abandon the plunder which he had seized.[8]

The Grand Master wrote to Francis I that he did not accept Suleiman's letter as a token of friendship but rather as a poorly veiled threat. If it was clear that an invasion would take place, Suleiman still did his best to hide when that would be. Shipping along the coast was kept in harbour and the roads patrolled to stop intelligence of the invasion reaching the island. Bourbon recorded that despite Suleiman's efforts: 'Howbeit so great apparel of an army could not be long kept close for the spies that the lord Great Master had sent to Turkey brought tidings to the Castle of St Peter [Bodrum] and to Rhodes of all that was said and done in Turkey.'[9] Some thought that the attack on Rhodes was another false rumour and an expedition, if there was one, would most likely attack Cyprus or the Albanian city of Kotor, also Venetian territory. The Grand Master took no chances and continued to strengthen the defences, completing the bastion of Auvergne and deepening and widening the ditches, work that he inspected twice or thrice every day.

The attack on Rhodes was felt necessary not just by Suleiman but by all true believers. Mustafa Gelal-Zada recorded the Knights' many iniquities. He thought that they were 'obstinate vipers' and the: 'worst of the sons of error, sent by Sheitan [Satan] and noted for cunning and artifice, outcasts, accursed workers of iniquity, expert seamen and outstanding navigators, possessed [of] great fortresses in all parts of the Mediterranean coast.'[10] Their depredations on trade and the enslavement and apostatising of the followers of Islam, made them trebly obnoxious and yet they were undefeated. Time was now ripe for the Padishah to conquer Rhodes and: 'Once more the shout is raised whose echo fills the earth. The Lord of Time

8 Eric Brockman, *The Two Sieges* (London: John Murray, 1969), pp.114–115.

9 Jacques de Bourbon, *Grande et Merveilleuse, & Tréscruelle Oppugnation de la noble Cité de Rhodes*, (London: 1524), page unnumbered.

10 Eric Brockman, *The Two Sieges* (London: John Murray, 1969), p.116.

goes to war. Old and young raise your hands in prayer. Rejoice, for all is prepared.'[11]

Ottoman Commanders

If the Hospitaller system tended to produce commanders of acknowledged ability, so did the Ottoman. Busbecq, who appears to have been an ardent Turcophile, admired and appreciated the advantages of their meritocratic system, with an implicit criticism of the aristocratic West. He described and explained how in the Ottoman Empire it was the Office that decided the importance of the man rather than the opposite! He explained this when observing the Sultan's court:

> The Sultan's hall was crowded with people, among whom were several officers of high rank. Besides these there were all the troopers of the Imperial guard, Spahis, Ghourebas, Ouloufedgis, and a large force of Janissaries; but there was not in all that great assembly a single man who owed his position to aught save his valour and his merit. No distinction is attached to birth among the Turks; the deference to be paid to a man is measured by the position he holds in the public service. There is no fighting for precedence; a man's place is marked out by the duties he discharges. In making his appointments the Sultan pays no regard to any pretensions on the score of wealth or rank, nor does he take into consideration recommendations or popularity; he considers each case on its own merits, and examines carefully into the character, ability, and disposition of the man whose promotion is in question. It is by merit that men rise in the service, a system which ensures that posts should only be assigned to the competent. Each man in Turkey carries in his own hand his ancestry and his position in life, which he may make or mar as he will. Those who receive the highest offices from the Sultan are for the most part the sons of shepherds or herdsmen, and so far from being ashamed of their parentage, they actually glory in it, and consider it a matter of boasting that they owe nothing to the accident of birth; for they do not believe that high qualities are either natural or hereditary, nor do they think that they can be handed down from father to son, but that they are partly the gift of God, and partly the result of good training, great industry, and unwearied zeal; arguing that high qualities do not descend from a father to his son or heir, any more than a talent for music, mathematics, or the like; and that the mind does not derive its origin from the father, so that the son should necessarily be like the father in character, but emanates from heaven, and is thence

11 Eric Brockman, *The Two Sieges* (London: John Murray, 1969), p.117.

> infused into the human body. Among the Turks, therefore, honours, high posts, and judgeships are the rewards of great ability and good service. If a man be dishonest, or lazy, or careless, he remains at the bottom of the ladder, an object of contempt; for such qualities there are no honours in Turkey![12]

Those chosen to serve Suleiman during the siege were tried and experienced commanders, whose command as Busbecq suggests were dependent on ability and not birth for promotion.

Suleiman was encouraged to continue with planning by his brother-in-law, Çoban Mustafa Pasha otherwise known as 'Mustafa Pasha the Shepherd', who was not a Turk at all but probably a Serbian who had been recruited into the ranks of the Janissaries as a boy. He rose through the ranks and gained both military and political experience and in 1511 was appointed as Grand Vizier. He married the sister of Suleiman and on her death a half-sister, placing himself, he might have thought, securely in the Sultan's closest circle. His rise exemplifies the points that Busbecq made above. Mustafa Pasha who was appointed the *Serdar-ı Ekrem* or vizier in commander of the land forces, boasted that Rhodes would be taken in fifteen or at most thirty days, a boast he would soon come to regret.

The command of the fleet was in theory in the hands of Pilaq Mustafa Pasha his chief-of-staff but the operational commander was the corsair Kurtoğlu Muslihiddin Reis. He was known in the West by many variations of his name, which included Cadoli, Kurtog Ali, or Cartalli (1487–1535?) but was feared in all of them. He had come to prominence in 1508 as the commander of 30 ships and 6,000 men launching raids against Liguria from his base in Bizerte. He led a naval force in the unsuccessful raid on Rhodes in 1509. The year after he had the temerity to challenge two papal galleys at the mouth of the Tiber and captured one. He went on to a successful and profitable career raiding Venetian and Genoese colonies taking prisoners for ransom and enslavement, as well as acquiring valuable loot.

Moving his operations to the Western Mediterranean he attacked shipping between Spain and Italy bringing it virtually to a halt for a time, as well as launching further attacks against Rhodes. In 1516 he outwitted a large fleet combining much of the naval power of Christendom, including papal and Rhodian vessels in an attack on Bizerte, before being called upon to command the Ottoman fleet in the conquest of Egypt. In 1521 he made his first full-scale assault on the island with 80 vessels. He had good reason to hate the knights as two of his brothers had been killed by them and a third was a prisoner on the island. His raid failed, although he captured a Venetian ship and sank ships in the port. He had attempted to capture the Grand Master travelling from Marseille in early 1522 and in June he

12 Ogier Ghislain de Busbecq (Charles Thornton Forster, trans.), *The Life and Letters of Ogier Ghiselin de Busbecq* (London: Kegan Paul & co, 1881), pp.153–155.

commanded the blockading fleet as well as providing reinforcements for the assault.

The land and sea commanders were experienced and determined opponents of the Order and Suleiman might have felt that the siege was in safe hands. As in 1480 the Ottoman ports were closed and all shipping requisitioned for the use of the assembled assault force. This was a policy that was not as unpopular as it might have been, as the merchants and sea captains of the empire understood the benefits of extirpating the Order from Rhodes. The decisive event in the decision to launch the attack, may have been the dream that the Sultan had of his dead mother, who promised the successful conquest of the island.

Preparations on Rhodes

The island which had been long expecting the siege now completed its final preparations. The outlying garrisons of the knights were brought in leaving only the slenderest of forces. Further supplies of food and munitions were supplied by Naples from the Romagna and wine was imported from Candia. Crete, a Venetian colony provided fifteen ships loaded with their precious cargoes of the best vintage, while some men were recruited, ostensibly as 'wine-porters .... under shadow of those wines,'[13] as the Venetians were unwilling to nail their colours publicly to the Rhodian mast and face Ottoman wrath. Signor Zuan Antonio di Bonaldi, a Venetian merchant, willingly gave the Order his support and 700 casks of wine: 'And during the siege the said captain behaved him worthily in his person. And put himself [forward to?] the places [of danger] as worthy men ought to be.'[14] Bourbon considered that more wine could have been acquired but for the discouragement of d'Amaral by: 'saying it was detestable to the turk whose part the said traitor held in his devilish heart.'[15] In fact it was not d'Amaral who was a spy but the merchant Bonaldi who was a Venetian agent. His arrival was entirely unplanned but like any good Venetian he sent reports back to Andrea Marzello the Venetian representative in Corfu, recording the preparedness of the defenders and then the invasion.

Domenico Fornari, a Genoese merchant, was less compliant then Bonaldi and had to be 'encouraged' to hand over his cargo of Alexandrian grain by a naval patrol sent by the Order. On Rhodes the civilian population repeated the plans of 1480: The crops in the field were harvested, even though the wheat was still only half-ripe and the food that could be was

13 Jacques de Bourbon, *Grande et Merveilleuse, & Tréscruelle Oppugnation de la noble Cité de Rhodes*, (London: 1524), page unnumbered.

14 Jacques de Bourbon, *Grande et Merveilleuse, & Tréscruelle Oppugnation de la noble Cité de Rhodes*, (London: 1524), page unnumbered.

15 Jacques de Bourbon, *Grande et Merveilleuse, & Tréscruelle Oppugnation de la noble Cité de Rhodes*, (London: 1524), page unnumbered.

stored, and what couldn't be was destroyed. The wells outside the city were poisoned and gardens destroyed, beginning with the Grand Master's own. Soil from the gardens was brought into the town as it was recognised that such material would become invaluable in a prolonged siege. The population was brought into the city from the villages as they could expect little from the Turks other than death or slavery.

Within the city, what was in effect martial law was enforced by a tribunal of four Grand Crosses of the Order who could pronounce death sentences on those brought before them. There was a clear division of responsibility for the different martial and civilian stores and it was reported that there was sufficient food and war reserves to sustain a siege of a year. The Knights were mustered, their arms and equipment inspected and all bore the cross of the religion on their persons. The militia were also mustered but company by company as a general muster would have revealed their full strength to the sultan's spies, who everyone knew were already within the walls. By May the preparations were complete. There was no possibility that the Ottoman armada could be stopped by the Order's galleys and only a few patrols were sent out to warn of its arrival. The galley port was closed by blockships, except for one small entrance, and the commercial port was closed with chains and booms.

In a final desperate effort to seek aid from the West, representatives were sent to announce the invasion to Pope Adrian VI, the Emperor Charles V and the Kings of France and England. In the short term nothing could be hoped for, as it would take months to raise and transport a sizeable force capable of assisting them. If within this time no Crusade had come to save them, then further resistance would be useless. Such a request was however an implicit criticism of those powerful leaders of Christendom who had failed to come to the aid of the Order in previous years.

The command structure of the Order was clear. Each Langue was responsible for their sector of the defences, with individual commanders appointed for each of the five main bastions. Four Grand Crosses commanded the reserves available for the sectors under their responsibility. The Tower of St Nicholas was placed under the command of Guidot de Castellac of Provence and Thomas of Beverley the Seneschal of the Grand Master was appointed to defend the palace of the Grand Master. Brother Didider Tholon, Bailiff of Monosaque, commanded all the artillery.

The distribution of commands was as follows:

Grand Cross d'Amaral

Raimond Rogier	Auvergne
Christopher Waldners	Germany

Bastion of Auvergne Tower, Jean de Mesnyl

Turcopolier, John Buck

William Weston	Post of England
Juan de Barbaran	Post of Aragon

Bastion of England/Tower of the Virgin Mary, Nicholas Hussey
Captain St Anthony's Gate Thomas Sheffield

Prior of Navarre, Gregoire de Morgut

Fra Raimond Ricard	Post of Provence
Giorgio Amari	Post of |Italy

Bastion of Provence, Jean de Brinquier de Lioncel
Bastion of Italy, Andreotto Gentile

Grand Prior Pierre de Cluys

Jean de St Simon	Post of France
Fernando de Sollier	Post of Castile and Portugal

Bastion/Tower of Spain, Tomas Escarrieros

The Germans and the Auvergnians almost came to blows over the command of the Bastion of Auvergne. This was a matter only resolved by the personal intervention of the Grand Master who ordered that his own banner and that of the Order should be flown from there and none other.

The Order had assembled the greatest force it could muster but once again the figures vary quite considerably. Bouhours provides a list of only 305 knights, organised by Langue:

> As to those of the Habit, there appear'd one and fifty of the Language of *Provence*; 26 of that of *Auvergne*; Sixty two of *France;* Forty seven of *Italy*; Fifty one of *Arragon*, *Catalogne* and *Navar*; Eleven of *England*; Six of *Germany*; Fifty seven of *Castile*; besides 13 others more that kept guard in the Castle of St *Nicholas*.[16]

The garrison may have numbered as many as 500–700 knights, four or five thousand men-at-arms as well as the local militia, mercenaries and the sailors from the fleet. Jacques de Bourbon gives a figure of 3,000 to 4,000 city militia and 1,500 to 2,000 more from the villages. A useful addition to the garrison was a body of four or five hundred Cretan archers.[17] De l'Isle Adam apparently wrote to the Venetian Senate that he had 16,000 men under arms, a figure apparently confirmed by Venetian agents. Jacobus Fontanus the legal administrator of the Order gave the authoritative number of 600 knights, 500 Cretans and 4,000 others. Del Carretto on his election in 1513 set aside 40,000 ecus to provide for the 550 Knights who were resident in the Convent at that time. Whatever the numbers there was evidence of high

16 Dominique Bouhours, *The Life of the Renowned Peter D'Aubusson*... (London: Geo. Wells, 1679), p.152.

17 Crossbowmen

morale among the defenders, who as Bourbon described vied with each other to present the bravest show:

> The more to give them good heart and give them courage and good will some Knights of the Cross decked [dressed] their men with colours and devices & took with them men of the town and strangers. And with great noise of trumpets & drums they made many [musters] as envying each other which should keep best array and order and have the [fairest] company. It was a great pleasure to see them all so well allied and so well willing.[18]

There was to be no aid from Christendom. The Venetians did mobilise a fleet, not to relieve Rhodes but to cover the possibility that the assault on Rhodes was merely a diversion from the real intent of the Turk, an invasion of Crete their own valued possession. They were not going to endanger their relationship with the Sultan, unless it was to protect their own interests.

Turkish Preparations

The Turkish invasion had to be delayed in order to deal with a small rebellion by Ghazali, the Governor of Syria. He was betrayed, defeated and beheaded, the offending head was sent to Suleiman who proposed to send it to Venice as a token of esteem. He was discouraged from this course of action and completed the collection of an invasion fleet. A final demand was sent to the Knights from Suleiman calling on their surrender and homage, thus avoiding the necessity for an invasion and their destruction.

> When the lord great master & his council had heard the tenor of the letter they would give him no answer to the great turk. But that he should be received with good strokes of artillery. So it to a foolish demand behoved no answer. And it was to believe it he would none have.[19]

In the Hospital at the heart of the convent, a Jewish Doctor acted as a spy for Selim and his successors. He reported that the morale amongst the Knights was poor, which was partly true. Some sought to return to Europe in search of lucrative appointments to Commanderies, while others considered that the only option for the order was to seek a settlement with Suleiman. Although they were many disputes within the brethren where

18 Jacques de Bourbon, *Grande et Merveilleuse, & Tréscruelle Oppugnation de la noble Cité de Rhodes*, (London: 1524), page unnumbered.

19 Jacques de Bourbon, *Grande et Merveilleuse, & Tréscruelle Oppugnation de la noble Cité de Rhodes*, (London: 1524), page unnumbered.

petty personal and national jealousies had always abounded, there was no discernible crack in their unity. The ultimatum from Suleiman came to Rhodes on 10 June 1522 by which time the Ottoman fleet was assembled.

The Order was all too aware of the impending descent of Ottoman might. A system of warning beacons alerted a patrolling vessel to a Turkish landing on Physcos and Jacob Jaxi was sent on shore. He was captured and tortured; it was said that he revealed the details of the defences of the city, though if he did, it didn't seem to help the Ottomans much. The first landing took place on Cos where the Turks were met by Prior John de Bidoux, who drove them back to their galleys, although some were injured in the action and the Prior's horse was killed.

In Constantinople 700 ships, 40,000 sailors and 20,000 Azabs had gathered ready for the invasion. Mustafa Pasha took the fleet to Gallipoli. It was joined by Pilaq and Kurtoğlu with more ships and men who reached Chios from where the combined fleet set sail for the anchorage at Marmaris on 16 June. The assembled fleet began an unopposed landing on 24 June, the feast of St John the Baptist, and an auspicious day for the Order. On 2 June the main fleet anchored in Kalitheas bay to the South of Rhodes on the East coast. The number of ships was impressive; according to one estimate it included 103 galleys, 35 galleasses, 15 *mahons* and numerous small craft. A Florentine ship's captain suggested sending fire ships into the assembled invasion fleet but this plan was abandoned, as it was felt that the costs outweighed the potential advantages. D'Aubusson might have made a different decision and de l'Isle Adam's decisions, if always sound, tended to avoid risky undertakings. The next month was spent with the Ottoman engineers finding and establishing the battery positions from which the city would be bombarded. The Ottoman camp had to be established, sources of water found and allocated, supplies unloaded and stored securely.

Suleiman followed the land route from Constantinople to Marmaris, where he was joined by the Janissaries and Ferhad Pasha who had defeated Ghazali. Ferhad had the leader of a neighbouring territory that had failed to come to his aid treacherously murdered, together with his four sons, and arrived at Suleiman's camp with all five heads. The Sultan was clearly not amused by a subject who had overstepped the mark by several heads. Ferhad's wife, Suleiman's sister, pleaded his case and Ferhad was sent into comfortable exile in the Balkans where his insubordination and insolence led to him losing his own head in 1524. The decisiveness with which Suleiman acted, even to a member of his own small family, demonstrated his intention to brook no insubordination. Suleiman arrived at Maramaris on 26 July and landed on Rhodes two days later with the force of Janissaries. He established his battle headquarters on the hill of San Stefano about a mile from the city walls, while the remainder of his entourage settled safely at Megasandra four miles away.

The Siege Begins – A Phony War

Inside the city there was considerable disquiet. There were many female Turkish slaves who worked as domestic servants in Rhodes. With the enemy landed and with an attack imminent, a rumour circulated that when the men of the town went to their posts, their slaves would set fire to their houses. There was no truth to it but one poor woman was hanged. Fear of spies and a slave uprising led to a climate of fear that would have serious consequences at the end of the siege. On 23 July the slaves working as pioneers were thought to have mutinied and a massacre began. Fortunately, the Grand Master heard of the slaughter and put a stop to it. There were too few labourers available already and any loss was keenly felt. Bourbon recorded their number and their important contribution: 'there were 15 hundred of them, the which slaves did great service in time of the siege. For they laboured daily to make our defences [....] & to cast earth out of the ditches & in all works they were necessary to our needs.'[20]

Although reinforcements from Christendom or from their Venetian neighbours were unlikely to arrive soon, the garrison did now receive a most important addition in the person of Gabriele Tadini da Martinengo. He was one of a new class of soldier/engineers who possessed the technical understanding that made them invaluable in a modern siege. They were the Renaissance men of warfare, able to design fortifications or besiege them, emplace and manage artillery, undermine a tower or countermine an enemy tunnel, construct a bridge across a fast-flowing river or design a siege tower.

The Governor of Candia (Crete) on hearing that the Grand Master had sought to entice Tadini to Rhodes, explicitly forbade it and threatened anyone who assisted with such an escape with condign punishment. Tadini, with the help of Antonio Bosio, hid the escape craft from Venetian patrols and at night set sail for Rhodes, after the initial Turkish landings but before an effective blockade had been established. He was welcomed by the Priors of St Gilles and Navarre, an indication of his status. On the first day of August, he was made a Knight of the Order by the Grand Master himself, and assured of appointment to the first priory that became vacant, as it surely soon would. Tadini was also given a 'pencyon' (salary) of 1,200 ducats a year. He was to prove himself of inestimable value and was personally responsible for prolonging the resistance. So valuable was he that when Rhodes surrendered, the Grand Master ensured his clandestine escape, as he felt that whatever promises Suleiman might give Tadini was too valuable an asset to be allowed to go free by the Turk.

It is impossible to provide an accurate assessment of the numbers in the Ottoman army and whether any numbers were fighting men or included

20 Jacques de Bourbon, *Grande et Merveilleuse, & Tréscruelle Oppugnation de la noble Cité de Rhodes*, (London: 1524), page unnumbered.

The moat from the bridge to the Gate D'Amboise. The moat surrounding the city did not correspond with those usually seen in western European castles. The Templar castle of Saone has an impressive rock hewn moat but nothing to compare with what is seen here. The moat was a killing ground, swept by artillery and small-arms fire. (Author's photograph)

support troops and camp followers. The figure of 100,000 is not unreasonable, considering the extent of the resources available to the Sultan, although Christian supporters gave a figure of 250,000 or higher. The Moslem army contained a very large number of Christians from Bosnia, Bulgaria and Wallachia, conscripted as pioneers. If one also considers that the Janissaries had been Christians until forced to apostatise and many of the soldiers were also Christian, then it gives a different colour to the conflict. Whatever the precise numbers and their present or past religious attachments it was a force that should have been able to crush the Order easily, especially after its triumph at Belgrade.

The principal Turkish artillery batteries were placed opposite the main fortifications. On the hill near the Church of Saints Cosmas and Damian[21] was placed the battery facing the post of England. Other equally powerful batteries faced the post of Provence and the Tower of Spain. Although the initial bombardment was impressive so was the counter-bombardment. The Order's guns were safely behind stone walls while the Ottoman guns were behind comparatively flimsy wooden mantlets and earth butts and the consequences of that soon became obvious. In the Ottoman camp it was considered that the early bombardment was ill-judged and that it was better to concentrate the bombardment of the heaviest guns on key targets.

Rhodes was now surrounded by a powerful and determined force, led by commanders who could not afford to lose face while directly under the eyes of their Sultan. To fail would be to risk losing more than their reputations. At sea, Kurtoğlu provided a strong blockading force and whereas the Order could expect no reinforcements, those for the Ottomans continued

21 The patron saints of surgery.

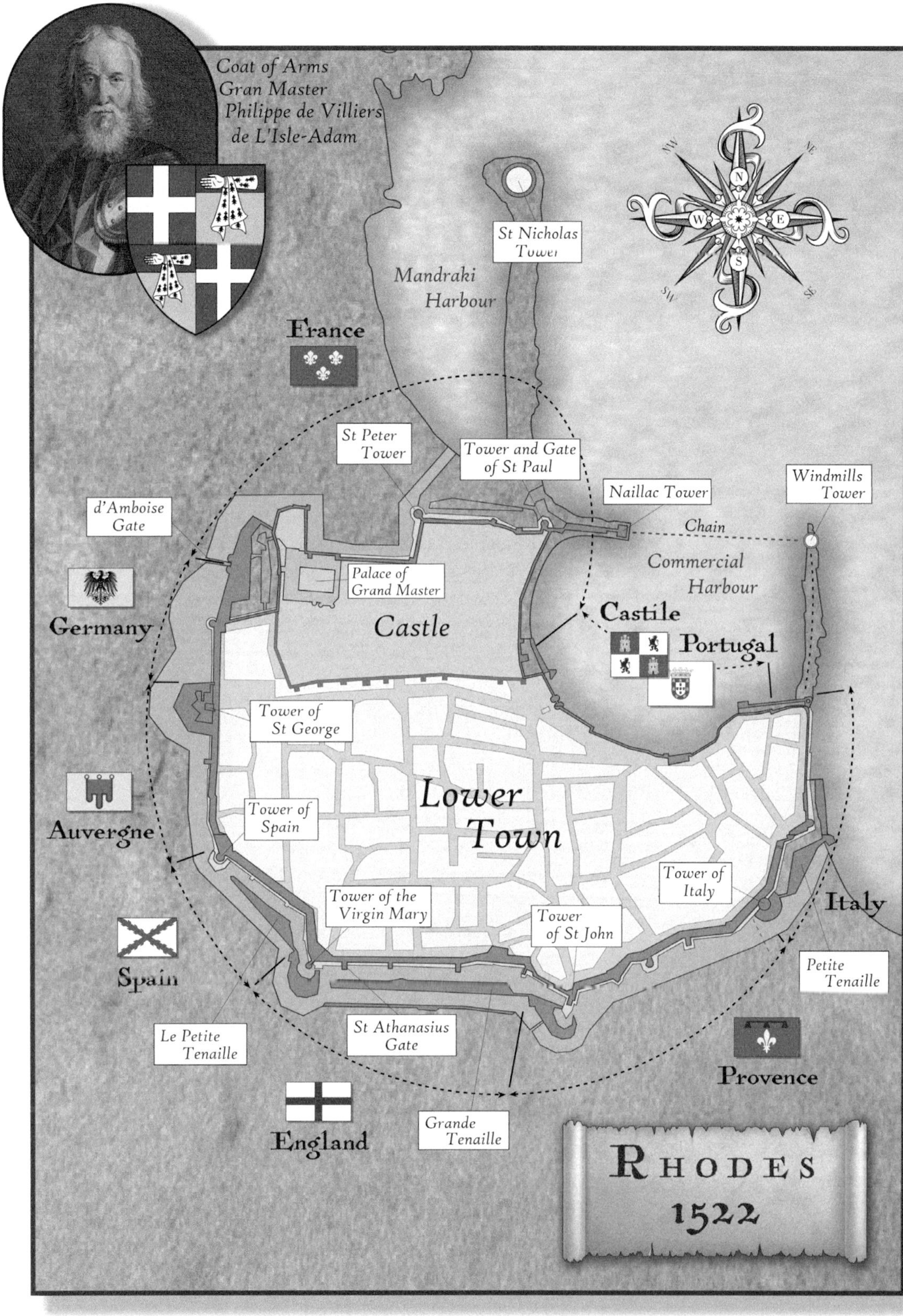
Coat of Arms
Gran Master
Philippe de Villiers
de L'Isle-Adam
St Nicholas
Mandraki
Harbour
France
St Peter
Tower
Tower and Gate
of St Paul
Naillac Tower
Windmills
Tower
d'Amboise
Gate
Chain
Commercial
Harbour
Palace of
Grand Master
Castle
Castile
Germany
Portugal
Tower of
St George
Lower
Town
Tower of
Spain
Auvergne
Tower of
Italy
Tower of the
Virgin Mary
Tower
of St John
Italy
Spain
Petite
Tenaille
Le Petite
Tenaille
St Athanasius
Gate
Provence
England
Grande
Tenaille
RHODES
1522

A painting of the *Agha* of the Janissaries and a *solak* of the Janissaries by Lambert Wyts in the 'Codex Vindobonensis Palatinus' of 1573. Although half a century after the siege the bow was clearly seen as an important symbol of martial skill and authority. What is surprising is that it does not seem to have played a larger part in the two sieges. The English archers at the siege of Leith in 1562, held by the French, had little or no impact on their foes either. Whether the finery worn by the men shown here would fare very well in a prolonged siege is doubtful, especially in the dreadful Autumn and Winter weather. (Public domain via Wikimedia)

to arrive. This included a force of Mamelukes and Janissaries who arrived from Syria and were immediately allocated to the forces of the Grand Vizier. In response to the deployment of the enemy close to the walls, the Grand Master moved his headquarters from his palace to the church of St Mary of the Victory, closer to where the main assaults had taken place in the previous siege.

Bourbon provided a detailed record of the scale and emplacement of the Ottoman artillery. He recorded a force of eighty large cannons but which was reduced by counter-battery fire and no doubt periods of maintenance, to a still formidable figure of roughly half that number. It was, for obvious reasons, relatively easy for the defenders to record the size of the projectiles that were shot at them:

> First there were 6 great guns cannons perriers of brass [bronze] that shot a stone of 3½ feet. Also there were 15 pieces of iron that stones of 5 or 6 spans. Also there was 14 great bombards that shot stones of about 11 spans. Also there was 12 Basilisks wherof they shot but with 8 that is to with 4 shot against the post of England and Spain [each] and 2 against the gate of Italy the other 2 shot sometime against St Nicholas tower. Also there was 15 double guns casting balls as basilisks [same diameter]. The mean [smaller] shot [guns] as sacres and passovalanti [falcon-falconet] were in great number. The handgun shot was innumerable and incredible. Also there was 12 pot guns [mortars] of brass [bronze] that shot upward, wherof 8 were set behind the Church of Sts Cosmas and Damien & 2 at St John of the Fountain towards the port of Italy & the other 2 afore the gate of Auvergne there which were shot night & day & there was 3 sorts of them wherof the greatest were of 6 or 7 spans about. And the said [stones] were cast in to the town to make murder of people, which is a thing very' inhumane and fearful, which manner of shooting is little used among Christian men. Howbeit by evident miracle thanked be [to God] the said pieces did no great harm and [slew] not past 24 or 25 persons: and the most part women & children.[22]

It is clear, that the Ottomans still depended to a great extent on comparatively low velocity stone projectiles, shot either from bombards or cannon-perriers. The 'smashing' artillery was concentrated in the double-cannons, which if they were equivalent to their western models shot iron projectiles weighing sixty to seventy pounds. In addition, there were *carcasses* (copper balls containing bitumen, sulphur and pitch) as well as fragmentation shot,

22 Jacques de Bourbon, *Grande et Merveilleuse, & Tréscruelle Oppugnation de la noble Cité de Rhodes*, (London: 1524), page unnumbered.

which scattered sharp iron shards which were known to cause infection. The mortars fired solid marble shot as well as hollow brass projectiles filled with wildfire but they appear to have done little damage.

Bourbon reported eighty mantlets, (wooden and earth defences for artillery pieces), placed around the town, many of which were destroyed by counter-battery fire. Four large pieces were placed against the bastions of Aragon and England and two large pieces opposite that of Italy. Bourbon also provided a figure of two thousand stone balls fired between 19 July and the end of August. If we accept this figure (and he should know), fired from forty pieces over thirty days this gives a paltry rate of fire of 1.67 rounds per day per gun. Bourbon also gave a figure of twenty five people killed during the entire month. These figures are almost inexplicable but considering the source, believable. It would suggest that there were perhaps very long pauses in firing and short periods of concentrated fire or a continuous rate of less than seventy rounds per day. It was reported that the post of Germany was bombarded for ten days from 1 August which destroyed the Tower of the Church of St John. It did not quieten the Order's counter-battery which in fact silenced the Ottomans as they returned fire with enthusiasm and, it seems, accuracy. This extremely low consumption of ammunition compares to the 100,000 rounds shot during the three-month long siege of Boulogne in1544 where the principal siege guns were provided with 360 rounds each. At the English siege of Therouanne in 1513 the Venetian merchant Bavarin was so impressed by the scale of Henry's artillery that he wrote: 'Hell itself could not resist so powerful a force.'[23] Hell was not unleashed on Rhodes, although eventually the siege would prove 'hellish' to both sides.

The Ottoman effort seems to have concentrated on the posts of Auvergne and Aragon and Italy, where a massive earthwork was being built, whose function was difficult at first to understand. The earth had to be brought from half a mile away and the losses amongst the pioneers completing the task were terrible. A Turkish speaking Rhodian named Basil Carapazio volunteered to discover the purpose of their efforts. He took a small boat with some friends, outflanked the besieging forces and infiltrated the enemy lines. They took a catch of fish with them and landed at the beach of Acandia just beyond the city where they inveigled three soldiers into a pleasant trip around the bay. On the boat two were subdued but a third, more troublesome was decapitated before the remaining pair were handed over. They revealed that the purpose of the Turkish efforts was to provide a motte or mount, an emplacement for an artillery battery, to fire into the bastion and clear it of defenders. The mount was constructed so that it came to the very brim of the ditch and was twelve feet higher than the defences it overlooked. This was hardly an unknown tactic: similar mounds were built during the siege of Boulogne to give the artillery a better field of fire.

23 Calendar State Papers Venetian, Volume II, 16 September 1513. Dated 2nd and 12th August 1513

Bourbon recorded the new dangers posed by the Turkish tactics and the attempts to counter the risks, especially from handguns:

> And it was against the gate of Auvergne and Spain and beat our men that were at the gates and bulwarks in such wise that none dare be seen til certain defences and repairs were made of planks and boards to cover our people and keep them from the shot. And at the gate of Italy was made such another heap [mound] & in no other part [of the defences]. When the trenches were thus made to the ditches the enemy made holes in the walls of the ditch outward where through they shot infinitely with handguns to our men as well on the walls as on the bulwarks and [slew] many of them.[24]

The purloined prisoners also reported that the Ottoman army was already dismayed at their losses and that only the presence of the Sultan with reinforcements could keep the army from mutiny. It is always surprising how prisoners seem to tell their captors what they want to hear. Spies also revealed that the Ottoman engineers were engaged in not only advancing a trench system towards the walls but digging tunnels to undermine them, a tactic that had helped in the capture of Belgrade. No doubt some of the spoil from these efforts was being used to build the mount. It was the digging of tunnels that would prove decisive in the history of the siege.

The Underground War

To the untutored eye very little of classical Rhodes remains above ground; underground the position is very different. Athanassios Migos has pointed to the very peculiar underground world that lay beneath the Hospitallers city and which made mining a key element in Ottoman strategy:

> It was possible to see the marks of the explosions where the walls had been rebuilt after the siege and these explosions had occurred with extraordinary regularity and were regularly spaced along the curtain walls. We know that under the streets and houses of the modern city lies the old regular street pattern of the Hellenistic city laid out in a grid pattern by the school of Hippodamus. We also know that beneath each street of the old city the Greeks had constructed large conduits to distribute fresh water and remove sewage. There were also large cisterns and interconnecting tunnels under the gardens of the old houses. Thus, Hellenistic Rhodes was honeycombed with tunnels and caverns. The knights must have been

24 Jacques de Bourbon, *Grande et Merveilleuse, & Trèscruelle Oppugnation de la noble Cité de Rhodes*, (London: 1524), page unnumbered.

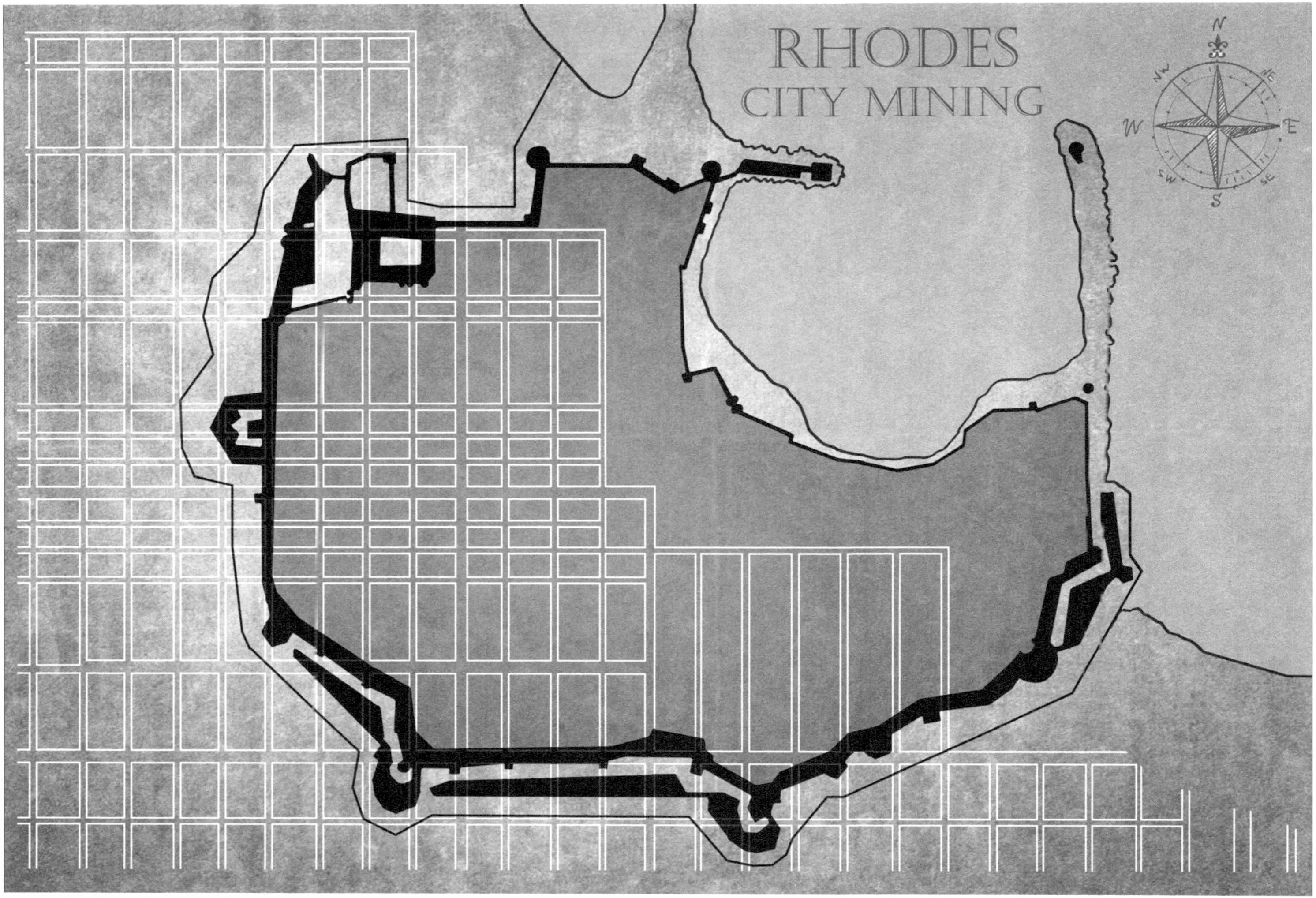

The Greeks and the Romans realised the importance of a reliable and safe water supply for their citizens as necessary for both health and prosperity. A sewerage system existed as well as a system of culverts and cisterns for the collection of fresh water. Such systems could operate for centuries, with only limited maintenance. I spent several weeks at Marqab relying upon a cistern system that had been in operation for almost a thousand years to provide cool, fresh and safe drinking water.

> aware of this as they would have struck some of the culverts and removed them when they dug the dry ditches outside the walls, but the tunnels would have continued beyond the counterscarp out into the countryside for the old city was much larger than that of the knights. One can still see some of the culverts, burrowing under the tenaille and running inland under the glacis.
>
> The street patterns of the modern city largely follow the grid plan of the older one and the fortifications are, in many places, built directly on the line of the ancient streets. Therefore, there are cross culverts running along the line of the fortifications and acting as countermine tunnels.[25]

Thus, although the fortifications were subject to mining, the same system that threatened the city also provided countermining galleries for Tadini. The underground war would be fought as bitterly as the one waged in the breaches of the city's defences.

Tadini's role in the defences was now proved crucial and was recorded in some detail by Giacomo Bosio (1544–1627), a Brother and historian of the Order:

> Because their [Turkish] captains were certain that a very great number of Turks would be slaughtered during the assault, knowing very well that our knights and soldiers were very able; before making the assault, as their principal hope was to capture the city, they used mines which elsewhere we have described. They were intent for many days in digging mines in such a way that, of the six sides of the city, in a very short time, five sides were mined under. Some say that the Turks dug fifty-four mines, others say forty-five, while others say only thirty-eight mines were dug. Most of them were ineffective because of the countermines dug by the industrious and most vigilant Fra Fabritio Tadino Martinengo. He had excavated underground a trench which encircled the Bastion of Auvergne, and on one side ran towards the walls of the Langue of Germany, on the other as far as the Bastion of England. He had another dug from the Bastion of Cosquino [St John], as far as the bastion built by the Grand Master Fra Fabritio del Carretto at the Gate of Italy. Thus most of the mines of the enemy came up against these countermines and were broken up when they were intercepted. Great diligence was used to pinpoint them. A large number of barbers' poles with little bells inside and very well covered drums were used continuously to listen for and more easily to pinpoint the Turkish mines. They were

25 Quentin Hughes & Athanassios Migos, 'Rhodes: the Turkish sieges,' *Fort*, vol. 21, 1993, p.14.

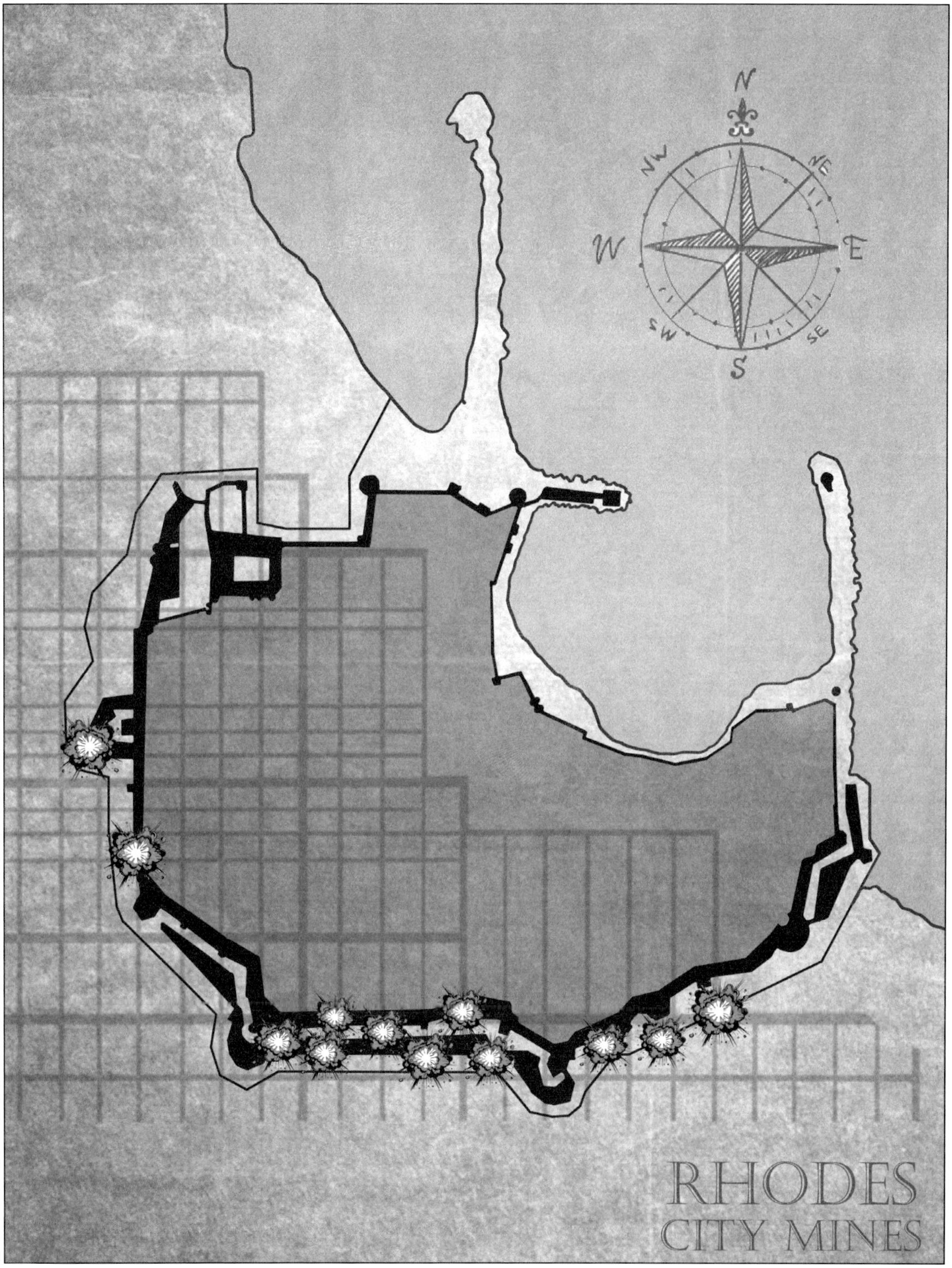

A plan of the city of Rhodes showing the ancient streets superimposed on Gabriel's drawing of the medieval city in 1522. The mine explosions follow the ancient street plan, especially along the fronts of England and Provence. (after Fort 21, p.9)

> used in the most dangerous places. As a result many mines were discovered and successfully intercepted.[26]

Tadini had expected such a strategy and had begun training Rhodians to use a mine detector, his famous *tambouri*. This was a tightly fitted parchment drum set on the ground and upon which pebbles were placed. The vibrations cause by mining would cause the drum to vibrate and the pebbles to bounce. According to Collado his system would be able to detect digging from up to fifty paces away. The alternative to the *tambouri* was a bowl of water, brim full, bedded into the ground to pick up vibrations. It would indicate not only whether a mine was being dug but in what direction. By triangulating with other mine detectors, the position and progress of the enemy could be gauged.

The Ground War

The ground war continued with an attack on the famous tower of St Nicholas, with the Ottoman batteries moved at night into position, itself an impressive operation. Bourbon recorded with some pride the resistance of the tower, which had been so thoroughly rebuilt to meet just such a challenge:

> The foresaid [Ottoman] mantlets were pointed [aimed] to beat [bombard] St Nicholas tower & by the space of 10 or 12 days they shot sore against it. But they had so sharp and vigorous answer that there was not one mantlet that abode whole [survived intact] an hour. The captain of the said tower and his folk did such diligence and busyness in shooting of their pieces that the enemy dared not set up any more mantlets by day and shot only by night while the moon did shine which is a thing worthy of memory of marvel and of praise.[27]

With more sense that had been shown in 1480, the bombardment was abandoned and the guns set against the posts of Aragon and England. This concentration ultimately proved more successful with breaches developing in the walls of the posts of England, Provence and Aragon. The collapsed walls would fill the ditches but also provided material for rebuilding, at a heavy cost in the lives of the Order's pioneers.

26 Dell'Istoria dell Sacra Religione, et ill.ma. Militia di S. Gio: Gierosol. no. di Iacomo Bosio, Rome 1630, Parte Seconda p.668C, in Hughes and Migos *Fort*, vol. 21, p.17.

27 Jacques de Bourbon, *Grande et Merveilleuse, & Tréscruelle Oppugnation de la noble Cité de Rhodes*, (London: 1524), page unnumbered.

The situation by the middle of August had become 'difficult,' with increasing losses being incurred by both sides. The Ottoman Chief Gunner, Mehmed, was badly injured when a culverin shot pierced the mantlet behind which he was observing the siege, it smashed the gun, killed five of its crew and the ball then struck off both his legs. Mehmed's loss was especially badly felt by Suleiman who declared, according to Bourbon, that he would rather lose any of his Pashas than his gunner. The defenders also suffered a grievous loss when the Spanish master Gunner Rostam was also killed. By 19 August the curtain wall of the post of Italy was breached and the Ottoman sappers were making a passage through the ruins towards the ramparts. The results of the bombardment proved impressive as Bourbon recorded:

> And this is touching the gunshot whereof I say not the third part because it is a thing considered idle to them that hath not seen it. For some days they shot with those great bombardes that were on the brim of the ditch and from the mantlets bent against the walls of England & Spain twenty or thirty times and more. And I believe verily that since the creation of the world such artillery and so great quantity was never bent and laid before any town as hath been against Rhodes at this siege. Wherefore it is no marvel if the walls been and have been be .... fell down and if there be brakes and clefts in many places.[28]

The garrison's response to the increasing effectiveness of the bombardment was to attack the attackers, spike their guns, collapse their mines and kill as many as possible for the smallest loss to themselves. This was not an uncommon tactic, especially when a confident and aggressive garrison saw that the alternative was to await an assault, that they could not hope to beat. Tadini led the first sally on 19 August against the sector commanded by the Grand Vizier. He attacked at the head of 200 mounted members of the Order, achieving their objective of causing the greatest possible amount of mayhem. Further attacks were launched on 20, 22 and 24 August against the Grand Vizier as well as Ahmed and Aya Pasha. The effect on the morale of the Ottomans must have been significant as up to this point it must have seemed that they were in control of events. The losses to the Order were not great but it was clear that even these could not be afforded and the sallies could not be repeated.

As August came to an end it was clear that that a major assault along much of the city walls was imminent. In some desperation Antonio Bosio was sent to Naples and Frater (Brother) Nicholas Hussey journeyed to Provence. They were to bring back supplies and reinforcements that could

28 Jacques de Bourbon, *Grande et Merveilleuse, & Tréscruelle Oppugnation de la noble Cité de Rhodes*, (London: 1524), page unnumbered.

help sustain the Order in its resistance for a little longer. Christendom was now aware of the scale of the siege, but how long would it be before a large force was mobilised to bring them aid? On the 24th a single ship commanded by Brother Emeric Depreaux with some supplies and a handful of knights from Europe, broke through the blockade and landed safely, it was a heroic gesture, but it was a gesture that was bought at considerable cost to Kurtoğlu. Suleiman frustrated and humiliated with the ease with which single ships could leave and enter Rhodes ordered his commander to be bastinadoed on the deck of his own flagship, *başkalarını teşvik etmek*.[29]

Tadini managed the defences well and responded to the breaches in the walls in the same way as had been done in 1480. The walls on either side of a breach would have guns mounted for enfilading fire and within the walls new fortifications were built. The civilian buildings behind the breach were fortified and well supplied with weapons and ammunition. Bourbon described the contribution of Tadini, or Martyningo as he called him:

> The capytayne Gabryell Martyningo prompt diligent & expert to give remedies to the needful places forthwith made to make the traverses upon the wall where as the breach was with good repairs & gonnes small and great which were set in the said traverses. The which only shot not at the breaches but to [....]he trenches & made great murder of enemies as well at the assaults that they made as every day. And beside the traverses the said captain made to lay small artillery as arquebuses & handgonnes upon certain houses within the town that stood open against the breach with good repairs. And from those places great slaughter of turks was made at the[ir] assaults.

The Ottoman mining efforts continued and by September almost the entire curtain wall had been undermined. Tadini countered with his line of countermines. On 9 September Tadini 'neutered' two charges beneath the post of Provence. As he knew where the mines were placed, he could dig vents referred to as 'spiral veins'. This allowed the force of the explosion to be directed harmlessly upward, rather than being contained, which would have thrown the fortification above up into the air. This failure by his miners drove Suleiman to distraction and it was rumoured led to their impalement, a fate that had been reserved for the Knights.

Tadini was not always so successful. On 4 September the Bastion of England had suffered a disastrous mine explosion, making a gap twelve yards wide in its face and which filled the moat with rubble giving the enemy a route in to the town. There was a sudden assault which brought the Ottoman banners to the very wall until a counter attack led by Tadini and Michel d'Argillemont, the Captain of the Galleys. The next reinforcement

29 *pour encourager les autres.*

came from the Grand Master himself, accompanied by his standard bearer, Henry Mansell, who brought the banner of the Crucifixion directly from a service at the church of Our Lady of Victories. The fighting was ferocious, with the Turks, after their first assault, withdrawing in some discord until rallied by their commander Mustafa. After two hours the Turks withdrew having suffered heavy losses, but so had the Order. The Captain of the Galleys died from an arrow to the eye and the Grand Commander Gabriel de Pommerols and Henry Mansell were also killed. Bourbon described the events and the role of the Grand Master, although all ultimately depended upon the intervention of 'our lord':

> And for to speak of the mines that had effect and damaged us it is to wit on the fourth day of September about four hours after noon the enemies fired two mines one was between the post of Spain and Auvergne which did no hurt but to the barbican. The other was at the bulwark of England that [the explosion] was so fell [terrible] and strong that it caused most part of the town to shake & cast down a great part of the said bulwark at the spring of the day. And by the earth & stones that fell in to the ditches the enemies came upon the bulwark with their banners & fought sore & mightily with our men not with hands but with shot of handgonnes. The lord Grand Master that had come fifteen days or more with his aid to the said bulwark went with his company to help them that fought. After that they had fought the for two or three hours the enemies repulsed and driven back by our men from the said bulwark and beaten with ordnance on every side withdrew them with their loss shame and damage. And this was the first victory that our lord [God] gave us [....] and there lay of our enemies a thousand and more.

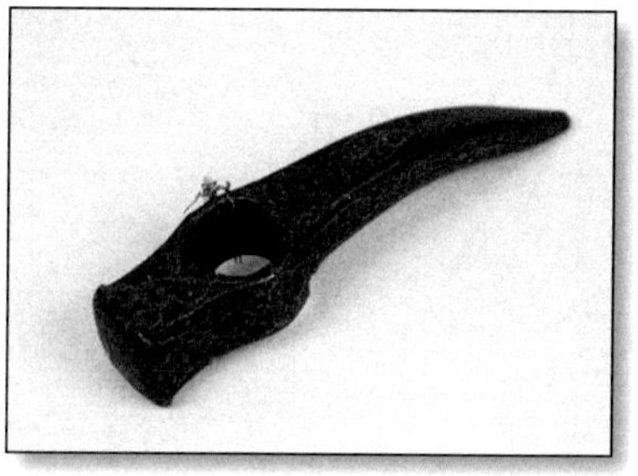

The head of a Janissary's war hammer, sixteenth century. The curved beak could penetrate armour plate, as trials of a similar western weapon have proved. The shape of the beak makes it much easier to disengage it from the plate than a straight point. The flat end would be of use in denting armour and causing devastating injuries to joints and hands. A hammer of a similar weight had a shaft 18 inches long.
Dimensions: H. 6 3/8in (16.2cm), W 1¼in (3.2cm), Wt. 15.1oz (428.1g).
(Metropolitan Museum of Art, public domain)

A smaller breach of the English Bastion on 9 September was accompanied by an attack, which collapsed yet again on the appearance of the Grand Master's banner. Enfilading fire from the gates of St John added to the confusion and the heavy casualties in the Turkish trenches. Mustafa used threats and his own example when he led the attack but yet again it produced nothing other than heavy casualties for the attacker:

> Then our men fought with moryspikes [pikes] & fired [hurled] spears [?] against them the space of 3 hours til at the last they being

well beaten with great ordnance and small on every side withdrew them. And of their banners our men got one for it was not possible to get any more. For as soon as any of our men went up on our repairs he was slain with small guns of the trenches & holes made in the walls of our ditches. And there was slain of our enemies 2,000 of mean men & 3 persons of estate which lay dead along the ditch with fair and rich harness [armour] .... And of Christian men of our part abode about 30 persons. And this was the second victory given to us by the grace divine.[30]

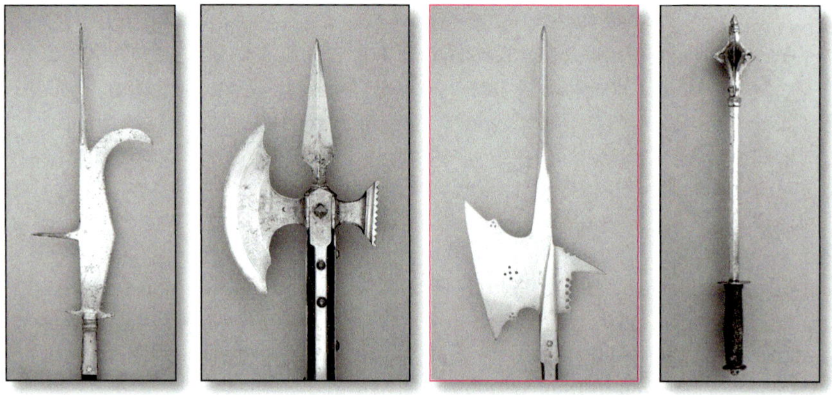

From left to right a Guisarme (Italian *c.* 1500, a pollaxe (Venetian *c.* 1475) a halberd (Swiss or German 1500–1525), and a late medieval mace probably from France. Hafted weapons, such as these, would be invaluable in the close quarter fighting experienced in the breaches made in the city's walls. The guisarme, like the English Bill has a vicious hook to drag an opponent down. The points and flukes on the halberd and guisarme could be smashed down on an enemy's skull. The pollaxe could smash, hack and stab at close quarters. The flanges on the mace could penetrate thin plate but would be of more use in crushing it, and the flesh beneath. Beautiful in the simplicity of their design, they were also deadly in the hands of a strong and determined soldier.

Guisarme: L. 8ft 4in (254cm), L of head 31¹/8in (79cm), W 7⁷/8 in (20cm); Wt 5lb 1oz (2,296.3 g).

Pollaxe: L 85in (225.9cm), L of head 13in (33cm), W 7 3/4 in (19.7cm), Wt 6lbs 7oz (2,920g).

Halberd: L 8ft 10in (269.1cm), L of head 24in (60.9cm). W 10¹/8in, (25.7cm), Wt 5lbs 14oz (2,660g).

Mace: L. of head 5½in (14cm); W. 2⁹/16in (6.5cm); Wt. 1lb 14oz (850g). (Metropolitan Museum of Art, public domain)

The pattern of bombardment and mining, counter-bombardment and counter-mining, followed by a bloody assault, repulsed with heavy losses was repeated, again and again. This took place against the post of England on 11 September and then the 13th and 14th in support of assaults from

30 Jacques de Bourbon, *Grande et Merveilleuse, & Tréscruelle Oppugnation de la noble Cité de Rhodes*, (London: 1524), page unnumbered.

Ahmed and Mustafa. The losses were heavy on both sides but those of Suleiman's could be replaced. Attacks on different sections on different days weakened the Order but did not overwhelm it. The strategy was to change only when there were simultaneous assaults on the post of Italy by Pir Pasha, followed by assault on the posts of Provence, England and Aragon which captured the Tower of Aragon and five Christian banners.[31] The counter-attack was as dreadful as the assault and accompanied with a far greater range of cruel weapons, especially incendiary weapons of all sorts which caused horrible injuries. The assault was repelled and the Tower of Aragon was back in Christian hands. Further mines and assaults took place later, against the posts of Aragon and Auvergne but the charges were dissipated using Tadini's 'veins'. The greatest casualties were to the Janissaries in the assault group who were struck by the back-blast from their own mine.

Individual assaults had failed, attempts at coordinated attacks supported by mining and artillery had failed. There was little left that Mustafa Pasha, the Grand Vizier, could offer his Sultan Suleiman in either strategy or tactics. The fate of Kurtoğlu was a terrible warning of the least he could expect from further failure. It was therefore essential that the next assault should be the final one. Suleiman was provided with an observation platform from which he could see his Janissaries sweep through the many breaches in the wall, raise their standards on the tops of towers and exterminate the tiresome Christians, who had frustrated his enterprise for so long. It was not to be.

The Ottoman force took a day of preparation for what should have been the decisive assault. On 23 September two mines were sprung against the posts of Auvergne and Spain. Both failed, in part due to Tadini's spiral vents and in one case to a natural fissure in the rock which achieved the same result in dissipating the blast. The attack would concentrate on the posts of Aragon, England, Provence and Italy. The bombardment which opened operations on 24 September was accompanied by a smoke screen intended to blind the defenders. On this occasion the *Azabs* and *Bashibazooks* would not be sent to fill the ditches and feed the cannon; it would be the Janissaries in all their glory led by their *Agha* who would spearhead this final push. The Bastion of Aragon was rapidly overwhelmed and to the delight of the Sultan their flags now flew there in profusion. Where a breach had been made Tadini had provided new trenches and palisades, just as had been done in 1480 and with the same result. Having crossed the breach, they would meet a murderous mixture of firearms, bolts, arrows and incendiary devices from all sides. There is also an account of the vengeful mistress of a dead English knight who killed her children, to avoid them being forced to apostatise, and then wearing his armour threw herself into the advancing Ottoman hordes, killing many and forcing others to flee in despair. Similar stories are told elsewhere, often, as in the case of the heroine of Corunna in 1589, with a fragment of truth to it.

31 Dates vary from different sources but the events seem to have taken place between 15 September and 20 September.

The Bastion of Aragon was recovered by Jacques de Bourbon using one of Tadini's lateral counter mines to enter it secretly. Mention must be made of the Rhodians, who supported the defence as best they could and of course the presence of the Grand Master and his banner which was as much a tonic to the defenders, as a discouragement to the attackers. After a day's fighting the exhausted defenders witnessed the withdrawal of the Sultan's best fighting men in dejection and disgrace. Bourbon described the day's events in some detail and attributed the victory to the presence of the Grand Master and the fortifications and firepower arranged by Tardini:

> And forthwith as the assault was given a great sortie of Turks entered in to the bulwarke of Spain and set up viii. or ix signs or banners upon it & drove our men out, … And they were lords of it [captured it] iii hours & more. Howbeit there was of our men beneath in the mine of the said bulwark the which bulwark so lost gave us evil hope. But incontinent [without any thought of the danger] the lord Grand Master being at the defence of the poste of England having knowledge of the said loss and that there was great fighting & resistance on both sides at the breach of Spain marched thither with the banner of the crucifix, … And the lord [Grand Master] mounted on the wall of Spain where as then began a great medling [melee] and every man laid his hands to the work as well to put the enemies out of the breach as to recover the bulwark that was lost. And the said lord sent a company of men in to the bulwark by the gate of the mine or by the barbican which entered at the said gate and went up where they found but few turks. For the artillery of the post of England right against the bulwark of Spain had so well met and scattered them that within a while our men had slain all them [that] were left. And thus the said bulwark was gotten and recovered again and with all diligence were made new repairs & strengths [reinforcements] to the said place And in likewise the enemies were put from the breach and few [of] them escaped and all their banners and signs were left with us. Surely it may be said that after the grace of god (the traverse of Spain & Auvergne and the small artillery set on the houses right against the said breaches as it is said with the coming and presence of the lord great master) hath given us this day.[32]

The disgrace of this abject failure was laid at the feet of Suleiman's commander Mustafa Pasha and his subordinates. The Sultan ordered that he should be shot to death with arrows as would Pir Pasha, who had bravely, but it seems foolishly, recommended mercy for his commander. Ayas Pasha

32 Bourbon uses the word journey, which derived from the French word for a day, *journée*.

who benefited from Suleiman's clemency, the Sultan having spent much of his ire on Mustafa, was with surprising generosity only to be placed in chains. Bourbon yet again seems to have had a good source of information in the Sultan's camp as he provides a vivid description of Suleiman's wrath directed at his commanders.

> During this assault the great turk was by his pavilion in a place that he had caused to be made & saw all the business & how his people were so sharply put back & the journey [day] lost on his side he was very sore displeased and half in despair. And sent for Mustafa Pasha with whom he was angry & chided him bitterly saying that he had caused him to come thither & had made him to believe that he should take the town in fifteen days or a month at the furthest & he had been there all ready three months with his army and yet had they done nothing. And after these words he was purposed to cause him [to] suffer death in the camp. But the other pashas showed him that he ought not to do Justice in the land of his enemies for it should consort [comfort] & give them courage whereby he did moderate his anger.

The executions were not carried out. And at least Suleiman did not hide in his tent for three days as his predecessor had done in 1480, but his subordinates' failures were as much his own. A greater leader would have acknowledged that.

The defenders had suffered terribly, having lost hundreds both killed and wounded. The wounded were considered those unable to stand, as almost all those in the battle would have received blows and cuts that would have compromised their ability to fight. William Weston for example had lost a finger of his sword hand to an arquebus shot, while Jean de Letoux had lost his arm to a cannon ball. Both sides were exhausted and in the case of the Ottomans they were running out of men willing to face their dreaded enemy and running out of ideas as to what to do next. Mining continued with eleven mines directed at the bulwark of England but these were defeated by Tadini's efforts.

Attacks on the bastions continued, designed to exhaust the defenders mentally as well as physically, in a new strategy of attrition. The Tower of Aragon now had only two guns left in action and only a few pieces in the gate of St John and the Bastion of Auvergne were left to counter the Ottoman attacks. Bourbon recorded the Ottoman troop dispositions around the siege as well as the rumours coming from the camp that the siege was to be abandoned. Bombardment and mining had failed and the assaults were proving too costly. Even the janissaries were on the verge of mutiny, or at least refusing to participate in any more murderous assaults. Bourbon considered that it was the information coming from traitors within the town that convinced the Great Turk to stay. He wrote of an Albanian who had: 'fled to the enemy's camp and warned them not to go for the gunshot was near wasted & that the most part of the knights and people should be theirs shortly.'[33]

Good news reached both sides as the end of the September came. To Suleiman the birth of a son was announced, which was accompanied by some much-needed collective celebration. Reports also reached the Knights of a relief force in Messina when Fra Jean de Bressolx arrived from Naples. Clearly even at this late stage, the Ottoman blockade was working no better than it had earlier. The weather was against a full-scale relief force, as the North Easterlies made navigation dangerous and although a single ship might slip past, a larger number would certainly fail. There were also disasters that would have gone unheard of to those at Rhodes. Fra Thomas Newport had organised a well-founded reinforcement to come from England. It got no further than the Bay of Biscay where the ship foundered with the loss of all on board. The worst news of all was the injury to the irrepressible and invaluable Tadini. When, in October, he was looking through a small embrasure to view the progress of the enemy he was shot through the right eye, with the ball passing out behind his ear. In only six weeks he returned to the fray, this time leading a raid against the Turkish sappers. This time he suffered a bad wound of a sword cut to his knee. In his absence the Lord Prior of St Giles supervised the engineering work.

The defences of the whole southern perimeter were now compromised by breaches and tunnels. The walls and bastions, of all except Aragon, still provided a defensive line and the breaches were provided with retrenchments that forced the Ottomans to build parapets in their own breaches! The besiegers were being besieged… A Venetian agent reported encouragingly that: 'On Rhodes they are in good spirits, they are not afraid of anything, and they do not wish for anything but 500 fresh men.'[34] Their losses had admittedly been grievous but the Ottomans were in a worse state and 'the Turk despairs.'[35] The greatest losses appeared to have been at the English Bastion where the casualty list had been great indeed. Of the knights recorded serving there, three were killed, twelve were wounded, with only one recorded as unwounded. So heavy were these losses that it was now manned by a mixed group of knights from different Langues, under the command of the Frenchman Jean Bin de Malincorne.

Mustafa Pasha in an attempt to restore his reputation launched three assaults on the bulwark of England between 3 and 5 October, after a bombardment of stone shot and incendiary carcasses – projectiles which were particularly feared. The assault troops eventually retired and their complaints were heard by some of the defenders, as they were speaking Greek.

33 Jacques de Bourbon, *Grande et Merveilleuse, & Tréscruelle Oppugnation de la noble Cité de Rhodes*, (London: 1524), page unnumbered.

34 Fabian Rieisinger, *Making an Island: the transformation(s) of Rhodes under early Ottoman rule* (1522–1560), MA Thesis, p.11.

35 Rieisinger, *Making an Island*, p.11.

> The troops returned in to their trenches evil contented and murmuring and swore by their Mahomet that Mustafa Pasha should not make them to mount any more to the said bulwark. And that it was great folly for them to make them be slain at the will and fantasy of one man.[36]

Despite the bad weather small reinforcements arrived on 14, 15, 16 and 20 October, who included Knights, gunners and sappers. What was lacking were labourers and munitions. To add to the shortage, a number of slaves were killed as it was thought they were mutinying. In fact, there were merely resentful of the unwarranted taunts and bullying of some younger knights. Bourbon highlighted the problem:

> By the will of our lord the enemy always in fear & dread would give no assault but continually shot against our repairs & made trenches for to pass forward in to the town. By the which trenches they shot infinitely with arquebuses and handguns and slew many of our folk especially of them that wrought and made the repairs that were broken & [razed]. And they put us in such extremity that we had almost no more slaves or other labouring people for to repair that they broke night & day which was a great hindrance for us & beginning of our perdition.[37]

Despite the passage of time and the work of successive teams involved in the restoration, and preservation and the partisan interpretation of the remains, there is considerable evidence of the fighting. The pock marks of small-arms fire seen here, would point to the intensity of the fighting and the fair degree of accuracy on the part of the Ottoman marksmen. (Author's photographs)

36 Jacques de Bourbon, *Grande et Merveilleuse, & Tréscruelle Oppugnation de la noble Cité de Rhodes*, (London: 1524), page unnumbered.

37 Jacques de Bourbon, *Grande et Merveilleuse, & Tréscruelle Oppugnation de la noble Cité de Rhodes*, (London: 1524), page unnumbered.

In addition to a shortage of labour there was a shortage of ammunition of all sorts and the order was given that firing at the enemy was to be at the discretion of the commanders and not the individual soldiers. The posts of Italy and Spain were now almost totally compromised by the skirmishes, assaults, trenches and mines. This meant that only Tadini's traverses, within the walls, still provided a perimeter of sorts for the garrison to defend.

Treachery Turns the Tide

Treachery was a feature of all military operations as each side sought to gain the upper hand through gathering intelligence, disseminating rumours and weakening the will of the enemy to resist. The citizens and defenders of Rhodes were expecting betrayal and treachery and they were to discover both. It was reported to the Grand Master that certain 'persons of quality' in the city were already communicating with the Turk. The first traitor to be uncovered was a Jewish doctor named Apella Renato who had been in place since the reign of Selim.[38] He had converted to Christianity and his work in the Hospital had earned him considerable recognition and praise. On 19 September he was discovered in the act of shooting a crossbow bolt into enemy lines, to which he had bound a message to Pir Pasha. It was his sixth effort to contact the enemy and reveal the increasingly parlous state of the garrison. He had already advised the besiegers that their mortar fire was useless and thus they had ceased wasting powder. His fate was inevitable he: 'confessed his evil & devilish doings and had his heed struck off.'[39]

In October when the situation had worsened, there were rumours of treason among the Rhodians who were becoming less willing to follow the Knights into disaster. Lucio Custrophilaca, a wealthy Rhodian merchant, was thought to have shot an arrow into the Turkish lines. He was arrested and tortured on the rack but admitted to nothing. Far more damage to the garrison followed when the treachery of Andrea D'Amaral, Prior of Castile and Chancellor of the Order was revealed. His servant Blasco Diaz, who was a *converse* – a Jew who had converted to Christianity, was discovered shooting a crossbow bolt into the Turkish lines with a message to Ayas Pasha. When Diaz was tortured, he naturally revealed all, although whether this was all, a fraction of all or all he could make up, it is now impossible to say. The message was apparently one of encouragement to the Turks to continue the siege as the condition of the garrison was pitiful. The defenders were reduced in number, short of munitions and the Rhodians were unwilling to offer themselves as martyrs to the Order's cause.

---

38 Bourbon gave him the name 'John the Baptist' and gives an earlier date for his discovery.

39 Jacques de Bourbon, *Grande et Merveilleuse, & Trèscruelle Oppugnation de la noble Cité de Rhodes*, (London: 1524), page unnumbered.

The Grand Master had D'Amaral arrested and placed in the Tower of St Nicholas, disgraced and facing a very uncertain future. The city and the garrison were in crisis and now others came to present their evidence of D'Amaral having sent more messages. Most damaging of all, a Knight from the same Langue declared that after D'Amaral had lost the election he had been heard to say that: 'He [de l'Isle Adam] will be the last Grand Master of Rhodes.' [40] Others claimed that he had said that he would sell his soul to the Devil, if he could encompass the ruin of the Order and the Grand Master with it. It is strange that, although apparently of dubious loyalty, he had been given a key role in the defence of the city and that no one had mentioned his multiple treacheries until after his arrest.

D'Amaral was unpopular, as the lack of support in the recent election showed, and he was certainly wayward and at odds with some of the brothers. He may have thought that maintaining a line of communication with the Turkish leader would be advantageous to him and the Order in the longer term. He was put to the question, probably by the special military tribunal set up at the beginning of the siege. He refused to admit any wrongdoing and declared: 'Am I, then, now to tell a lie and to sell my honour to save my old limbs from the pain of the rack.'[41] At a time when the Order and the citizens needed to discover the enemy within, someone who was the cause of all their woes, D'Amaral was the ideal candidate. He could be cruelly disposed of without damaging the Order as he was quite clearly not 'one of them,' despite of course having spent forty years as a Hospitaller!

The Grand Master was convinced of his guilt. It was clearly d'Amaral's treachery that had been one of the causes of all this suffering. As he wrote to Anne de Montmorency, the Maréchal de France and his nephew, on 13 November 1522:

> I tell you, my Nephew, that I have not been at war only with the Turks, but with one of the most senior members of our Council who, by reason of envy and a thirst for power, had long conspired to bring the Turk here and had promised to surrender this city to him. The matter has been divinely revealed and confirmed and he has been executed.[42]

Bourbon did not doubt his guilt, which was worse than that of Judas. Judas had betrayed Christ, an act which had led to the Resurrection, while D'Amaral had connived at the loss of Rhodes, from which no good could come. A Venetian citizen or spy – they performed both roles – reported on D'Amaral's treachery and asserted that all was not lost by any means.

40 Eric Brockman, *The Two Sieges* (London: John Murray, 1969), p.140.
41 Eric Brockman, *The Two Sieges* (London: John Murray, 1969), p.142.
42 Eric Brockman, *The Two Sieges* (London: John Murray, 1969), p.145.

> It is true that they have little wine left; but they have enough ammunition, bread, rice and water, and they wait for the west wind to pass, and they are hostile towards the Turks, of whom they say they will not let them go in any more, and they want to cut them all and burn their fleet; which is in the worst possible shape. They have discovered an act of treason committed by a Portuguese friar [d'Amaral], who used to be the first man of Rhodes, and he had been outdone by the current Grand Master, by two votes, and they cut his head off. And everyone inside is in good spirits.[43]

Suleiman had made the decision not to abandon the siege but to continue it, a resolution he announced to the full war council on 31 October. This was despite dreadful weather in October, with North-Easterly gales bringing rain and later hail. Mustafa Pasha passed over his (failed) command to Qasim Pasha in order to take up the post of the Governor of Egypt, where he died of natural causes and therefore with his head on his shoulders. All now asked how would the siege be ended? De l'Isle Adam seemed to have considered a fight to the bitter end, a very bitter end indeed. Every Brother and every citizen, would have to be prepared to die, rather than to surrender and apostatise. By doing this the Order might still survive and thrive and Christendom might be inspired to pursue another era of crusades.

This was not an attractive option to the citizens of Rhodes, who had up to this point followed their masters loyally. Nor was it attractive to many of the knights and brethren, who in the circumstances thought that an honourable retreat would be more likely to save the Order, as well as their own lives. In November a few vessels continued to arrive with a tiny number of reinforcements and stores but nothing to change the fundamental situation. Mining and countermining continued but the shortages of wood, gunpowder and labour made it impossible to match the efforts of the tens of thousands of Ottoman pioneers and miners. Meanwhile dreadful weather made the lives of both besieger and besieged miserable.

Major attacks on the Bastions of England and Italy were beaten back, again with cost to both sides, on 21 November. On 29 November there was one more major bombardment with 150 large shot smashing the repairs that constituted the last line of defence of the town. The last major general assault was to take place on post of Spain on 29 November.[44] Bourbon provided a vivid description of the fighting that took place and the collapse and flight of the Ottomans. Even the foul weather aided the Christians!

> in the morning the 29th day of the same month the vigil of Saint Andrew at the spring of the day the enemies went through the breach with their banners and entered in to the repairs with greater

43 Rieisinger, *Making an Island,* p.12.

44 Or the 30th as accounts differ.

> number of people than they did at the great battle in September hardly and furiously for to fight with us. But at their coming in the artillery of the traverses and the handgonnes and the gunshot of the [wind]mills found them so well and so sharply that he that came in was at once dispatched and overthrown and there abode above 2,000 of the Turks slain. The other that came after seeing their fellows so evilly welcomed as people that were astonished and lost they turned again to their trenches, to whom the artillery of the mills [Windmills Mole?] shot vigorously and hastened them to go a pace. And by report from the camp there died six thousand or more that day. The which day might be called very happy and well fortunate for us thanked be god. For there was none that thought to escape that day but to have died all and lost the town. Howbeit the pleasure of our Lord was by evident miracle to have it otherwise and the enemies were chased and overcome. And it is to be noted that the same day the rain was so great and so strong that it made the earth to sink a great deal that they had caste into the ditches for to cover them from the shot of Auvergne. And the said earth being so sunken the artillery of the said bulwark (unawares to them) smote them going and coming and made great murder of the said dogs.

Sir Nicholas Roberts reported that 180 of the garrison were slain along with 11,000 Turks, both figures that should be treated with caution but certainly point to a very bloody engagement. One horrible feature of the day's fighting was that the rain and blood turned the mud at the bottom of the ditch red, an event too oft repeated in the annals of warfare. After this there were no more Turkish assaults. The numerous tunnels meant that the Turks were now effectively within the walls but they were no longer willing to put the issue to a final assault. Suleiman and his Janissaries must have been almost as frustrated and exhausted as the Knights. Sir Nicholas reported the desperate condition of the defenders who had little or no hope of surviving the siege:

> Most of our men were slain, we had no powder nor manner of munitions nor victuals, but only bread and water; we were as men desperate determined to die upon them in a field rather than be put upon the stakes, for we doubted he would give us our lives considering there were slain so many of his men.[45]

45 Desmond Seward., *The Monks of War* (London: Penguin 1995), p.263.

An Exit Strategy for Both Parties?

For the siege to end the garrison, and above all the Grand Master, had to be presented with an option that could be justified to themselves and explained to Christendom. For them to sue for peace after so much suffering, would have seemed like a betrayal of those who had died. Suleiman could also not appear to his side to be weakening, or negotiating from a position of weakness, although he was still outside the walls with little real hope of getting into the city. A way was found to begin negotiations through the employment of a Genoese merchant, one Girolamo Monile. He appeared before the gate of St John under a flag of truce hoping, he claimed, to speak to another Genoese merchant who lived in Rhodes. He was sent on his way but returned and was then followed by an Albanian also seeking entrance. He had left the town for the Ottoman camp and now sought to return. It was clear that Suleiman meant to negotiate with the Grand Master and a letter had been prepared for him. It was rumoured that Rhodians were promised that their lives, property and religion would be respected.

De l'Isle Adam appeared to be hostile to these entreaties from these dubious messengers: 'to whom no words were spoken nor answers made for the lord great master as wise and prudent considering that a town that will hear entreatying is half lost.'[46] He was also aware that the toing and froing would be noticed by the Rhodian population at large. The Rhodians recognised the possibility of a negotiated settlement and called upon their Catholic and Orthodox bishops to present their case to the Grand Master, through Knights of the Grand Cross. The Grand Master presented himself as implacable in resisting a negotiated settlement and: 'the said lorde [Grand Master] showed many things for his honour and the religion. And that no such things ought to be done nor thought for any thing in the world but rather he and they to die.'[47] The lords who presented the case for the civilian population, who preferred life under the Turk to martyrdom, also pressed the argument that this would be best for the survival of the Religion.

The Grand Master was now in a position where he could argue that he was forced to summon the Council in the face of Rhodian dissent.[48] At this dramatic point, as if carefully choreographed, the Rhodians began to batter on the Council chamber doors, urging that they be admitted to plead their case. Their case was a simple one. As Nicholas Roberts reported:

> The commons of the town hearing this great proffer (of the great Turk to give us our lives and our goods) came to the Lord Master and

46 Jacques de Bourbon, *Grande et Merveilleuse, & Tréscruelle Oppugnation de la noble Cité de Rhodes*, (London: 1524), page unnumbered.

47 Jacques de Bourbon, *Grande et Merveilleuse, & Tréscruelle Oppugnation de la noble Cité de Rhodes*, (London: 1524), page unnumbered.

48 Eric Brockman, *The Two Sieges* (London: John Murray, 1969), p.150.

> said that considering that the wall and strength of the town is taken, and the munitions spent, and most of your Knights and men slain, and also seeing there is no succour ready to come, they determined [to take] this Partido that the Great Turk giveth upon the lives of our wives and children.[49]

The Great Master was not to be outdone in the drama of the moment he swooned, recovered his wits and finally agreed to consider the arguments of the civilian population. The Master remained unhappy with the arguments, especially the presentation made by the 'richest of the town' and: 'the said lord and his council were abashed and evil content as reason would seeing that it was but a coarse game.'[50] The reality was that the enemy were already within the gates. It was reported that: 'They came into the town by trenches in so much, they made many great trenches, and in a space of a month did come almost to the midst of the town, in as much as there lay nightly within our town many thousand Turks.'[51]

The Grand Master could now call upon the Council for their opinion and especially of those two most responsible for the continuation of the siege:

> The said lord [Prior] of Saint Giles arose saying & affirming upon his honour and his conscience that almost all the slaves and labourers were dead and hurt. And that scantily there was folk [there were too few people] .... now to remove a piece of artillery from one place to another & that it was impossible without folk any more to make or set up any repairs the which every day were broken and crushed by the great furious and continual shot of the enemy's artillery. As for [gun]powder the said lord said that all that was for store in the town was spent long ago. And of that that was newly brought was not to serve and furnish [repel] two assaults. And he seeing the great advantage of the enemy being so far within the town without power to put or chase them away for default [shortage] of men was of the opinion that the town would be lost and that there were no means to save it.
>
> The words of the said lord finished the captain Gabriel Martingo [Tadini] for his charge said and declared to the reverend lord and them of the council that seeing and considering the great beatings of shot that the town had suffered and after seeing the entering that the enemy had [made] so large and they were within the town by their trenches both endelonge and overthwart [both

49 Eric Brockman, *The Two Sieges* (London: John Murray, 1969), p.150.

50 Jacques de Bourbon, *Grande et Merveilleuse, & Tréscruelle Oppugnation de la noble Cité de Rhodes*, (London: 1524), page unnumbered.

51 Eric Brockman, *The Two Sieges* (London: John Murray, 1969), p.178.

> surrounding and entering the town?]. Seeing also that in two other places they were at the foot of the wall and that the most part of our knights and men of war and other were slain and hurt and the powders wasted [spent] & that it was impossible for them to resist their enemy any more that without doubt the town was lost if there came no succour to help and resist the siege. The which opinions and reasons of these two worthy men and expert in such feats understood and pondered by the lord great master and the lords of the council they were most part advised for to accept and take treaty if it were offered for the safeguard of the common people and of the holy relics of the church.[52]

The Grand Master was still of the opinion that death was preferable to surrender but the general opinion of the Order was clear:

> …whereby they did conclude that it were better and more agreeable to God for to take the treaty if it were proffered than for to die as people desperate and without hope.[53]
>
> 'Wise men surrender to necessity. No matter how praiseworthy our death, let us consider whether it may not be more damaging to the Holy Religion than our surrender.'[54]

The Grand Master was still unhappy with accepting defeat but it was clear that Rhodes could not resist further assaults. If no peace was made, the priceless relics of the Religion would be lost and so could be the Order itself. The women and children would suffer most, with rape, murder, enslavement and forced conversion. The inevitable dreadful fate of the Rhodians meant that he could end further resistance, not to save his skin but to save theirs. He could be free of any opprobrium directed at him – he had not been defeated by the Turk but by the 'commonalty.' Bourbon also pointed out that Suleiman would lose face, if he was forced to take the town by treaty, rather than storm.

The surrender proceedings began on 10 December, with white flags raised and envoys exchanged. The Turkish offer was a generous one in the circumstances: the Order could leave with all their personal property as well as could any Rhodians who chose to depart, or the garrison and city would face a massacre. The Council agreed to the terms and sent a delegation to the red tent of the Sultan and allowed some days for the detailed arrangements

---

52 Jacques de Bourbon, *Grande et Merveilleuse, & Trèscruelle Oppugnation de la noble Cité de Rhodes*, (London: 1524), page unnumbered.

53 Jacques de Bourbon, *Grande et Merveilleuse, & Trèscruelle Oppugnation de la noble Cité de Rhodes*, (London: 1524), page unnumbered.

54 Jacques de Bourbon, *Grande et Merveilleuse, & Trèscruelle Oppugnation de la noble Cité de Rhodes*, (London: 1524), page unnumbered.

to be agreed upon. The Rhodians were still unsure about what their fate would be and asked the Grand Master to seek clarification as to their fate after the departure of the Knights. The negotiations did not prosper, perhaps because the Grand Master expected miraculous assistance and to speed the process on Suleiman ordered a continuation of the bombardment on 15 December. On 16 December, relief did arrive, in the form of a ship loaded with wine from Candia, seized by Nicholas Fairfax and diverted from its voyage to Flanders from Crete. The cargo may have raised the spirits of the Knights, who for the preceding two months had nothing to drink other than water, but it could not affect the final outcome.

Although the Rhodians were still mobilised and 'stood to' along the walls, there was little enthusiasm for continuing the struggle. One poor young man was hanged for leaving his post but this had little effect on the majority of his fellow citizens. They might stand guard but no longer had they any stomach for a fight, if a generous peace was on offer. A half-hearted attack on the posts of Aragon and England also fizzled out, as both sides realised that enough blood had been spent already, the siege was at an end and those who survived it wished to live. The Rhodians sent their own envoys to Suleiman and it was clear that Rhodes had surrendered, even if the Knights still had not. Relations were still tense. Two of the garrison carrying earth to reinforce the post of England, against the rules of the truce, were captured and had their noses, ears and fingers cut off.

Suleiman was very keen to see the end of the siege. Bourbon suggests that he thought that the information regarding the strength and reserves of the garrison was suspect and that they could continue to put up a fight, with further heavy losses to the besiegers. Suleiman was also aware that the siege had gone on too long and if the town was taken by storm all discipline may have broken down in his army. The Grand Master finally agreed to surrender the city on 20 December.

The ending of military operations on Christmas Eve was accompanied by a final and very generous agreement. The Knights and all those who wished would leave in twelve days, in Ottoman ships if not enough space could be found in their own vessels. The civilian population were to be protected from rapine and any abuse and could choose to leave either then or at any other time over the next three years, if they found Ottoman rule not to their liking. Forty-six hostages were sent to Suleiman's camp: twenty-four Knights and the remainder civilians; an occupation force of only 400 janissaries was to be admitted into the city. The Turkish army could now celebrate a hard-won victory:

> Today, by the grace of God, at the time of the noon prayer, in the noble name of the inspired ruler, the sultan's muezzins recited the call to prayer in the Arab tower and the red and yellow standard of the janissaries was hoisted on the same tower and many times the imperial band played, and festivities took place. And Ferhad Pasha

> came crossing the sea and met with the army. And the call to prayer with cries of Allah Allah filled every corner of the castle.[55]

A further force of 24,000 or 25,000, including Janissaries, now arrived from the mainland. They were to be the assault troops if the siege was to be continued, as the troops on the island were clearly considered unreliable. It was these 'fresh' troops that entered the town raped and attacked civilians, ransacked and desecrated the churches, including the Hospital of the Order, from which they stole the silver vessels used by the patients. Order was eventually restored and the evacuation continued. The Janissaries blamed the Sipahis and their commanders were 'dressed down' and their men returned to their tents.

The Grand Master met Suleiman on three occasions, with the formal surrender and exchange of gifts taking place on 26 December. Relations between the two were cordial: the Grand Master exchanged a present of gold coin for a fine cloak. It was reported that, in conversation with Ibrahim Pasha, that Suleiman had said that: 'It saddens me to be compelled to cast this brave old man out of his home.'[56] Suleiman entered the city through the gates of St John on the next day without his bodyguard, as he said that the word of the Grand Master was safety enough.

The city itself was undergoing great changes. The churches were converted into mosques and the occupying troops in some cases clearly behaved badly. The misbehaviour was not as extensive as it could have been and hardly a fraction of what would have been visited on the city if the great assaults that took place in earlier months had succeeded. Ahmed reportedly punished some of those committing excesses and returned property to the Order. The fine bronze guns were left, some taken as trophies to Constantinople but others remained in situ. There they remained until they were given as gifts to Napoleon III. Far more valuable to the Order were the religious relics, including the right hand of St John himself, which were collected and carried aboard ship with suitable veneration. They would make the long and slow voyage with the Order around the Mediterranean, until finding a resting place in Malta.

There were some loose ends to be tied up. The remaining islands that owed allegiance to the Order and the Castle of St Peter in Bodrum had to be handed over. Murad the son of Djem had been an honoured guest of the Order but his fate was sealed. Suleiman could not allow a nephew with any claim to the throne to live. He was protected by the Knights in the Castle of Feraklos, which held out for some months after Rhodes had fallen. Murad was quietly killed and his family and household sent to Constantinople; the Knights and the rest of the garrison were murdered. The Grand Master with the remaining Knights and their company departed on 1 January 1523

55 Rieisinger, *Making an Island*, p.14.
56 Eric Brockman, *The Two Sieges* (London: John Murray, 1969), p.153.

in the carrack *Santa Maria*. This ship flew the Banner of the Sorrowing Virgin, which bore the words *Affictis tu spes unica rebus* (In all which afflicts us thou art our only hope) and had the Icon of Philermos affixed to the mainmast for additional protection. The ship carrying the Grand Master was commanded by the Englishman Sir William Weston; accompanying him was a young knight Jean Parisot de Valette.

Tadini with the approval of the Grand Master escaped, as he feared that his skills might be highly valued by the Sultan who would seek to detain him or worse. He did not worry about the prospect of facing Venctian wrath for leaving Crete, against the prescribed orders of its Governor for as 'by defending the land, he defends the State of his Most Illustrious Lady' [Venice].[57] He had also acted as a spy for *il Serenissima* since from as early as July 1522 he had become the principal source on the island for Sanuto his Venetian 'handler'. Suleiman who must have been heartily sick of this cold, wet and now blood-soaked small island did not remain longer than was necessary, having achieved what would be a memorable victory.

> Making the Church of Saint John a mosque and a place of worship he [Sultan Suleiman] cleansed it from being a place of idols and the devil. He performed the Friday prayers there, that is at Saint John. Then, having achieved his goal, he headed towards Constantinople with blissful inspiration.[58]

Why Was Rhodes Lost?

> Most wars are fought under the mistaken hypothesis that their conduct will be a repetition of previous ones. In this respect, defence is particularly vulnerable as often the defender has to assume a static role and it takes considerable time to put the pieces into place. Once there, they are often immutable and their efficiency will depend upon the attacker doing what he is expected to do. Victories are won by those who do not. However, the role of the attacker is equally hazardous and prone to miscalculation. If he attacks the wrong object with the wrong forces at the wrong time, the success of his project is doomed.[59]

It could be argued that the loss of Rhodes was inevitable considering the massive forces sent against it, what really mattered was how it was lost. Bourbon was quite clear about the reason: it was due to the presence of

57 Riesinger, *Making an Island* p.15.
58 Riesinger, *Making an Island* p.26.
59 Quentin Hughes, 'Errors of Judgement: The Sieges of Rhodes and Malta', *Fort, The Journal of the Fortress Study Group* vol.31, (2003), p.61.

the Great Turk himself: 'For his coming his presence and continual abiding in the field is & has been cause of the victory that he has had.'[60] In 1480 a subordinate commander could make the decision to cut his master's losses, in the face of the collapse of his own morale and that of his men. Suleiman on the other hand was riding high, he had recently captured Belgrade and he was next clearly fated to capture Rhodes. It would confirm his new reign as one of conquest and witness the reversal of previous humiliations. He was, after all, the son of Selim and had at his disposal a well-honed military machine, recently returned from foreign victories. The size of his army was 'big enough' for the task and he could, and did, call upon considerable reserves. It was reported from sources within his camp that he had lost over 60,000 men in action and a further 40,000 from disease. Although unlikely figures, it suggests that the numbers of casualties were irrelevant, as Rhodes was to be taken whatever the cost.

In 1480 the Ottoman force abandoned the siege at the end of the traditional campaign season, which Rhoads Murphey has established began on 21 March,[61] and ended on 6 November which was called the *Ruz-i Kasım* (Day of Division). In 1522, Suleiman's determination led to the continuation of the campaigning season until the end of December. It was clear that there would be no relief for the besieged from Christendom whereas the Ottoman Army could remain there indefinitely as they were close to their supply lines and potential reinforcements.

De l'Isle Adam and Carretto had been warning of an imminent attack upon Rhodes ever since Selim had begun his successful aggressive campaigns. It was clear from the continual re-fortification of the town that a siege was expected, when time permitted. It was also increasingly clear, that the defence of Rhodes was not high on the agenda in Rome, or with the secular powers of Christendom. Generous benefactions were made for the defence of the town but there was never going to be a Crusade, or a Christian armada bringing relief. The Order was itself compromised by those secular and ecclesiastical powers that envied its wealth and influence, which meant that it could not even fully mobilise its own resources.

The Grand Master had to defend Rhodes but he also had to ensure the survival of the Religion. He could not abandon the town, nor could he surrender it ignominiously, however prolonged the siege. I am struck by a comparison with Admiral Cunningham who when required to sacrifice scarce and valuable ships for the withdrawal of the British army from Crete was reported to have said: 'It takes the Navy three years to build a ship. It will take 300 years to build a new tradition.' Rhodes had to be held, until there could be no criticism of the Order, even better, its defence could add a new glorious chapter in its history – it did.

60 Jacques de Bourbon, *Grande et Merveilleuse, & Tréscruelle Oppugnation de la noble Cité de Rhodes*, (London: 1524), page unnumbered.

61 Rhoads Murphey, *Ottoman Warfare*, (New Brunswick: Rutgers University Press, 1999).

The Grand Master and his predecessors especially d'Aubusson had done their best to refortify the town as far as resources and technology permitted. The town and the garrison were well provisioned and all that could be done in that respect was done, although assistance from the Venetian republic would have helped. The Order had collected as many men and as much firepower as possible and with the aid of Tadini in 1522 the defences were managed brilliantly. The enemy failed to make one disastrous mistake which perhaps the defenders had counted on. This was an expensive and futile assault on the massively reinforced Tower of St Nicholas, attacks which had drained the morale and manpower of the Ottoman Army in the first siege. Even without making this mistake the enemy bombardment and mining generally proved far less effective than they would have hoped. This was because of the resilience of the fortifications, the work of Tadini in counter-mining and the quality of the defenders. The Knights and the citizens rallied to defend the rubble and fought the enemy assault troops to a standstill. Bourbon stressed the importance of artillery and firearms, especially from the traverses and the fortified houses within the walls, but ultimately it was not a battle between guns and stone but a battle of wills.

The Ottoman Army certainly had brave commanders, who fought and died at the head of their men, rallying them bravely. The defenders had the Grand Master under his standard by which his presence could be seen. Bourbon described the part that de l'Isle Adam, no longer by any means a young man, played in the fighting, 'For often times he puts himself farther in the press [of battle] than needed for the unquietness of his person. But he did it for to hearten and strengthen the courage of his people being so well willing to defend and die for the [f]aith.'[62] The Grand Master played a chess grand master's game throughout the siege. As Bourbon noted the victory for Suleiman was barely a victory at all. He had to call for strong reinforcements, as his own men could no longer be made to face the Knights in battle. The withdrawal of the Order was by treaty and forced by the civilian population on an unwilling commander. The Religion would survive and thrive, together with its most precious relics, to face and defeat a final assault by Suleiman over forty years later. It was in some sense a victory. The best epitaph on the siege were the words of the emperor: 'Nothing in the world was ever so well lost as Rhodes.'

62 Jacques de Bourbon, *Grande et Merveilleuse, & Tréscruelle Oppugnation de la noble Cité de Rhodes*, (London: 1524), page unnumbered.

10

After Rhodes?

It is easy to assume that because of the siege of 1522, the Knights would have emerged as the heroes of Christendom and be free to settle and prosper wherever they wished but this was far from the case. The news of their defeat was met with disbelief by Charles V, as reports had reached the West that the Ottoman forces had retreated after their defeats in late October. As late as May 1523 it was reported that the English Court did not believe the news of the loss. Francis I seems to have welcomed the news; although the French predominated in the Order, his rivalry with the Empire dominated his own strategic thinking. It was hoped that the heroic defence of Rhodes would reinvigorate the idea of the Crusade across Christendom and produce a universal peace between aggressive monarchies. Pope Adrian VI suggested this in a letter to Katherine of Aragon, and in April 1523 he issued a Bull for a universal peace and preparation for a Crusade, together with a new papal tax to pay for it. This proposal would never have gained support while France and the Empire were at each other's throats, in the struggle over Italy. Despite his protestations, Henry VIII was more concerned with subsuming the Order in England into his own grasping hands than assisting it.

The Order left Rhodes in three galleys, four barque, one large galleon, one smaller galleon, one carrack and numerous smaller craft. They had first to bring their wounded to a place of safety. They were also encumbered by loyal Rhodians, who either saw no future under Ottoman rule or possibly hoped to prosper with their knightly overlords. The ships of the Order first found landfall on Crete. The Grand Master now vented his fury on the Serene Republic and especially Agnadello, the Governor of Crete, for his role as Pontius Pilate washing his hands of the Order and allowing their slaughter. From Crete they made their way first to Brindisi and then Syracuse, a property of the Empire. They travelled from Messina to Cumae from there to Civita Vecchia and Viterbo. The Order settled in Viterbo from 1524–1527 where the Convent was formally established. In 1527 they were re-established in Villefranche in territory of the Duke of Savoy. This created serious legal issues relating to the separate status of the Order and its followers including the Rhodians.

What added to their problems was that this was a time of plague and of famine so overwhelming that it even brought the Italian wars to a brief halt. In 1527 Rome itself was sacked by German Protestant troops of the Catholic Emperor, adding to the general air of chaos and despair. The Italian wars created serious tensions between the members of the Order, who were without an external enemy to fight and now had the luxury of bickering amongst themselves. In 1527 the first full Chapter meeting was held since the fall of Rhodes. The Ottoman threat had also increased with their decisive victory at the battle of Mohacs in 1526, which was followed by the capture of Budapest and the siege of Vienna in 1529. The Order's enemies were to be found among Christian monarchs as well. In 1527 Henry VIII declared the English Langue independent and gave it the task of defending Calais against the French. The Grand Master journeyed to England in 1528 and with honeyed words and by granting Henry the dubious title of 'Protector of the Religion', preserved its independence. The Order in England was dealt its death blow in 1534, by Henry's denial of the authority of the Pope and as with the suppression of the monasteries, the Order was dissolved, with those unfortunate enough to publicly oppose, suffering martyrdom.

The Grand Master had received the title of Defender of the Faith from Pope Adrian VI and he gained almost legendary status for his defence of Rhodes. He spent the next few years trying to find a European King or perhaps the Emperor himself to give the Order refuge. His absence on his long diplomatic expeditions caused even more disquiet within the Order, with rumours of his death and even abduction. The Order was so short of funds that it couldn't even refit escort vessels for the Grand Master's peregrinations; it was now entirely dependent upon the generosity of others. Henry VIII gave 20,000 gold crowns after his ego had been thoroughly massaged by the Grand Master and Cardinal Farnese provided prisoners to fill the rowers' benches in the Order's few remaining war galleys.

The independence of the Order remained paramount; it had to be sovereign in its own territories, it could never happily settle on another's land. To become dependent upon another sovereign would compromise their purpose, as they would inevitably become embroiled in the politics of their new overlord. In 1524 Charles V offered Malta, Gozo and Cosimo as well as Tripoli (captured in the Spanish Crusade of 1510), and additionally a gift of 100,000 ducats. Commissioners were sent by the Order to inspect the proposed 'gift' and were not overly impressed by the properties on offer and the demand that they would be required to swear an oath of fealty to The Emperor. At the same time, the French King encouraged the Grand Master (who was French) to reject the offer, as it would help his rival, The Emperor, to further control the western Mediterranean.[1] The initial demands made by Charles V were considerable as the Venetian Ambassador reported:

1 *Calendar of State Papers Relating to English Affairs in the Archives of Venice*, volume 3, 14 May 1520 (London: HMSO, 1869); Sanuto Diaries, v xxxvi, p.242, 824, Marco Foscari to the Signory.

> [He] Has been told by Gabriel da Martinengo, that besides the other demands made by the Emperor of the Order of Rhodes for the grant of Malta and Tripoli, he requires the knights to take upon themselves the defence of Tripoli; a responsibility which Martinengo expects the Order to ponder and hold in great account. The Emperor also insists on their paying the fourth of the revenues of the priories and commanderies in his dominions, according to the concession made to him by Pope Adrian of all the ecclesiastical benefices in his realms. The knights apologise for not acceding to this demand, alleging the expenses incurred by them in the present war against the Turks, besides what they will have to disburse [pay] before they can domicile themselves in safety; but they would come to some compromise on this point, were the proposal to defend Tripoli cancelled.[2]

An idealised portrait of Jean de Valette, the hero of the Great Siege of Malta in 1565. He was born in 1495 and experienced the full horrors of the 1522 siege. He would have heard the tales of the earlier siege told by the older brethren. The lessons of the importance of the futile Ottoman attack on the Tower of St Nicholas may have been important in deciding his strategy in 1565. It may explain his determination to sustain the Fort of St Elmo, prolonging its siege and draining his own manpower. (Public domain via Wikimedia Commons)

The Knights hoped initially to return to Rhodes. The population of Rhodes could be encouraged to rebel but the Ottomans suppressed any plotting. In addition, a large expedition in support of the Order, organised amongst Christian powers, was unlikely. It was hoped to establish another base in Greece but they failed to capture the city of Modon, despite several attempts. Rhodes meanwhile should have become one of the key naval

2 *Calendar of State Papers Venice*, February 1 1524; *Original Letter Book*, Letter no. 251, St. Mark's Library.799. Gasparo Contarini to the Signory.

bases for Ottoman power in the region and its governor, one of the small number of influential and strategically important 'sea governors.' In fact, this did not happen and Christian piracy would continue unhindered and unabated. The focus of Suleiman's efforts was now turned towards Hungary and towards Iraq and not seaward.

De l'Isle Adam finally accepted the Emperor's offer of Malta as a fief of the Empire. In return an annual payment of a single falcon was demanded – the famous Maltese falcon. It was to be delivered to the Viceroy of Sicily on All Saints' Day, every year. In 1532 it was reported that the Grand Master had written to The Emperor seeking to abandon Malta for the safety of Syracuse; the Pope suggested Otranto or Ancona but The Emperor demurred. The Grand Master accepted the perpetual fiefdom not because of Malta but because of Tripoli. Tripoli was a wealthy, populous city of strategic importance and an excellent base from which to attack the trading routes along the North Africa coast; its loss in 1551 meant that the Order had for the first time to accept Malta as their permanent home, since Malta, whatever its limitations, was the only option left to them.

Malta was (is) arid and treeless, without either rivers or streams: a hellishly hot rock of 122 square miles in area, it seemed as much a prison as a base. Its 20,000 inhabitants had more in common with the Moors than good western Christians It already possessed an alien aristocracy made up of arrogant and obstreperous Aragonese and Sicilians and a *Città Notabile*, the capital, Mdina. In its favour, its climate permitted two harvests per annum, the first barley and the second cotton. It also produced olives, honey and flax. The port at Birgu had an excellent harbour and an ancient fortress. It was already a haunt of what were, in all but name, pirates, so in that respect the Order should have felt at home. The Order set about establishing itself on the island with a massive programme of fortifications based on the most modern system of angled bastions known as the *Trace Italienne*. However, it would not be long before they would face their third and most famous siege at the hands of their old enemy.

Colour Plate Commentaries

A.

1. Portrait of Sultan Mehmet II

Portrait of Sultan Mehmet II, (1432–1481) Gentile Bellini (1480). (Victoria and Albert Museum, London)

With supreme irony, whilst we have no contemporary portrait of d'Aubusson, we have a magnificent Renaissance portrait by Gentile Bellini of his great enemy Mehmet II, the conqueror of Constantinople. It is the portrait of a man who has experienced much and would now appear to fear little. His face shares the hardness of many of those renaissance portraits of condottieri, merchant princes and assorted menacing autocrats. The eminent historian Sir Steven Runciman described him as, 'handsome, of middle height but strongly built. His face dominated by a pair of piercing eyes under arched eyebrows, and a thin, hooked nose that curved over a mouth with full red lips. In later life his features reminded men of a parrot about to eat ripe cherries.' (Steven Runciman., *The Fall of Constantinople 1453* (Cambridge: Cambridge University Press, 1990), p.58) (Wikimedia Commons, Public Domain)

2. Portrait of Selim 'the Grim'

A Portrait by Nakkaş Osman of Selim 'the Grim' but rather disappointingly he is not even looking a little bit grumpy. He had rebelled against his father Bayezid II before succeeding to his throne, and his brutal treatment of his brother and cousins was intended to stop them rebelling against him. A successful military commander, he expanded Ottoman possessions by almost three-quarters by area and could claim to be the first Ottoman Caliph. He controlled Jerusalem as well as Mecca and Medina after the defeat of the Mamluks. His acquisition of the Prophet's own battle flag gave him tremendous kudos in the Islamic World. His premature death, after prolonged successes, led to the West breathing a sigh of relief. Unfortunately, his successor would turn his eyes to the West, rather than primarily pursuing further conquests in Muslim lands. (Wikimedia Commons Public Domain)

B.

1. Detail of a Cavalry Action

Detail of a cavalry action, from 'Bahram Recovers the Crown of Rivniz', folio 245r from the 'Shahnama of Abu'l Qasim Firdausi' by Abu'l Qasim Firdausi. The painting attributed to Qadimi Iranian *c.* 1525–30

The description of Ottoman cavalry by Busbecq and others highlighted the versatility of this force. The main figure on the right has just killed his opponent with a light lance, upon which he now displays his enemy's helmet/cap. He has a bow and arrows in a bowcase/quiver overlaying his sabre. In the bottom left a standard bearer is wielding his sabre, while his neighbour to his left, has just hit an enemy soldier with his characteristically shaped mace. At the top of the image, two combatants with sabres and shields are fighting. The shields were light and made from cane but, as can be seen here, provided only limited protection. With such an array of weapons and levels of skill it is unsurprising that firearms played little part in cavalry warfare. Skill at arms and personal bravery were greatly admired by the Turks but their lack of plate armour would prove a grave disadvantage during the sieges. (Metropolitan Museum of Art, public domain)

2.

Detail from the 'The Battle of Pashan Begins', folio 243v of 'The Shahnama of Shah Tahmasp' by Abu'l Qasim Firdausi. The painting is attributed to 'Abd al-Vahhab Iranian *c.* 1530–1535. This is a fine demonstration of the horse archery of the period. The short horn and sinew bows were designed to be used on horseback. A thumb loose is being used, with the arrow shot from the right side of the bow and supported on the thumb of the bow hand, a very different style from the western, so-called, 'Mediterranean' method. The horse archer excelled in snap-shooting, aiming instinctively and able, as demonstrated here, to shoot in all directions. The archers could also loose many arrows in a minute. It is hardly surprising that illustrations in Caoursin show the Knights and their allies well-armoured in the face of such archery excellence. (NB please ignore the white elephant in the picture). (Metropolitan Museum of Art, public domain)

C.

1.

Tower on the curtain wall of the city. This photograph is of one of the towers and wall sections that underwent little change as a consequence of the first siege, protected as it would then be protected by the *grande tenaille*. The wall of the *fausse braye* (greatly restored) is very apparent, as is its relationship to the curtain wall. It is easy to see how the 'independent' tower was joined to the main wall after 1480 by building a relieving arch, which was later infilled. A new embrasure on the new connecting section would provide enfilading fire along the *fausse braye*. I cannot understand why the Order did not build round towers, which were generally considered superior to square towers, especially in a zone subject to strong earthquakes. (Author's photograph)

2.

Hospitaller 'Bombarde-mortier'. One of the most remarkable survivals is a 'bombarde-mortier,' a hybrid type, capable of both low and high angle shooting. The gun has the heraldic device of the Grand Master and in the inscription F PETRVS DAUBUSSSON M HOAPITALI HEER, and could have been used in the siege of 1480, as he became Grand Master in 1476. It does not have a representation of the Cardinal's hat that he was awarded in 1489. In 1862 when it was given by the Sultan, together with its ammunition, it was still emplaced in the German Langue according to the Swedish doctor Hedenborg who was resident on Rhodes in 1848. It is 1.93m in length with a bore of 58cm slightly longer than half the overall length and a sub-calibre powder chamber 23cm in diameter. The granite projectile would have weighed about 261kg. It has trunnions which were probably developed for mortar pieces while at the same time it has two slotted rings at mouth and breech ends of the type associated with conventional bombards. The slots could be used to insert wooden or iron levers to assist the movement of what is a very heavy piece – it weighs approximately 3,325kg. J. B. De Vaivre proposes that this feature and the lower quality of the casting suggests that it was of Rhodian manufacture. (Author's photograph)

D.

The Attack on the Tower of St Nicholas. The Tower of St Nicholas in this image although somewhat battered, is still well garrisoned. The broken pontoon bridge stretching from the Ottoman camp was a bold but flawed enterprise. The Turkish artillery can be seen emplaced on the ground, rather than on wheeled mountings, and protected by wooden mantlets. The importance of the *fausse braye* is also made clear in the depiction of the Rhodian defences. It was worth noting the angled bastions placed before two of the towers are an indication of future developments. The two vessels belonging to the Order are a nice addition here but played no part in the defence of the Tower. The defenders are all well supplied with armour, appearing to wear sallets and in some cases full plate armour. (Master of the Cardinal de Bourbon, 'Gestorum Rhodiae Obsidionis Commentarii', *c.* 1483. Wikipedia, public domain)

E.

The final Ottoman assault of 1480. A gruesome depiction of the defeat of the final Ottoman assault and the Order's counter-attack. The extensive damage to the defences is clear, especially to the Tower of Italy, as is the use of barrels filled with earth to reinforce the walls. The Order's guns are in fixed emplacements and wrought iron guns (shown as black) alternate with bronze pieces. There is no attempt to hide the bloody nature of the fighting, with some Rhodian defenders lying dead on the battlement although greatly outnumbered by their enemy. (Master of the Cardinal de Bourbon, 'Gestorum Rhodiae Obsidionis Commentarii', *c.* 1483. Wikipedia, public domain)

F.

The defences on the flank of St John's Tower of the Post of Provence, seen from the moat. The successive lines of defence, pierced by gun loops of different sizes, would have proved a serious obstacle to any attack by infantry, however disciplined or motivated by religious zeal or a desire for loot. Although no doubt diminished by artillery fire and mining, the toll such defences would take of any attacking force would have been substantial. By the end of the siege and in the winter weather the moat would be a welter of mud, rank and carmine with the blood of the slaughtered. (Author's photograph)

G.

Grande Tenaille. What has been termed the 'grande' tenaille, stretching from Tower of the Virgin Mary to the Tower of St John. It is not a minor addition to the defences but a massive bulwark against which any enemy assault would break. Any infantry would be funnelled into the 'kill zone' at either end. There was only one way to enter the city and that was by tunnelling, a solution that it took some time for the besiegers to realise. The moat wall is also sheer, making any descent hazardous. It is only at the Tower of Italy that the ground slopes away to sea level. It is difficult to appreciate the sheer scale of these additions to the fortifications, when standing beside it I was reminded of the massive steel hull of a large ship. (Author's photograph)

H.

The Carretto Tower. There are clear similarities between the Carretto Tower and the Device Forts of Henry VIII of two decades later. There is no obvious direct connection between them and their purposes were different. This tower was defensive in nature while the Device Forts were meant to cover anchorages and harbours with their offensive firepower. They were however both attempts to exploit the opportunities and resist the challenges created by the artillery revolution. The Tower was fully integrated into the older curtain wall and *fausse braye* and was connected as well with the newly developed *caponier* and the *petite tenaille.*

I

The Tower of St Nicholas. The Tower of St Nicholas had become transformed into a major fortification after the first siege. It proved a match for the only artillery battery which attempted to reduce it in 1520. It would have proved nearly impossible to make a landing at the base of the walls and the heavy gun armament, some of which remained *in situ* until sent as a gift in 1862, would have made such an assault suicidal. It is unsurprising that no major effort was made to bombard it, let alone take it.

J.

1.

Suleiman the Magnificent. This is the only surviving portrait of Suleiman from the three that were 'by the hand of Titian' and can probably be more accurately attributed to Titian's workshop. Suleiman stood upon the shoulders of others, great or greater than himself. Selim the Grim's achievement gave Suleiman the resources and the impetus to finally rid himself of the worrisome warrior monks on Rhodes. He continued his predecessors' conquests in the Moslem world but was forced to retreat from Vienna in 1529. He was married to a red-headed Ruthenian who was an Orthodox Christian until her conversion and she was as exotic and intriguing to the West, as Suleiman was terrifying. Although the conflict can be characterised as Islam versus Christianity the Ottoman Empire was culturally and religiously very diverse. Suleiman's extraordinarily large turban was probably as big as it is portrayed here. It was decreed than no turban should exceed in size and magnificence that of the Sultan and it therefore had to be of a monumental size. The material for the turban was wrapped around a cone-like frame which rested upon his head, it was then decorated with feathers and jewels. It would have been worn every Friday when he attended services at the Mosque – hats maketh man! (Titian - Kunsthistorisches Museum Vienna. Public domain)

2.

Portrait of Tadini da Martinengo. There is surprisingly no portrait of Phillipe de l'Isle Adam although he was the hero of Christendom and after the siege a regular visitor to European courts. Tadini da Martinengo was fortunately immortalised, five years before his death, in a portrait by Vecello. He proudly displays the cross of the Order on his gown, with his perky little red codpiece peeking out below. He has not hidden his mutilated eye socket as that was clearly as much a badge of honour as the cross on his chest and the magnificent gold collar about his neck. The impressive artillery park in the landscape reflects his skills as gunner and engineer. I would have hoped for a representation of the siege of Rhodes in the background but perhaps his scarred face was all that was needed to remind viewers of the part he played. He was born in the castle of Martinengo which belonged to his grandfather, and learnt his trade as an engineer under the tutelage of a Frenchman. He entered the service of the Serene Republic in 1509 with the rank of Captain and fought in the Italian wars, when he was captured on one occasion. He was appointed 'Engineer General and Colonel of Infantry' and was also, as were all Venetians, a spy for La Serenissima. As a Knight of the Order he was appointed Prior of Barletta which had a healthy income from its subordinate Commanderies. (Portrait of Gabriele Tadini by Tiziano Vecelio, 1538. Public domain via Wikimedia Commons)

K.

Ottoman depiction of the siege of Rhodes in 1522. The Siege of Rhodes, illustrated in the 'Süleymanname' of the 1550s, which recounts the life and achievements of Suleiman I. Suleiman is portrayed observing the progress of the siege and protected by his *solaks*. He has brought with him his flags, including according to Konstantin Mihailovica, a white flag indicating the Sultan's presence at the siege. The Janissary arquebusiers are much in evidence, equipped with long bronze-barrelled pieces with flared muzzles. Behind them are the infantry, who are prepared to launch an assault. There are also some archers depicted with their bows shouldered. In the left-hand corner can be seen a representation of miners digging furiously at numerous tunnels, an acknowledgement of the part they played in the siege. What is noticeably absent is any image of the siege artillery. This might simply have been an artistic decision, or perhaps it is an acknowledgement that, as important as artillery was, it would be the miner and not the gunner who would decide the outcome. The fortifications of Rhodes and its defenders are presented in a highly stylised fashion. (Public Domain via Wikipedia)

L.

Hospitaller Heraldry

The Hospitallers' banners and pennons were decorated with a simple white cross on a red background (L1+L2). This could be combined with a rather etiolated Maltese cross on a gold background (a cross formy couped gules) in four quarterings (L3). The same variations were to be found in the long swallow-tailed pennons (L4). There is no evidence for personal heraldry being flown in battle. The Langues clearly had their own heraldry as there was a bitter dispute over whose flag should fly over the Bastion of Auvergne.

M.-N.

Flags of the Langues

M1. Provence, the arms of Jerusalem (argent, a cross potent between 4 crosses or).
M2. Langue of Auvergne, being yellow with a blue dolphin.
M3. France, azure, 3 fleurs-de-lis .
M4. Italy, black with the word 'Italia' embroidered across it in gold.
N1. Langue of Aragon, comprising Aragon (paly, or and gules) impaled with Navarre (gules, a cross, a saltire and an orle, of chains linked together or, the centre pierced vert).
N2. England, the arms of England.
N3. Germany, the arms of Germany (argent, a 2-headed eagle displayed sable).
N4. Castile, the arms of Castile with the arms of Portugal.

D'Aubusson's personal standard loomed large in the narratives as well as appearing in a number of the pictorial records. This standard displayed the figure of Christ Crucified, with Mary and the Disciple, John, both standing at the foot of the Cross, either as a vexillum (H5)[1] or as here a banner. In the example given in the Caoursin images it is painted on a blue background, although the representation is very small. Detail from De Casuregis *Zyzymy* (The case of Sultan Djem) printed in Ulm by Ioannem Reger, in William Caoursin's *Obsidionis Rhodiae Urbis Descriptio* (1496). Detail from f.12v

1 Vexillum is a banner hanging from a transverse pole attached to a staff.

O.

Grand Masters' Arms

Gabriel Albert identified 151 separate coats of arms in Rhodes from the period of Hospitaller occupation on the defences, mostly those of the Grand Masters (GM 1-5) but also donors. On the Tower of St Nicholas can be found dedications to Philip the Good, Duke of Burgundy, and Grand Master Zacosta responsible for the construction of the tower that so frustrated Turkish efforts in 1480. The later periods of construction on the Tower have dedications to Pierre D'Aubusson.

This excellent survival from the street of the knights has (left to right) the Arms of: England, Grand Master Helion de Villeneuve (1319-1346), the cross of the Hospitaller Order, Grand Master Dieudonne de Gozon (1346-1353), the Royal House of Edward III (1350).[2] The English Auberge is nearby but not on the street itself and it is difficult to explain why the English devices are found here. (Author's photograph)

The knights were discouraged from personal ostentation but that would not extend to their shields where their family arms could be displayed. All the members of the Order wore a red tabard, called a *supraveste*, with a white cross. This either hung loosely or was tied at the waist. Those not of the Order wore a similar tabard, usually blue, and embroidered or lettered as they wished.

P.

Ottoman Heraldry

The principal colours of the flags of the Ottoman Army were red, white, green, yellow and black. The armies of Mohammed had white and black flags: black if led by the Prophet in person and white if led by one of his subordinates. The Ottomans had acquired what was believed to be Mohammed's own flag, the *Sancak-ı Şerif* (or Great Flag). It had been

2 I am indebted to John Sneddon and Anthony Portelli of the Facebook group *Medieval Heraldry* for providing me with this information.

captured by Selim I during his conquest of Egypt in 1517 and was taken to Istanbul where it remains in the Topkapi palace. The possession of the flag gave considerable kudos to the Ottomans but it was only in the late sixteenth century that it was permitted to accompany military expeditions. It remain furled, as it is thought that it will only be opened at the end of days. Green flags symbolised the Islamic faith and were associated with a religious as well as political confrontation.

Konstantin Mihailovic served as a Janissary a little time before the first siege and provided a description of the principal Ottoman flags:[3]

> There are four imperial banners, which belong to the Sultân's court. The first one is white with letters of gold written, and it is above all others, because it signifies that the entire imperial power is there, and they call it *alemsançak*, that is, the flag of the empire. The second flag is red - for the *kapıkulu* (royal court, central government) cavalry. The third is green and red, the fourth is yellow and red, and these are the Janissary court footmen. And whenever those four banners are unfurled, the Sultân is among his entourage.[4]

The flags varied in colour, although red, white yellow and green in single colours or various combinations seem to have predominated. Illustration of Janissary and artillery flags show the colours green over red and red over yellow/gold respectively. Subordinate commanders were given their standards by the Sultan, from which their title of *sancak bey* (Lord of the Standard) derived. These varied in shape and size including rectangular and swallow tailed designs, and were often decorated with the crescent and Koranic script, with the colours red, blue, white and yellow predominating.

The sultans in this period had their own, red, flags, a colour associated with the origin of the Ottomans as Steppe warriors. Murad I (1361-1389) was the third Ottoman ruler and claimed the title of Sultan for the first time (S.1). Murad was responsible for extending Ottoman territories into the Balkans and it was at this period that the recruitment of Janissaries began. Sultan Mehmet II changed the Ottoman flag after the capture of Constantinople and included the famous crescent (S.2). Bayezid II added further crescents to the flag in 1499 (S.3). Selim I, after he had conquered Persia and Egypt, altered the flag by placing the three crescents into a green oval and this flag was retained in use until 1844 (S.4).

There are two remarkable survivals from this period. The first is the original war standard of Selim I of 1519, now in the collection of the Topkapi

---

3 Konstantin Mihailovic served eight years as a Janissary (1455-1463) before being captured and released by Christians. He wrote his memoirs probably in the last decade of the fifteenth century.

4 Memoirs of a Janissary or Türkish Chronicle by Konstantin Mihailović, 1490 (Academia edu), p.35.

Museum in Istanbul, which has a representation of the *Zülfikar* sword of the legendary Caliph Ali ibn Abi Talib, which was a common motif on Ottoman war standards and which was misinterpreted and developed into the Masonic insignia. The second is a war standard from the field of Mohacs (1526) which has remained with the Sehagic family, relatives of the original owner. It is decorated with Islamic script as well as a lyric poem extolling the virtues of its original owner.[5]

In addition to the cloth banners were horse-tail standards or *tug*, again a reminder to the Ottomans of their origins as horsemen of the East. The Sultan would have six or seven horse tails borne before him, and five would be placed before the palace of the commanding general, if it was not to be the Sultan himself. The senior leaders of the army would have three horse-tails placed before their residences. The imperial tents also had emblems placed on top of them, these were made from copper, iron and even gold - they were engraved with inscriptions from the Koran as well as floral designs.

The most important flag for the Janissaries was the *Yeniçeri Alay Bayrağı* (Procession Flag of the Corps). It was the principal flag and contained three important symbols all in white on a red background. The first was the *Zülfikar* (the double-edged sword of Caliph Ali). The second was the open hand with five fingers or *pence* which represented the 'Holy Five.'[6] The word *Pençik* (penchik, one of five) was applied to individual janissaries who were ostensibly recruited from captured Christians with the ratio of one child being chosen from every five. The final symbol was the white disc or *moncuk* representing the full moon, an ancient good luck symbol.
Every Orta had its own symbol which was placed at the entrance to its barracks and which was carried into battle by the *Bayrakdar* (Bannersman). The Janissaries would have this insignia tattooed on their bodies to demonstrate their allegiance to the Orta. The artillery boasted a distinctive yellow and red flag with edges embroidered in yellow, including a picture of a ball embroidered with white sequins on a red background and with three cannonballs on its rim.

5 Currently in the care of the Museum of Tesanj, Bosnia-Herzegovina

6 Prophet Muhammed, Caliph Ali, Ali's wife Fatima, and Ali's sons Hasan and Husein

Bibliography

A note about the quotations from sources: where appropriate, I have modernised spellings and interpreted the meanings of some of the words.

Primary Sources, printed

Agricola, Georgius, *De Re Metallica*, (New York: Dover Publications Inc., 1950)

Biringuccio, Vannoccio, *The Pirotechnia*, (New York: Dover Publications Inc., 1990)

Bouhours, Dominique, *The Life of the Renowned Peter D'Aubusson, Grand Master of Rhodes containing those two remarkable sieges of Rhodes by Mahomet the Great and Solyman the Magnificent, being lately added to compleat the story adorn'd with the choicest occurences in the Turkish Empire at that time*, (London: Geo. Wells, 1679)

Bourbon, Jacques de, *Grande et Merveilleuse, & Tréscruelle Oppugnation de la noble Cité de Rhodes*, (London: 1524)

Bourbon, Jacques de. *The Begynnynge and Foundacyon of the Holy Hospytall, [and] of the ordre of the knyghtes hospytallers of saynt Johan baptyst of Jerusalem*, (London: 1524), Oxford Text Archive

Bueil, Jean de (Craig & Jane Taylor, trans.), *Le Jouvencel*, (Woodbridge, The Boydell Press, 2020)

Busbecq, Ogier Ghislain de (Charles Thornton Forster, trans.), *The Life and Letters of Ogier Ghiselin de* Busbecq, 2 volumes (London: Kegan Paul & co, 1881). Project Gutenberg eBook.

Caoursin, Guillaume, *The Siege of Rhodes*, (London: *c.* 1482)

Corneweyle, Robert, *The Maner of Fortifications of Cities, Townes, Castelles and other Places*, (London: 1559)

Guicciardini, Francesco, *The History of Italy*, (Princeton: Princeton University Press, 1984)

Lad, John, 'A Rule of Gunners Art 1586 (his notebook)', pp18–36. Published in. Caruana, Adrian B,*Tudor Artillery 1485–1603* (Museum Restoration Service (Canada), 1992)

Mihailović, Konstantin (Željko Zidarić, ed.), *Memoirs of a Janissary or Türkish Chronicle,*1490, (Academia edu)

Smythe, John, *Certen Instructions, Observations and Orders Militarie, Requisit for all Chieftaines, Captaines*, (London: 1594)
Pisan, Christine de, (Charity Cannon Willard ed.. Sumner Willard trans.), *The Book of Deeds of Arms and of Chivalr*, (Pennsylvania State University Press, 1999)
Tartaglia, Niccolo, *Three Bookes of Colloquies Concerning the Arte of Shooting in Great and Small Pieces of Artillerie* (Cyprian Lucar, trans.), (London: 1588)

Secondary Sources, Books

Adams, Nicholas and Pepper, Simon, *Firearms & Fortifications: Military Architecture and Siege Warfare in Sixteenth-Century Siena* (Chicago: University of Chicago Press, 1986)
Ágoston, Gábor., 'Ottoman artillery and European military technology in the fifteenth and seventeenth centuries' *Acta Orientalia Academiae Scientiarum Hungaricae* , 1994, Vol. 47, No. 1–2, pp. 15–48
Ágoston, Gábor. *Guns for the Sultan: Military Power and the Weapons Industry in the Ottoman Empire*. Cambridge Studies in Islamic Civilisation. (Cambridge University Press, 2005)
Brown, R. R. and Smith, R. D., *Bombards – Mons Meg and her Sisters* (Leeds: Royal Armouries, 1989)
Barber, Malcolm (ed.), *The Military Orders: Fighting for the Faith and Caring for the Sick*, (Aldershot: Ashgate Publishing Ltd, 1994)
Brockman, Eric, *The Two Sieges*, (London: John Murray, 1969)
Carr, John, *The Knights Hospitaller: A Military History*, (Barnsley: Pen & Sword Military, 2016)
Davies, Jonathan, *The Tudor Arte of Tudor Warre, 1558–1603,* volume 3, Retinue to Regiment series no.22, (Warwick: Helion & Co, 2023)
Davies, Jonathan., *The Medieval Cannon* (Oxford: Osprey, 2019)
DeVries, Kelly and Smith, Robert Douglas, *The Artillery of the Dukes of Burgundy* (Woodbridge: The Boydell Press, 2005)
Duffy, Christopher, *Siege Warfare: the Fortress in the Early Modern World. 1494–1660* (London: Routledge Kegan Paul, 1979)
Gabriel, Albert, *La Cité de Rhodes, 1310–1522 : Topographie, Architecture Militaire*, · volume 1, (Paris: E. de Boccard, 1921), volume 2, (Paris: E. de Boccard, 1923)
Gille, Bertrand, *The Renaissance Engineers* (London: Lund Humphries, 1966)
Guilmartin, J. F., *Galleons and Galleys*, (London: Cassell and Co, 2002)
Guilmartin, J. F., *Gunpowder and Galley*, (Cambridge: Cambridge University Press, 1974)
Hale, J. R., *Renaissance Fortification. Art or Engineering?* (London: Thames & Hudson, 1977)
Hale, J. R., *Renaissance War Studies*, (Hambledon & London: Hambledon Press, 1983)

Hall, Bert S., *Weapons and Warfare in Renaissance Europe*, (Baltimore: The Johns Hopkins University Press, 1997)

Karcheski, Walter and Richardson, Thom, *The Medieval Armour from Rhodes*, (Martlesham: Boydell & Brewer, 2003)

Luttrell, Anthony, *The Hospitallers in Cyprus, Rhodes, Greece and the West, 1291–1440*, (Titchmarsh: Variorum, 1979)

Lyber, A. H., *The Government of the Ottoman Empire in the Time of Suleiman the Magnificent*, (Cambridge: Harvard University Press, 1913)

Mattingly, Garret, *The Defeat of the Spanish Armada*, (London: Jonathan Cape, 1960)

Murphey Rhoads, *Ottoman Warfare*, (New Brunswick: Rutgers University Press, 1999)

Napoleon III, *Études sur le Passé et l'Avenir de de l'Artillerie*, (Paris: J Dumaine, 1846)

Nicholson, Helen, *The Knights Hospitaller* (Martlesham: Boydell Press, 2001)

Nicolle, David, *Armies of the Ottoman Empire: 1775–1820*, Men-At-Arms series no.314, (Oxford: Osprey Publishing, 1998)

Nicolle, David, *Knight Hospitaller: 1306–1565*, (Oxford: Osprey Publishing, 2001)

O'Neil, Brian Hugh St John, *Castles and Cannon: A Study of Early Artillery Fortifications in England* (Westport: Greenwood Press, 1975)

O'Malley, Gregory, *The Knights Hospitaller of the English Langue* 1460–1565 (Oxford: OUP, 2005)

Partington, J. R. A., *History of Greek Fire and Gunpowder* (Cambridge: W. Heffer & Sons, 1966)

Oswin, Tony, *Rhodes. A-Z Travel Guides*, (Bury St Edmunds: Arima Publishing, 2022)

Phillips, Simon (ed), *The 1522 Siege of Rhodes: Causes, Course and Consequences* (London: Routledge, 2022)

Porter, Whitworth, *A History of the Knights of Malta or the Order of St. John of Jerusalem* (London: Whitworth Porter, 1883)

Riley-Smith, Jonathan, *Hospitallers: the History of the Order of St John* (London: Hambledon Press, 1999)

Runciman, Sir Steven, *The Fall of Constantinople 1453*, (Cambridge University Press, 1990)

Seward, Desmond, *The Monks of War*, (London: Penguin Books, 1995)

Smail, R. C., *Crusading Warfare*, (Cambridge: Cambridge University Press, 2008)

Smith, Robert D. & De Vries, Kelly, *Rhodes Besieged – A New History*, (Cheltenham: The History Press, 2011)

Smith, Robert D. & DeVries, Kelly, *The Artillery of the Dukes of Burgundy*, (Martlesham: Boydell Press, 2005)

Spiteri, Stephen C., *On the Study of Military Architecture Part 1. The significance of military architecture, why it deserves to be studied and how* (ARX Occasional Papers Issue 5/2015) Valkana, Annina, *The Knights of Rhodes* (Peristérion: Editions M. Toubis, 2006)

Vertot, Abbe René-Aubert, *The History of the Knights Hospitallers of St John of Jerusalem: Styled Afterwards, the Knights of Rhodes, and at Present, the Knights of Malta* (Dublin: J Christie, 1818)

Zoitou, Sofia, *The Hospitallers' Institutions in Staging Holiness: The Case of Hospitaller Rhodes (ca. 1309–1522)*, (Leiden: Brill, 2021)

Wernham, R. B., *After the Armada – Elizabethan England and the Struggle for Western Europe* 1588-1595 (Oxford: Clarendon press, 1988)

Secondary Sources, Articles

Ágoston, Gábor, 'Behind the Turkish war machine: gunpowder technology and war industry in the Ottoman Empire, 1450-1700', Chapter 4 in *The Heirs of Archimedes: Science and the Art of War through the Age of Enlightenment*, Brett D. Steele (ed.), pp.101–133

Ágoston, Gábor., 'Ottoman artillery and European Military Technology in the Fifteenth and Seventeenth centuries' *Acta Orientalia Academiae Scientiarum Hungaricae* , 1994, vol. 47, No.1/2, pp.15–48

Ágoston, Gábor,' Firearms and Military Adaptation: The Ottomans and the European Military Revolution', 1450–1800, *Journal of World History*, Vol. 25, No. 1 (March 2014), pp 85–124, published by: University of Hawaii Press on behalf of World History Association

Ágoston, Gábor, 'Habsburgs and Ottomans: Defense, Military Change and Shifts in Power', *Turkish Studies Association Bulletin,* Vol. 22, No. 1 (Spring 1998), pp.126–141

Ágoston, Gábor, 'Ottoman Military Organization' (up to 1800), at *Academia edu*

Ansani, Fabrizio, 'This French artillery is very good and very effective.' Hypotheses on the Diffusion of a New Military Technology in Renaissance Italy', *The Journal of Military History* 83 (April 2019): pp.347–378.

Ardali Fehmi, 'Food for the army in the Ottoman Empire', at *Academia edu*

Badoud, Nathan, 'Early Explorers of Rhodes 1342–1853' in *Documenting Ancient Rhodes: Archaeological Expeditions and Rhodian Antiquities.* In *Acts of the International Colloquium held at the National Museum of Denmark in Copenhagen*, February 16–17, 2017, pp.35–50

Borekçı, Günhan, 'A contribution to the Military Revolution Debate: The Janissaries use of volley fire during the long Ottoman-Habsburg war of 1593–1606 and the problem of origins', *Acta Orientalia Academiae Scientiarum Hungaricae*, Vol. 59, No. 4 (2006), pp.407–438

Brown, Ruth Rhynas, 'Troncks, Rockets and Fiery Balls: Military Fireworks of the Early Modern Period', *Journal of the Ordnance Society*, Vol. 17 (2005), pp.25–38

Brummett, Palmira, 'The Overrated Adversary: Rhodes and Ottoman Naval Power', *The Historical Journal*, Vol. 36, No. 3 (Sep, 1993), pp.517–541

Bury, J. S, 'The early history of the explosive mine', *Fort, The Journal of the Fortress Study Group*, vol.10 (1982), pp.23 –30

Capwell, Tobias, 'A Cursed Abominable Device? The True, Shared History of Knights and Firearms', *Bulletin of the American Society of Arms Collectors*, (2019), pp.29–43

DeVries, Kelly, 'Gunpowder Weaponry and the Rise of the Early Modern State', in *War in History*,V (1988), pp.127–145

Finlay, Robert, 'Politics and History in the Diary of Marino Sanuto', *Renaissance Quarterly* vol. 33, no.4 (Winter, 1980), pp.585–598

Charles Ffoulkes, On Italian Armour from Chalcis in the Ethnological Museum at Athens *Archaeologia* 62, part II, 2nd Feb, (1911) https://www.gonderzone.org/Library/Armour/chalcis.htm

Ffoulkes, Charles, 'Pallisadoes and other Defences', *Journal of the Society for Army Historical Research*, vol. 19, no.73, Spring, 1940, pp.2–8

Fuess, Albrecht, 'Sultans with Horns: The Political Significance of Headgear in the Mamluk Empire', *Mamlūk Studies Review*, vol. 12, no.2, 2008 (Chicago: University of Chicago Press, 2008), pp.71–94

Grant, Jonathan, 'Rethinking the Ottoman "Decline": Military Technology Diffusion in the Ottoman Empire, Fifteenth to Eighteenth Centuries', *Journal of World History* vol. 10, no. 1 (Spring, 1999), pp.179–201. Published by: University of Hawaii Press on behalf of World History Association Stable

Guilmartin, J. F., 'Ideology and Conflict: The Wars of the Ottoman Empire, 1453–1606.' *The Journal of Interdisciplinary History*, Spring, 1988, vol. 18, no.4, in *The Origin and Prevention of Major Wars*, (Cambridge, Mass: MIT Press, 1988), pp.721–747

Hacker, Barton C., 'Mounted Archery and Firearms, Late Medieval Muslim Military Technology Reconsidered', *Vulcan* 3, 2015 (Washington D.C., Journal of the Smithsonian Institution, 2015), pp.42–65

Haksever, Cengiz, 'Supply Chain & Logistics of the Ottoman Army' (1300–1566),

International Journal of Supply Chain Management (IJSCM), vol. 9, no.5, October 2020 pp.46–59

Hale, J R, 'Men and weapons: The fighting potential of sixteenth-century Venetian galleys',

War in History, vol. 5, no.2 (1998), pp.309–334

Hall, Bert S. (review), *The Book of Michael of Rhodes: A Fifteenth-Century Maritime Manuscript* (Alan M. Stahl, ed. and trans.) in *Isis*, vol. 103, no.1 (March 2012), pp.151–154. Published by: The University of Chicago Press on behalf of *The History of Science Society*

Hall, Nicholas, 'Building and firing a replica *Mary Rose* port piece'. *Royal Armouries Yearbook*, vol. 3 (1998), pp.57–66

Hall, Nicholas, 'Casting and firing a Mary Rose culverin', *Royal Armouries Yearbook*, vol. 6 (2001)

Harris, John, 'Sarzana and Sarzanello: traditional designs and Renaissance designers', *The Journal of the Fortress Study Group*, vol. 37 (2009) pp.50–77

Hasluck, F. W, 'Heraldry of the Rhodian Knights, Formerly in Smyrna Castle', *The Annual of the British School at Athens*, vol. 17 (1910/1911), pp.145–150

Herzfeld, Michael, 'New Light on the 1480 Siege of Rhodes', *The British Museum Quarterly*, Autumn 1972, vol. 36, No.3/4, pp.69–73

Hughes, Quentin & Migos Athanassios, 'Rhodes: The Turkish Sieges', *Fort, The Journal of the Fortress Study Group*, vol.21 (1993) pp.3–18

Hughes, Quentin, 'Errors of Judgement: The Sieges of Rhodes and Malta', *Fort, The Journal of the Fortress Study Group* vol.31, (2003), pp.61– 80

Hughes, Quentin, 'The siege of Fort St Elmo 1565', *Fort, The Journal of the Fortress Study Group*, vol.10 (1982), pp.71–92

Kasdagli, Anna-Maria & Manoussa-Della, Katerina, 'The defences of Rhodes and the Tower of St John', *Fort, The Journal of the Fortress Study Group*, vol.24 (1996), pp.15–36

Jones, Dorsey D, 'The Janissaries-unique fighting men', *Social Science*', vol. 6, no.4, (October, 1931), pp.399–401

Kahraman Sakul, 'Military Engineering in the Ottoman Empire'. Chapter 7 in *Military Engineers: The Development of the Early Modern European State* (Bruce P. Lenman ed.), published 17 July 2013

Katić Tatjana, On the Origin of Konstantin Mihailović, Author of the Turkish Chronicle, *Recueil du Kosovo et Metohija* 9 (Dragan Vojvodić ed.) (Belgrade: 2022), pp.81–93

Lamberini Daniela, 'Practice and Theory in Sixteenth Century fortifications,' *Fort, The Journal of the Fortress Study Group*, vol. 15 (1987), pp.5–20

Latham, J. D., 'Notes on Mamlūk Horse-Archers', *Bulletin of the School of Oriental and African Studies*, University of London, vol. 32, no.2 (1969), pp.257–267

Long, Priscilla, 'Michael of Rhodes', *The Antioch Review*, vol. 75, no.2, Spring 2017, pp.38–40

Lugatism, *Headwear and footwear in the Mamluk Sultanate* posted JUNE 22, 2022
https://lugatism.wordpress.com/2022/06/22/headwear-and-footwear-in-the-mamluk-sultanate/

Luttrell Anthony, 'Smoke and fire signals at Rhodes 1449', pp.125–130 in Peter W. Edbury (ed), *The Military Orders Vol.*, (Farnham: Ashgate publishing Ltd, 2012)

Luttrell, Anthony, 'Venice and the Knights Hospitallers of Rhodes in the Fourteenth Century', *Papers of the British School at Rome,* vol. 26 (1958), pp.195–212

Morris, Robert, 'Coins of the Grand Masters: of the Order of Knights Hospitallers of St John of Jerusalem', *American Journal of Numismatics, and Bulletin of the American Numismatic and Archaeological Society*, vol. 17, no.2 (October, 1882), pp.31–38. Published by American Numismatic Society

Nicolle, David C., 'Cresting on Arrows from the Citadel of Damascus', *Bulletin d'Études Orientales*, 2016, T. 65, Mélanges en mémoire de

Djamel Eddine Kouloughli (2016), pp.247–286, Institut Francais du Proche-Orient

Özgüven, Burcu H., 'Early Modern Military Architecture in the Ottoman Empire', *Nexus Network Journal*, volume 16 (2014), pp.737–749

Paterson W. F., 'The Archers of Islam', *Journal of the Economic and Social History of the Orient*, vol. 9, no.1/2 (November 1966), pp.69–87

Pepper, Simon, 'Castles and Cannons in the Naples campaign 1494–5', in David Abulafia, David, *The French Descent into Renaissance Italy, 1494–95: Antecedents and Effects*, (London: Routledge, 2016)

Pepper, Simon, 'Firepower and the design of Renaissance fortifications', *Fort, The Journal of the Fortress Study Group*, vol. 10 (1982), pp.93–104

Pepper, Simon, 'The Face of the Siege: Fortification, Tactics and Strategy in the Early Italian Wars', in Christine Shaw (ed.), *Italy and the European Powers: The Impact of War, 1500–1530*, (Leiden: Brill, 2006)

Pepper, Simon, 'The underground siege,' *Fort, The Journal of the Fortress Study Group*, vol. 10 , (1982), pp.31–39

Phillip, Simon D., 'The shining virgin, sappers and silent night assaults: comparisons with the precursors to the 1565 siege' in *Besieged: Malta 1565*, vol.1. (Valetta: Heritage Malta, 2015), pp.107–116

Purton, Peter, 'Ancient, medieval and modern: continuity and change in siege warfare.' at *Academia.edu*

Pyhrr, Stuart W., 'European Armor from the Imperial Ottoman Arsenal', *Metropolitan Museum Journal*, vol. 24 (1989), pp.85–116

Radushev, Evgeni, '"Peasant" Janissaries? *Journal of Social History*', Winter, 2008, vol. 42, no.2, pp.447–467

Scaglia, Gustina, 'Franceso di Giorgios' chapters on fortresses and on war machines', *Fort, The Journal of the Fortress Study Group*, vol.10, (1982), pp.40–69

Schierup, Stine (with the assistance of Hoffmann Sanne), 'Documenting Ancient Rhodes: Archaeological Expeditions and Rhodian Antiquities', *Acts of the International Colloquium held at the National Museum of Denmark in Copenhagen*, February 16–17, 2017, (Aarhus: Aarhus University Press)

Shmuelevitz, Aryeh, 'Capsali as a Source for Ottoman History, 1450–1523', *International Journal of Middle East Studies*, vol. 9, no.3 (Oct, 1978), pp.339–344

Smith, Robert D, 'All manner of peeces: artillery in the late medieval period', *Royal Armouries Yearbook*, vol. 5 (2002), pp.130–138

Smith, Robert D, 'The reconstruction and firing trials of a replica of a 14th Century cannon,' *Royal Armouries Yearbook*, vol. 4 (1999), pp.86–94

Smith, Robert D, 'The technology of wrought-iron artillery,' *Royal Armouries Yearbook*, vol. 5 (2000), pp.68–79

Soucek, Svatopluk, 'Naval Aspects of the Ottoman Conquests of Rhodes, Cyprus and Crete', *Studia Islamica*, no.98/99 (2004), pp.219–261

Stefanidou, Alexandra, 'The Medieval Town of Rhodes based on Johannes Hedeborg's manuscript (1854)', *Mediterranean Archaeology and Archiometry*, vol. 1, no.1, pp.69–77

Tomkinson, John, 'Dürer's Artillery Fortifications: a New Look at his Designs', *Fort, The Journal of the Fortress Study Group*, vol. 42 (2014), pp.30–35

Trim, D. J. B., 'Medieval and Early-Modern inshore, Estuarine, riverine and Lacustrine warfare' in *Amphibious Warfare 1000–1700* (Leiden: Brill, 2006), pp.357–419

Vann, Theresa M, 'Battlefield Tourism: A description of the 1480 siege of Rhodes', in Edbury, Peter W (ed.), *The Military Orders Vol.5* (Ashgate publishing Ltd, 2012), pp.141–145

Veinstein, Gilles, 'On the Ottoman Janissaries (fourteenth-nineteenth centuries)', in *Fighting for a Living: A Comparative Study of Military Labour1500–2000'*, Erik-Jan Zürcher (ed.) (Amsterdam: Amsterdam University Press, 2014), pp.115–134

Theses and Dissertations

HO Group, *Casting and testing a 15. Century Bronze cannon,* The HO report no 15, February 2016 (September 2020)

López-Martín, Francisco Javier, *Historical and Technological Evolution of Artillery From its Earliest Widespread Use Until The Emergence of Mass-Production Techniques,* a thesis presented in the Sir John Cass Dept. of Art, Media & Design, for the degree of Ph.D, London Metropolitan University (June 2007)

Riesinger Fabian, *Making an Island: the transformation(s) of Rhodes under early Ottoman rule* (1522–1560), MA Thesis in Late Antique, Medieval and Early-Modern studies. Central European University Private University, Vienna 2012

Other titles in the From Retinue to Regiment series:

No 1 *Richard III and the Battle of Bosworth* Mike Ingram

No 2 *Tanaka 1587: Japan's Greatest Unknown Samurai Battle* Stephen Turnbull

No 3 *The Army of the Swabian League 1525* Doug Miller

No 4 *The Italian Wars Volume 1: The Expedition of Charles VIII into Italy and the Battle of Fornovo* Massimo Predonzani & Alberici Vincenzo, translated by Irene Maccolini

No 5 *The Commotion Time: Tudor Rebellion in the West, 1549* E.T. Fox

No 6 *The Italian Wars Volume 2: Agnadello 1509, Ravenna 1512, Marignano 1515* Massimo Predonzani & Alberici Vincenzo, translated by Rachele Tiso

No 7 *The Tudor Arte of Warre Volume 1: The Conduct of War from Henry VII to Mary I, 1485-1558* Jonathan Davies

No 8 *The Ethiopian-Adal War 1529-1543: The Conquest of Abyssinia* Jeffrey M. Shaw

No 9 *The Ōnin War: A Turning Point in Samurai History* Stephen Turnbull

No 10 *One Faith, One Law, One King: French Armies of the Wars of Religion 1562–1598* T J O'Brien de Clare

No 11 *The Italian Wars Volume 3: Francis I and the Battle of Pavia 1525* Massimo Predonzani & Alberici Vincenzo

No 12 *On the Borderlands of Great Empires: Transylvanian Armies 1541-1613* Florin Nicolae Ardelean

No 14 *The Art of Shooting Great Ordnance: A History of the Development, Manufacture and Use of Artillery, 1494–1628* Jonathan Davies

No 15 *The Italian Wars Volume 4: The Battle of Ceresole 1544 - The Crushing Defeat of the Imperial Army* Massimo Predonzani & Simon Miller

No 16 *The Men of Warre: The Clothes, Weapons and Accoutrements of the Scots at War 1460–1600* Jenn Scott

No 17 *The German Peasants' War 1524–26* Douglas Miller

No 18 *The Tudor Arte of Warre Volume 2: The conduct of war in the reign of Elizabeth I, 1558–1603: Diplomacy, Strategy, Campaigns and Battles* Jonathan Davies

No 19 *The Kalmar War 1611–1613: Gustavus Adolphus's First War* Michael Fredholm von Essen

No 20 *Hojo: Samurai Warlords 1487–1590* Stephen Turnbull

No 21 *The Battle of Castillon 1453: The Death Knell for English France* Peter Hoskins

No 22 *The Tudor Arte of Warre Volume 3: The Conduct of War in the Reign of Elizabeth I 1558-1603: The Elizabethan Army* Jonathan Davies

No 23 *Sweden's War in Muscovy 1609-1617: The Relief of Moscow and Conquest of Novgorod* Michael Fredholm von Essen

No 24 *'Of Kerns and Gallowglasses': Irish Armies of the Sixteenth Century, 1487-1587* Robert Gresh

No 25 *'The Italian Wars Volume 5:The Franco-Spanish War in Southern Italy 1502-1504* Massimo Predonzani

No 26 *The Sieges of Rhodes 1480 and 1522* Jonathan Davies